'At last, a simple and accessible guide which makes the massive world of wine seem smaller and more approachable' JAMIE OLIVER

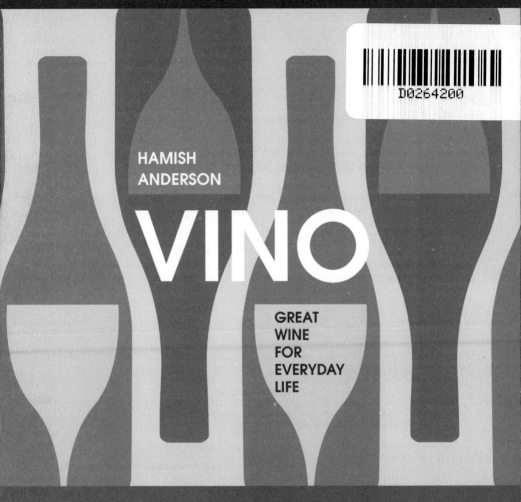

HAMISH
ANDERSON

VINO

GREAT
WINE
FOR
EVERYDAY
LIFE

'An intelligent, well designed book for those who want to increase their knowledge of the complex subject of modern wine.'
ROSE GRAY, The River Cafe

'*Vino* is a lively, fun and informative read, written by an excellent young sommelier.'
ANTHONY WORRALL THOMPSON

Available now from all good bookshops

CENTURY
An imprint of The Random House Group Ltd
www.randomhouse.co.uk

GRANTA

GRANTA 84, WINTER 2003
www.granta.com

EDITOR   *Ian Jack*
DEPUTY EDITOR   *Matt Weiland*
MANAGING EDITOR   *Fatema Ahmed*
ASSOCIATE EDITOR   *Liz Jobey*
EDITORIAL ASSISTANT   *Helen Gordon*

CONTRIBUTING EDITORS   *Diana Athill, Gail Lynch, Blake Morrison, Andrew O'Hagan, John Ryle, Sukhdev Sandhu, Lucretia Stewart*

ASSOCIATE PUBLISHER   *Sally Lewis*
FINANCE   *Geoffrey Gordon, Morgan Graver*
SALES   *Frances Hollingdale*
PUBLICITY   *Louise Campbell*
SUBSCRIPTIONS   *John Kirkby, Darryl Wilks, Anna Tang*
PUBLISHING ASSISTANT   *Mark Williams*
ADVERTISING MANAGER   *Kate Rochester*
PRODUCTION ASSOCIATE   *Sarah Wasley*

PUBLISHER   *Rea S. Hederman*

Granta, 2–3 Hanover Yard, Noel Road, London N1 8BE
Tel 020 7704 9776 Fax 020 7704 0474
e-mail for editorial: editorial@granta.com

Granta US, 1755 Broadway, 5th Floor, New York, NY 10019-3780, USA

TO SUBSCRIBE call 020 7704 0470 or e-mail subs@granta.com
A one-year subscription (four issues) costs £26.95 (UK), £34.95 (rest of Europe) and £41.95 (rest of the world).

Granta is printed and bound in Italy by Legoprint. The paper used in this publication meets the minimum requirements of American National Standard for Information Sciences — Permanence of Paper for Printed Library Materials, ANSI Z39.48-1984.

Granta is published by Granta Publications.
This selection copyright © 2003 Granta Publications.

Design: Slab Media.

Front cover photograph: 'United Nations fight for Freedom' by John Rous, c.1941 courtesy of Library of Congress, Prints and Photographs Division [LC-USW36-473]
Back cover photograph: taken in New York, March 2003 by Anthony Suau

ISBN 0-903141-64-7

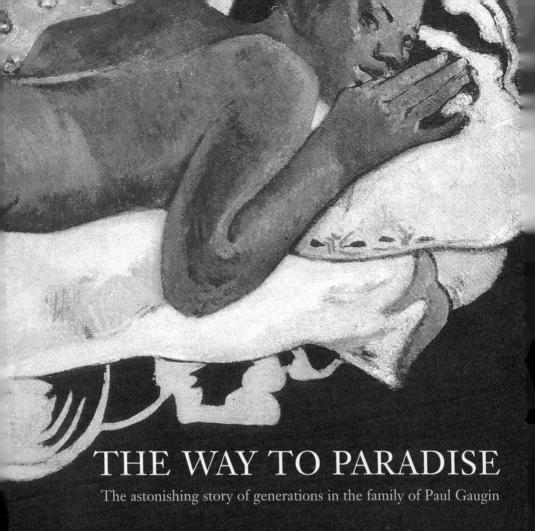

THE WAY TO PARADISE

The astonishing story of generations in the family of Paul Gaugin

Mario Vargas Llosa

'He is a great storyteller, who combines high seriousness with lightness of touch' *The Times*

OUT NOW

ff

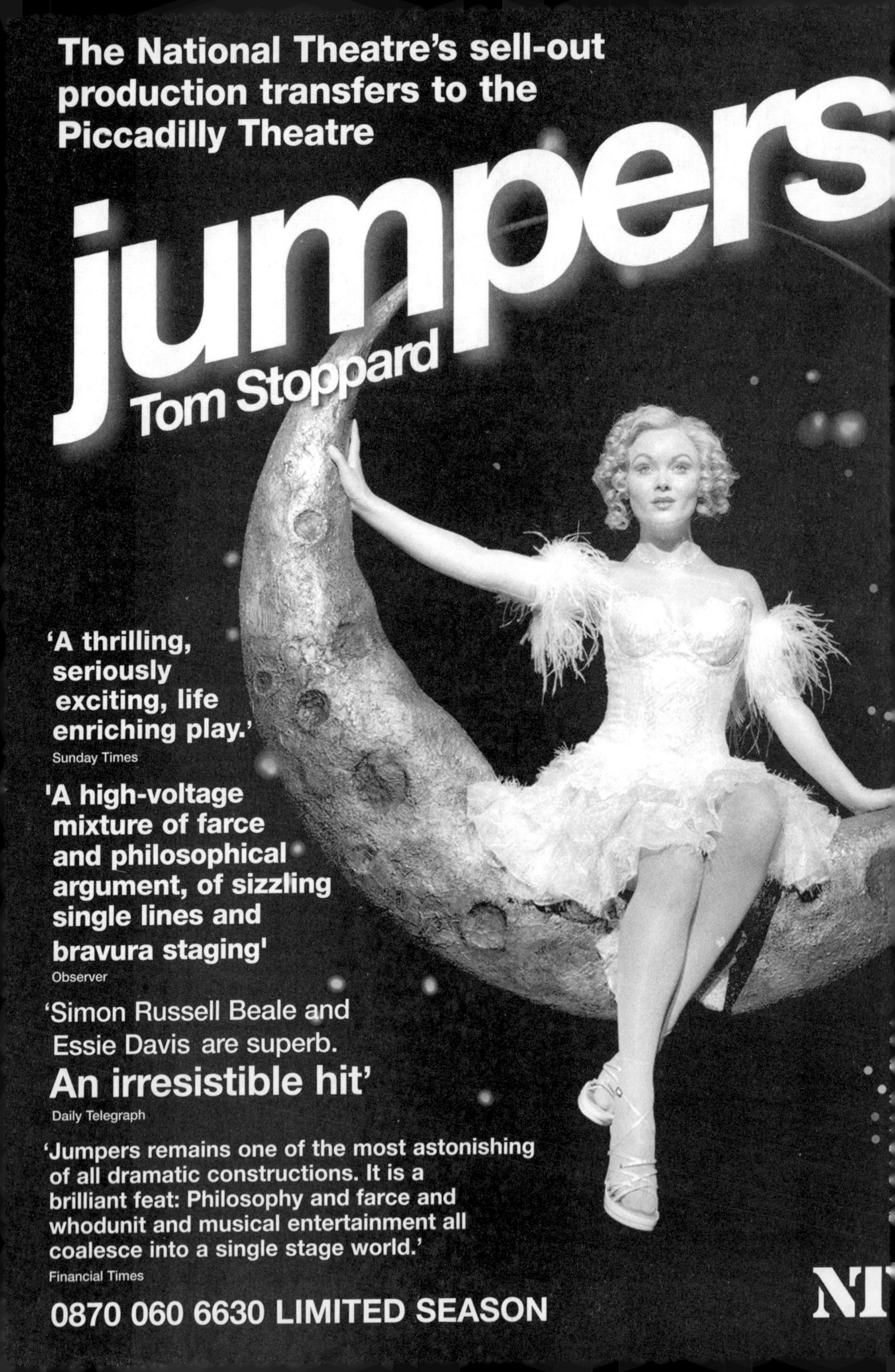
The National Theatre's sell-out production transfers to the Piccadilly Theatre
jumpers
Tom Stoppard
'A thrilling, seriously exciting, life enriching play.'
Sunday Times
'A high-voltage mixture of farce and philosophical argument, of sizzling single lines and bravura staging'
Observer
'Simon Russell Beale and Essie Davis are superb.
An irresistible hit'
Daily Telegraph
'Jumpers remains one of the most astonishing of all dramatic constructions. It is a brilliant feat: Philosophy and farce and whodunit and musical entertainment all coalesce into a single stage world.'
Financial Times
0870 060 6630 LIMITED SEASON
NT

GRANTA 84

Over There
How America Sees the World

RECOLLECTIONS AND FORECASTS FROM TWENTY WRITERS
Tom Bissell, Gardner Botsford, Paula Fox,
Nell Freudenberger, Paul Fussell, Charles Glass, Chris Hedges,
Adam Hochschild, A. M. Homes, Chalmers Johnson,
Murad Kalam, J. Robert Lennon, Jacki Lyden, Todd McEwen,
Darryl Pinckney, Eric Schlosser, Gary Shteyngart,
Studs Terkel, Paul Theroux, Joel Turnipseed

INTRODUCTION

Two years ago, in the wake of September 11 and the invasion of Afghanistan, this magazine asked writers across the world to describe how America had influenced their lives: how it had affected them and the countries they lived in—culturally, politically, economically, for good or ill. The results were published in *Granta 77*, an issue entitled 'What We Think of America', and they showed a variety of experience and opinion at a time when attitudes to America were on the cusp of changing from widespread sympathy to an anxiety, among many states and individuals, over what America would do next. Now we know: Iraq has been invaded and incompletely conquered under the doctrine of 'preventive' war—a doctrine outlined by President George W. Bush in his West Point speech of June 1, 2002, when he said that America 'must take the battle to the enemy...and confront the worst threats before they emerge'. The old policies of containment and deterrence were out, Bush said: 'In the world we have entered, the only path to safety is the path of action. And this nation will act.' Opinion polls suggested that a majority of Americans believed that Iraq's ruler, Saddam Hussein, was the hand behind the terrorist outrages of September 11. The Bush administration said it had evidence which showed that, though not the actual perpetrator, Saddam was at least in partnership with al-Qaida and its leader, Osama Bin Laden. Neither was true. Nor does it seem to be true—the research furiously continues at the time of writing—that Iraq possessed weapons of mass destruction which were an imminent threat to the United States (or to any other country, including America's only important military ally, Britain).

None the less, Iraq has been occupied by American and British troops at the cost of several thousand lives, without the sanction of the United Nations, and with no clear plan for its future. America, or at least its present government, is determined to rearrange the world to its own satisfaction, come hell or high water. It refuses to sign or ratify international treaties, including those which would reduce carbon emissions or bring war criminals to trial. For more than two years, it has held 650 men and boys captured in Afghanistan at a prison camp at its military base in Guantanamo Bay, Cuba, denying them access to lawyers or tribunals and breaching the Third Geneva Convention. It has somewhere between 240,000 and 340,000 military personnel based abroad on combat or peacekeeping duties. It is the world's supreme power: uncontestable.

How much does imperious America know of the world it wants to shape? As a state with such lavish resources—financial, diplomatic, technological, scholastic—at its disposal, it should know a great deal. Then again, there are those reports (gleefully seized on by the rest of us) that show, for example, how most pupils at a Texan high school believe that Rome is the capital of France or that India is in Africa, while official intelligence of pre-war Iraq, including the expectations of the welcome it would extend to its liberators, suggests that that kind of ignorance may not be confined to high schools. (Recently an American academic who specializes in the Middle East told me that he had been asked by a Washington intelligence department if he would care to write a paper which could answer their question: 'Why Arabs Lie'.)

Anyone who knows America will recognize that these accounts don't represent the complete picture, and that our relish of them is partly brewed by envy, resentment, and most recently, fear (aka Shock and Awe). As Europeans in Old Europe we enjoy the sentence in Graham Greene's *The Quiet American* about Pyle, the do-gooding and consequently do-badding idealist in French Vietnam: 'I never knew a man who had better motives for all the trouble he caused.' On the other hand, did Pyle ever die? Anyone who knows America will also know that many and perhaps most of its people seem to believe that they have got life 'sorted'; that their way of living and thinking is the most perfect to be attained on this earth; that other ways are inferior; that theirs is the model to be copied everywhere else. Increasingly, there seems an almost religious dimension to US citizenship, not just because America is a remarkably Christian state led by a man who peppers his rhetoric with the words 'good' and 'evil', but because the sheer fact of being American is for many Americans to be part of an evangelical, patriotic faith—to be one of the elect, to be one of the saved.

Can America be so immune to the rest of the world, how it lives, what it thinks? For this issue we turned *Granta 77*'s question around and asked American writers how they had encountered countries other than their own, how the experience had affected them, if it had changed them or their views of their homeland. This was a trickier proposition than discovering what non-Americans felt about America. For one thing, 'abroad' or 'over there' is, other than for Native Americans, the site of every American's ancestry or birth—in some, often dark department of familial memory 'abroad' is what they fled. For another, it proved difficult to find an outright expression of contempt ('Went there once. Awful food. Showers didn't work. No democracy, no liberty, not much free-enterprise. Quicker we get Gigantic Oil Co in there the better.'), even though contempt may form some (only slightly) submerged part of the new foreign policy.

Our contributors and their mixture of episode and opinion are all more thoughtful than that about what the rest of the world means to them. They are, of course, only writers—people almost invisible to America's popular or political eye. But their differences give the lie to the idea of America as a monolith. The frequency of their dissent suggests that the new empire will sooner or later be in trouble at home as well as abroad—or rather, in more trouble than it is already.

Ian Jack

GRANTA

OVER THERE

Over there, over there/ Send the word, send the word over there/
That the Yanks are coming.../ So prepare, say a pray'r/
Send the word, send the word to beware/ We'll be over, we're coming
over/ And we won't come back till it's over/ Over there.

from 'Over There', popular First World War song by George M. Cohan

Tom Bissell
b. 1974, Escanaba, Michigan

Americans, speaking of foreign lands, often say, 'It's a nice place to visit, but I wouldn't want to live there.' Somewhere in that cheery sentence is an insult—especially if you live in the place being dismissed—but few such speakers would acknowledge it. To many, it just seems obvious: why *would* anyone want to live anywhere else?

A Muslim is a Muslim to most Americans, and Central Asia morphs into the Middle East which somehow becomes the Indian subcontinent. All of whose people hate us, we imagine. We, in turn, hate them back, though in a far lower key. The famed American tolerance becomes self-righteous American indifference. *The rest of the world can rot. If you are not with us, you are against us.* We still do not wish to live anywhere else, but many no longer even want to visit.

I would be lying if I did not admit to occasionally feeling this way myself. I nearly deoxygenated myself arguing with the European journalists I met in Afghanistan who believed the whole endeavour was one big pipeline-construction scheme, or that America was the world's biggest sponsor of state terrorism. What I have seen of the world has brought me close to innumerable victims and many scoundrels but frustratingly few arch-villains. It is now a dog-eared trope of the Left that the troubles in Afghanistan are the sole responsibility of covert American malefactors, when actually Pakistan and Saudi Arabia were major contributors. Our attempt to bolster Saddam Hussein's regime during the Iran–Iraq war of the 1980s (a time when few in the Reagan administration had any illusions about Hussein) is now evidence that we 'created' the neo-Stalinist dictator, when, in fact, Hussein's regime came to power largely thanks to the hernias and spasms of Ba'athism, a movement independent of American foreign policy. In addition, France and Germany sold Hussein's regime millions of dollars' worth of weapons, some of which were used genocidally. Hatred of America, like love of America, is primarily founded upon the notion that only America affects the world in any meaningful way. But the idea that the lava of worldly power flows from a lone volcano in the heart of an American Mordor is a dangerous simplification. George W. Bush and Noam Chomsky are not as distant in their turns of mind as one

ABBAS/MAGNUM

11

might initially suspect. Not only does unblinking belief in American supremacy, however it is regarded, intellectually paralyse one's view of the world, it helps create a self-fulfilling prophecy of an America run amok.

In Uzbekistan I was told by a devout Muslim that while many hated America, just about everyone loved Americans. (This was followed by his insisting that his countrymen loved Russia but hated Russians.) As a traveller, I have been the beneficiary of foreigners' kindness and hospitality, though often after being compelled to sit through a point by point discussion of why America's unilateral actions were wrecking the world. There is much to learn from people whose minds are not calcified by 'either/or' determinism, who can disapprove of America and invite an American to tea. Such people know the world is far more complicated than Al-Jazeera or CNN care to admit.

Still, one has to be some kind of anti-genius to nullify the massive surge of support the United States enjoyed on September 12, 2001; to move against a monstrous dictator and manage to outrage the world. The rhetorical disaster of proclaiming war on terror—rather than on al-Qaida or even on Islamist terrorists—is now becoming clear. The world is filled with terror, just as it is filled with beauty and kindness. It can never be exterminated, only borne. Every traveller knows this—every traveller expects it—because an understanding of our world's shifting ambiguities is travel's most mysterious gift.

The enemies of the United States can be defeated but the war on terror cannot be won. What, then, can we in the United States hope for? I myself have a hope, which is that the Bush administration abandons its absurd, misguided crusade against abstract 'terror' and addresses the American people as thinking adults about the specific terrors we face.

'Oh, America,' D. H. Lawrence wrote in 'The Evening Land', 'The sun sets in you/Are you the grave of our day?' American actions will not plunge the world into its grave—at least, not without a good deal of multilateral assistance. But current American actions could leave the United States a place where no human being with a conscience would care to visit, much less live.

Gardner Botsford
b. 1917, New York, New York

Late one evening in May 1944, I was having a final cup of tea with Mr and Mrs George Coward and their daughter Pamela in the living room of their semi-detached house in the outskirts of Blandford, Dorset. I was their new tenant. I had been in the UK since October, but always swaddled in the cocoon of the American army. A couple of weeks earlier, I had been assigned to the headquarters of the First US Infantry Division, now occupying a big mansion nearer the centre of town, and this allowed me to break free of the cocoon and take my first dip into civilian living since I had been a civilian myself. On the morning of our tea, I had rented the room vacated by the Cowards' son Everard, now serving with the British army in the Middle East. Mr Coward, a retired office worker, was about sixty-five, Mrs Coward a bit younger, and Pamela a pouty young woman of twenty or so who worked in the post office and was visiting her parents for the evening.

I was delighted with my new situation; I wanted to get as far away from the army as I could, and this was a long way away. The room we were sitting in could have served as the stage setting for Agatha Christie's Miss Marple mysteries: the teapot in its cosy, the photographs of the children in twisty, artistic frames, the souvenir plate from the Brighton Pavilion, the brace of last year's Christmas cards stuck in the mirror over a sideboard. The only thing seriously out of place and scale was the table we were sitting at. It was much too big for the room— six or seven feet long and four feet wide—and was draped in a cloth that reached to the floor on all four sides. It was also very solid, as unforgiving as stone when I put my teacup down on it. 'Steel,' Mrs Coward said, reading my thoughts. 'It's a Morrison table. Government model. We have no cellar for a shelter, so this is the next best thing.'

Mrs Coward was pouring her husband another cup when the air-raid sirens went off. 'Damn!' said Mr Coward. 'We could have used a bit of sleep tonight.' He got up and went to a closet in the hall where he started taking down his air-raid warden's steel helmet, a flashlight, and other warden's gear. There was a powerful thud that caused the whole house to shudder slightly. 'Damn!' Mr Coward said again.

'Oh, dear!' said Mrs Coward, sliding from her chair to the floor.

'Down by the warehouse, I'd guess,' said Mr Coward. He was a rotund man, quite short, and in his air-raid warden's steel helmet he looked a bit like Tweedledum in his saucepan hat.

'Don't forget your sandwiches, George,' said a subterranean voice at my feet. 'They're in the fridge.'

I looked down, but all I could see was Mrs Coward's rump, sticking out from under the tablecloth. The rest of her was under the table, plumping up pillows, from the sound of it. 'Pammy, bring the thermos.' With that, the rump itself disappeared under the table, followed by Pammy with the thermos. There was another thud, farther away.

'Well, I'll see you when I see you,' said Mr Coward, and disappeared through the blackout curtains at the front door.

'You can join us until the all clear if you'd like, Lieutenant,' Mrs Coward said to me from her cave. 'You can have George's place. He may not be back until morning.'

'Thanks, but I think I'll stay out here and take my chances,' I said. 'Are you comfortable in there? Not a bit crowded?'

'Mr Coward and I sleep here every night, just in case,' Mrs Coward said. 'And sometimes Pammy does, too, when it's real bad, like it was during the Blitz.'

It was a queer conversation we were having—she invisible in the depths of her lair, I sitting on my chair with my chin on my knees talking down to listeners I couldn't see.

'The enemy bombers flew right over us on their way to London,' Pammy said. 'They would drop bombs on us by mistake, or for practice or just bloody-mindedness.'

'The whole house would shake so hard that I wondered if the table would really save us if the roof and walls fell in,' Mrs Coward said. 'The government said it would, but at times like that you wonder. Poor Mr Coward—I don't think he got a real night's sleep for weeks on end.'

'He was nearly killed when a fireman's ladder fell on him,' Pamela said.

'It was very bad,' Mrs Coward said. 'But things will be better soon. It won't be long before our troops land in France, and that will set things straight. Pammy, you cannot go to Charlotte's tomorrow with your hair looking like that. Let me brush it out.'

'Oh, *mother*!' Pamela said.

'Mr Coward tells me you're from New York,' Mrs Coward said, fending off further comment from Pamela. 'I'd be scared to death. All those people rushing about.'

'London is just as big as New York,' I said.

'Oh, but London is in *England*,' Mrs Coward said.

Ten days later, I left the Cowards for good, without even saying goodbye. They would have asked where I was going, and I couldn't tell them. It was the biggest secret of the whole war. Where the First Infantry Division and I were going was to France on June 6, to try to set things straight for the Cowards and a number of other people.

Paula Fox
b. 1923, New York, New York

I was in my early twenties when I first went to Europe, full of shadowy imaginings of the countries where I was going to live, only aware at moments of unearned and questionable convictions about Europeans. I had not thought of the United States as a country in the world. It was the place where I came from.

It was the early spring of 1946, and I'd crossed the Atlantic in a partly reconverted troop carrier. I was in London and looking for work. What little professional experience I had had in the United States was in Hollywood, reading Spanish manuscripts and novels to see if they had film possibilities. I went first to the London office of Twentieth Century-Fox and got a few novels to read, then to the publisher, Victor Gollancz, at 14 Henrietta Street. His long-time reader had been knocked to the pavement by an aggrieved Irishman whose manuscript, crammed with Irish mythology and legends, she had had the temerity to reject.

With that assault in mind, Mr Gollancz advised me not to mention to anyone in what capacity I was employed by him. A month or so later, I was hired as a stringer, the lowest rung on the journalistic ladder, by a British peer who had begun a small news service.

Soon I was sent to Poland. Warsaw was a destroyed city, its ruins covered with the thick accumulation of months of snow. It was said to be the coldest winter in Europe in twenty years. As I made my way daily to the Foreign Ministry for news conferences or handouts, I wore sheets of newspaper for warmth beneath my borrowed fur coat.

I stayed in the Centralny, one of the three hotels left standing by the bombings and the Warsaw uprising. A fourth hotel had been hastily erected to accommodate delegates to the Polish Parliament which was elected during the winter months. The Centralny had been a four- or five-storey hostel for country people during the years Warsaw had been known as 'the Paris of the East'. The rooms were cells, furnished with cot, chair, a narrow wardrobe, a small basin with one working tap, and a window opposite to the door.

There was a bathroom on each floor at the end of the corridors. Marie, the hotel drudge, filled the tub for me once a week, dragging several pails of hot water, one at a time, up the stairs from the hotel cafe.

I wrote several stories about the first election to take place since the end of the war and the uprising. The outcome was a foregone conclusion: Boleslaw Bierut, a Communist and a citizen of the USSR, was elected President. From the Parliament House, I and other journalists watched as he rode in the back seat of an open Mercedes-Benz between two rows of Polish cavalrymen, mounted on restive horses, during a light snowfall on a January morning. In the afternoon I joined a large crowd at a celebratory party in a palace on the outskirts of the city. Polish ham, caviar, Tokay wine, and other delicacies were set out on a long table beneath windows through which I could see a snow-covered expanse of fields and woods.

I sent the reports to the wire service by post since the war had disrupted the usual lines of communication. Privileged journalists were patched through by telephone to their home offices in Western Europe and England.

Before I left Poland, I asked Marie for her last name so that I could leave her an envelope of my few remaining zlotys. She stared at me with an expression of utter dread as her hands flew to her mouth. Then she fled from my room.

A few minutes later I ran into a British reporter who was also staying at the Centralny. I asked him what had given her such a fright. 'You asked for her last name,' he replied. 'She was sure you were going to report her to the political branch of the police for some offence.'

A few months later I went to Spain. Franco and the Falange were still in charge of the political and social life of the country. I exchanged the hundred dollars I'd managed to save on the black market in Barcelona, where I stayed for several days with Tio Antonio, my grandmother's only surviving brother. From his apartment on one of the Ramblas, I left for Madrid. On the train I was in a third-class compartment along with a Guardia Civil, a doctor unable to practise medicine because he had been a Republican, an old woman, and several other passengers. When we crossed the Ebro river, the doctor whispered to me, 'Here many brave men died.' He glanced at the Guardia Civil who was, at that moment, taking out a canteen from his kit. He began his meal of a cold potato omelette and bread. A beggar woman came to the door of the compartment and held out her hand when she saw him eating. He tore off a bit of bread and placed it on her palm.

'What a richness he gives her!' the old woman exclaimed with an ironic smile. The Guardia Civil grunted without looking at her.

The doctor told me he saved vials of penicillin and other medicine to take to the mountains on weekends where hundreds of Republican families had sought refuge after the Spanish Civil War.

When the train stopped briefly at a station in New Castile, everyone in the compartment looked at me, their expressions full of pride. The old woman said, 'This is the birthplace of Miguel de Cervantes Saavedra.'

Eventually I boarded a freighter at Calais and returned to the United States. I had enough money left to afford a taxi which I found on the wharf. As we drove to the baggage department a few yards away, I heard the taxi driver ask the baggage clerk, 'Does she speak English?'

'I do indeed,' I said icily.

I understand better now that politics, customs, histories, are no more, no less, than direct aspects of human temperament. It is a small understanding.

I recollect the people in the Spanish train compartment, their faces guileless as they told me about Cervantes's birthplace at the station where we paused; Red Lion Square in London on a foggy evening where I felt at the centre of the world as I gazed at lighted windows, aware of the mysterious lives that were enacted behind them; the Jewish mayor of a Polish town, pausing as he led journalists, me among them, on a path in the snow, to a sign left by the Nazis. It read: NO JEW WILL EVER WALK THIS PATH AGAIN.

But what I remember most vividly these days is Warsaw, a skeleton of a great city lying beneath snow, the work of man.

Nell Freudenberger
b. 1975, New York, New York

We were in a noodle shop in Nambak in northern Laos. The shop was like the others on the road: six or eight wooden tables, a few crates of dusty soft drinks, and a glass case, empty except for one red slab of meat hanging from a hook. Perhaps it was a bit cleaner than the others, popular with out-of-towners. While we were eating, a large party of expatriate Lao pulled up in two white minivans, emblazoned with the crest of a fancy hotel: HÔTEL DE LA PRINCESSE, LUANG PRABANG.

The ladies giggled at the primitive surroundings; one of them approached our table. Her skirt was traditional woven cloth, but she wore it with a pale-pink silk sweater set and a gold necklace with semi-precious stones: garnets, amber, tourmaline. She leaned over our table. *'Qu'est-que-c'est que ça?'*

My friend Maya, who grew up partly in Paris, responded neatly in French: *'Sais pas—des legumes?'*

We were Americans, on vacation from teaching jobs in Thailand. We had chosen Laos because we would be able to use our rudimentary Thai, and in order to see Pi Mai, the Lao New Year, when people douse each other with water and line the streets of the old capital, Luang Prabang, for a spectacular parade.

In Luang Prabang, you can sit along the river and watch the orange sun ease into the Mekong like a big animal bathing. In the morning, the palm trees cast long purple shadows on the dusty roads. It was the hot season, but it rained, and the rain turned the roads to mud and puddles and, underneath the stilted houses, made shallow lakes, which choked up immediately with lime-coloured moss and lilies. Civil servants and schoolchildren paddled from home to the road in two-person wooden skiffs. In all of the government offices, the telephone exchange and the state airline, we saw calendars: VISIT LAOS YEAR 1999 and LAOS: YOUR NEW LOVE.

It was only 1998, but we loved Laos already.

The party of tourists in the noodle shop took up so much space that at first we didn't notice the tall foreigner who had come in just behind them.

'Can I sit with you?' he asked.

We made room at the table, and Peter introduced himself. He told us he was an agronomist, doing development work for the European Union. He was tall, with green eyes and Nordic features; he spoke heavily accented, nearly perfect English.

'Are you German?' I guessed.

Peter opened his eyes wide, in exaggerated surprise. 'Danish.'

I'd made that mistake before: the first time was even worse, with a group of backpackers who turned out to be Israeli.

'Are *you* German?' he said, teasing us.

When we told Peter that we were Americans, he raised his eyebrows. 'Why do you speak languages then?'

Before we met Peter, we had visited one village. We arrived by boat, in the evening, and wandered through the thatched houses, trailed by children and wild pigs. The children took us to the temple, with its one gap-toothed monk, and to an abandoned school, where the blackboard was mottled and cracked from humidity and the chairs, stacked upside down on the tables, looked as if they'd been looted from time to time for firewood. Spiders were colonizing what was left with dense, white webs.

The village on the riverbank was poor, but charming—the place Peter took us was just poor. We arrived in the middle of the day, when there was no shade. The houses seemed to cling to the side of the road; occasionally a truck would speed by, whipping up dust. Young men lay on the porches of the grey houses in the middle of the afternoon, resting. It was the kind of place, Peter said, where people ate enough rice to keep going, but not enough to do much more than that. The villagers had moved down from the hills after the government dammed the river, to create a picnicking waterfall for tourists.

We were going to hike to the home village. While Peter talked to the headman, Maya and I waited by the trail head. There was a particularly squalid-looking small hut, set apart from the other buildings, which looked like an outhouse. I needed an outhouse badly.

'Use that,' Maya joked.

I looked at Peter, whose attention was focused on the headman. Unlike a lot of NGO people, he was able to be both passionate about his project and a little self-deprecating. When he talked to the Lao, he made fun of himself as the hapless, bumbling foreigner. Clearly, he was the opposite. Everywhere we went people seemed to know him; the women flirted, and the men fought to talk to him. When he tried to make the traditional gesture of respect, people clustered around him and insisted on shaking his hand.

I imagined what he must think of us: babies, from America, bewildered by the smallest hardships—and I decided I could use the hut. In retrospect, I remember a skull and crossbones over the door. I remember two men watching me with interest, or concern. It was difficult to get inside (I had to crouch down and almost crawl) but once I'd begun, it seemed humiliating to turn back.

Inside, it was surprisingly dim and cool. There was a dry, shallow impression in the dirt. Next to this was a clean tin bowl—also, strangely, dry. I peed on the dust, keeping an eye on the little door. I felt exposed, but it wasn't unpleasant in there. In fact, in the shade, it was much better than outside. There was no smell at all.

When I came out, one of the two men had wrapped a sarong around his waist and stood up. He was looking in my direction, shading his eyes with his hand.

'It was fine,' I told Maya, but I knew I'd done something wrong.

Peter, immersed in his conversation with the headman, hadn't noticed anything.

'They promised a water project for them here. That's why they moved.' He shook his head. 'It's been a year, and still no project.'

'Is that the outhouse?'

'What?'

I pointed.

'The toilet?' Peter looked at the hut and raised his eyebrows. 'I hope so,' he said.

We were part of an experiment, Peter said: sample ecotourists. The government was considering a suggestion by Western ecologists: that Laos could best develop by remaining backward. This was an idea about which Peter was deeply sceptical.

'Is this interesting for you?' he would ask us periodically. 'Would you pay to do this?' 'Is this fun?'

We followed the ravine into the hills. On our left was a stream, and on our right, a few cultivated rice paddies. In the water alongside the paddies, submerged water buffalo flared their nostrils and stretched their necks to look at us.

'Stop,' said Peter, and a moment later we heard a dry rustling sound. Three little boys were coming along the path. The biggest was carrying a trio of dead birds, tied by their feet on a string.

'Hunting?' Peter asked them. The boys nodded.

'To eat?' Another nod. Peter examined the birds: they were very small, white with black speckles. 'Not much meat.' The children nodded politely, and moved on.

Just before we entered the canopy of monsoon forest, Peter pointed out a rusted canister in the grass. 'Some of the caves up there are still full of these things from the war.'

'The Vietnam War?'

'Well, they don't call it that,' Peter said.

'They were fighting here too?'

'Didn't you learn about this in college?' Peter asked.

I looked at Maya. 'Vietnam, a little—not Laos.'

He gave us some of the statistics: 200,000 dead, 580,000 American air sorties, two million tons of bombs dropped, or more than two tons for every inhabitant—an average of one planeload of bombs every eight minutes for nine years.

'You didn't learn about that?'

'No.'

Peter looked at us with something like awe.

When we got back to the village, Peter remembered to ask the headman about the outhouse. The man frowned, and shook his head vehemently. Peter indicated that we should go back to the jeep.

'Not the toilet?' I asked him, although I already knew.

'No.'

'What was it?'

'I didn't understand the word,' he said. 'It was an old word—for a ceremonial kitchen, maybe. Or a crematorium.'

'I'm so sorry,' I said. I wished he would say something then, or even get angry. 'I feel like I sabotaged your development project.'

Peter looked at me in the rear-view mirror.

'It's not my development project,' he said gently. 'It's theirs.'

After Peter left us that day, I developed an ache just below my ribcage. I had trouble sleeping.

'It was an accident,' Maya told me. 'You didn't know.' She couldn't help smiling. I knew there was something absurd about this situation—a story about public (or at least semi-private) urination—but I couldn't see it. I took long walks by myself. I had the sort of anxiety that makes you want to keep moving, as if it were possible to walk away from yourself.

One afternoon, a few days later, I came back to the guest house and the woman behind the desk handed me a message. On a piece of paper from the best hotel in town:

Girls who would like to see a village should get up early. If you aren't outside at seven on Friday, I will leave without you—Peter.

On our last day with Peter, we reached the plateau: about a square mile of dry grass, surrounded by low grey boulders. In the crevices between the boulders were the caves where might still be unexploded ordnance. In the distance some farmers were building a house, or a barn: they had only erected the skeleton, but the sun had bleached the bamboo so white that you had to squint to see it against the sky.

We had been walking for two hours before I got up the courage to tell Peter how sorry I was.

'I know,' he said.

'Have you ever made a mistake in one of these places?'

Peter smiled. 'Once I drank too much *lao-lao* at a wedding, and fell asleep in the family shrine. They had to sacrifice some chickens.'

'That's better than what I did.' I was hoping he would contradict me.

Peter smiled. 'For you it'll be a buffalo.'

He was trying to cheer me up, but somehow that made me feel worse. 'Couldn't I make a contribution?'

'You could devote your life to development work in Laos.'

It was sometimes hard to tell when he was kidding.

We finished our hike at the waterfall, where Thai teenagers were drinking Singha beer, and eating roast chicken with papaya salad. They wore bandannas and carried boom boxes on their shoulders. They took photographs in front of the falls. We stopped to get something to eat at one of the stands, and when we turned around, Peter was gone.

I waited in vain for another note. The last time we saw Peter was at one of the New Year's parades, which he'd obviously been invited to join. He was at least two heads taller than anyone around him, and he was walking with his eyes closed, carried along by the movement of the crowd. Somehow this didn't look silly or pretentious. He looked like he was where he belonged.

It wasn't so much the numbers Peter told us on the trail, but the fact that we hadn't known them, that made the statistics horrifying. (I find it very hard to remember history or geography unless I've been to the place in question; I'm not sure whether this is a personal failing or an American one.) If it weren't for a noodle shop in Nambak, I would probably never have thought about what 'we' did in Laos; it was an accident that I learned to feel anything at all about the Secret War.

But then, ignorance is no excuse. It's obvious to me now that you can do a terrible thing by accident.

Paul Fussell
b. 1924, Pasadena, California

Granta's invitation to join this silent round table deployed the term 'world' as if it carried a simple meaning understood and accepted by all, as in 'the world beyond the USA' and 'the rest of the world'. The world is a lot more varied, irrational, and inexplicable then those easy phrases imply. I would warn especially against expressions like Secretary of State Colin Powell's favourite, 'the international community', which in its optimistic misrepresentation carries only the authority of top jargon. Languages alone divide 'the world' into hundreds of jurisdictions notable for not understanding the idiom of even their closest neighbour, and idiom includes much more than spoken or written words. It includes everything ignored by American language study, like hand gestures, eye movement, and eyebrow elevation as a signal of disbelief. We can ask: How many top dogs now busy in Iraq know enough of the local languages and, as important, the appropriate gestures even to tell a successful dirty joke?

My 'world' includes Germany, France and England where I have managed to live during periods of American national disgrace, like the Vietnam War and Richard Nixon's crimes and non-punishment. And I'm familiar with at least the folkways in Turkey and Iran, Russia and Lithuania, China and Hong Kong, Japan and India and Egypt and Israel, enough to be sceptical of any simplifying version of a sensible, unified 'world'. In my eighty years, I have noticed enough things outside America to sense that what is good in Sierra Leone is not necessarily beneficial in Pakistan, and to observe preeminently that with languages, expecting exact translation is naive and likely to be dangerous. The current attempt to impose US-style 'democracy' on the Middle East by means of language is not just vainglorious and economically cynical. It is preposterous and intellectually disgusting.

The military survivors of the Second World War who saw the world in ruin have a right to sense that they have witnessed the end of European pretences to cultural authority. For them, Europe remains a place perhaps to travel to but is now stained so deeply by folly and cruelty as no longer to justify the reverence Henry James and others once lavished on it as an immutable guide to manners and intellectual technique.

It seems true that first impulses are the strongest and magically most able to survive what follows. My first impression of the world outside America was delivered at Marseilles when the US Army caused me to enter France in 1944, and shipped me into a less genteel and stylish port than Calais. Marseilles and environs are still powerfully attending on me and I feel a distinct ally of Cyril Connolly who recalls 'sizzling down the long black liquid reaches of Nationale Sept, the plane-trees going sha-sha-sha through the open window...she with the *Michelin* beside me, a handkerchief binding her hair.' It happens that I knew the Mediterranean world and its appeals and usages before I was acquainted with London or Paris, and it was to that version of the world that after the war I escaped whenever possible. This is to say that the world outside America opens itself to me as more hedonistic and aesthetic than diplomatic or moral-political or intellectual.

This is my confession of hopeless Mediterraneanism and of the undemocratic feeling that America's extensive future is now nowhere near reposing in my hands, or even anxious for my opinions. At the same time, as one who has been roughed up at the airport at Tehran, and in Egypt stoned as an unwanted foreigner by perfectly nice people, I'm aware that the religious intensities propelling anti-American violence are unlikely to melt away into a universal peaceable secularism. But it's not world uniformity that I want. It's variety and oddity and unfamiliarity. And I cannot avoid saying that my experience of abroad has in the long run deepened my fondness for America, with its nice toilets and showers and its precious First

Amendment, encouraging writers to praise and damn without fear of arrest. For that, I'm willing to bear any amount of national ignorance and stupidity.

Charles Glass
b. 1951, Los Angeles, California

Fidelina, my stepmother's loyal maid from El Salvador, packed the fried chicken in tin foil and put it into a basket with Californian apples and slices of cake. Suspicious of food provided by airlines and expecting Lebanon's cooks to poison me, she laid on enough food for a week. At Los Angeles I boarded Pan Am One, the American flagship's round-the-world flight, in the late summer of 1972, for what was to have been a year of graduate study. America was never home to me again.

It was dark when a taxi driver at Beirut airport deposited my Samsonite suitcases in the back of an old Mercedes and delivered them and me to a hotel, the Astra, that he recommended near the Rue Hamra. The room was small and squalid, concrete walls and bare tiles, the shower a mere spigot in the ceiling that dripped water straight on to the bathroom floor.

I went outside and found a bar, where a woman sat next to me and ordered champagne. The bartender charged me ten dollars for the beer and a hundred dollars for her champagne. I refused to pay, and he poked a snub-nose .38 into my head. I returned to the hotel and ate Fidelina's southern fried chicken. A few days later, the chicken pieces, my last taste of America, were gone.

The world looked strange through my eyes—my conservative, Republican, privileged, Christian eyes. The life I had left—early and bitter parental divorce, maternal depression and suicide, childhood memories of hanging on to a pendulum that whirled between wealth and penury—was less certain than my political orthodoxy. My friends in Lebanon knew nothing of family break-ups and psychiatry. Instead, they were terrorized. Rashid Hamid was born in Ain Zeitoun, a village near Safad in the Galilee, that the Israeli army razed when he was two. I used to visit his family in their refugee camp, Ain el-Hilweh, in the south. I was there on the day that Israeli warplanes, manufactured in and donated by the United States of America to which I had pledged my allegiance, dropped a 2,000-

pound bomb on the school where his brothers and sisters studied. Ten children and two adults slept in one room, over which the Lebanese government prohibited the construction of anything more substantial than a tin roof lest the Palestinians become permanent residents. In 1972, the Hamids had already been there for twenty-two years. Ten years later, Israeli invasion forces bulldozed every house, including theirs, in the camp. It was around that time that Rashid, whose life made him the best political analyst I ever met, predicted that Lebanese Christian militiamen would massacre Palestinians when Yasser Arafat's commandos evacuated Beirut.

Antebellum Lebanon was a playground for the international riff-raff who added it, after the Alps and the Côte d'Azur, to their seasonal migrations. The allure of the country rested, however, on local dissidents and political exiles. There were old White Russian ladies who taught piano; thousands of Armenians scarred with memories of Eurasia's first modern genocide; rebels from southern Sudan, who could not live under the treaty their leaders signed with the Arab north; ancien régime Syrians and Egyptians longing for the restoration of their nationalized properties in what had become socialist republics; guerrillas from Eritrea fighting to break out of Haile Selassie's Amharic empire; Kurds demanding independence for their people in Turkey or Iran or Iraq and trying to warn the world about Saddam Hussein; Palestinian poets who dreamed of taking coffee on the stone verandas of houses that were no longer standing; Yemeni royalists and republicans; communists escaping torture and summary execution in Iraq and Iran; a few democrats from Saudi Arabia who feared assassination at home. They had their beer halls and coffee houses, where they intrigued and argued and despaired and let naive American kids listen. A friend of mine hijacked an airplane. No one died. A few years later, he married, had twins and took an executive job with an American corporation. Lebanon was like that then.

When I boarded Pan Am One, I knew nothing except for what the nuns and priests and culture of California and its corporations had taught me. A twenty-one-year-old quiet American, I learned slowly the political intricacies of countries that my teachers had never mentioned. I shared an apartment with an Afghan girl and hosted evenings of Afghan politics, music and food. I shed belief after belief, some of which the boy on Pan Am One would have died, and probably killed, for. It took time. As late as April 1975, I was unhappy to see the American flag lowered from the embassy in Saigon. There was no single epiphany, but over the years came knowledge that running out of Fidelina's chicken would not leave me or the world hungry.

I used to resent hearing the word 'American' combined with 'imperialism'. It is now the fact rather than the epithet that causes revulsion. America dispatches its armies to most of the world, but its other exports dominate as well: corporate logos, security guards, medical companies, accountants, bankers, contractors, computer wizards, advertising agencies, evangelical missionaries, television channels, Hollywood films, baseball caps, T-shirts, Cokes and hamburgers. The flag's shadow falls dark on foreign climes, and the nation's boot-step digs deep. America killed two million Vietnamese. How many Arabs will go? Ours is an empire without borders, without limits, without the restraining hand of a rival. It is military, cultural, economic, psychological. It standardizes—standardize is itself an American neologism from the industrial era—man on the American model. A good Arab—or African or Chinese—is one who speaks English and studied at Harvard, an honorary American, almost one of us.

While empire treads on its dominions, the metropolis acquires colonial characteristics. The English eat curry, French women boil couscous. American plutocrats learn from the example of colleagues in Colombia and Mexico that life protected by bodyguards and kidnap insurance is at least as desirable as diminishing their wealth. Thus the *laagers* of white South Africa and the barricaded enclaves of Bogotá become the gated communities of Orange County.

Joseph Roth, that elegiac chronicler of the fading Austro-Hungarian Empire, wrote in one of his short stories, 'Towards the end of the nineteenth century, the people of my native place were of two sorts: they were either very poor or very rich. To put it another way, there were masters and servants.' It did not last.

Chris Hedges
b. 1956, Johnsbury, Vermont
In May 2003, New York Times correspondent Chris Hedges gave the Commencement Address at Rockford College in Rockford, Illinois. During the speech students in the audience climbed the stage

to disrupt him, and he was escorted out by the police before the ceremony concluded. Subsequently the president of the college apologized to students for having invited Hedges, and the New York Times *sent Hedges a letter of reprimand. This is what Hedges said in Rockford:*

I want to speak to you today about war and empire.

The killing, or at least the worst of it, is over in Iraq. Although blood will continue to spill—theirs and ours—be prepared for this. For we are embarking on an occupation that, if history is any guide, will be as damaging to our souls as it will be to our prestige, power and security. But this will come later as our empire expands. And in all this we become pariahs, tyrants to others weaker than ourselves. Isolation always impairs judgement, and we are very isolated now.

We have forfeited the goodwill, the empathy the world felt for us after 9/11. We have folded in on ourselves, we have severely weakened the delicate international coalitions and alliances that are vital in maintaining and promoting peace. And we are part now of a dubious troika in the war against terror with Vladimir Putin and Ariel Sharon, two leaders who do not shrink in Palestine or Chechnya from carrying out acts of gratuitous and senseless acts of violence. We have become the company we keep.

The censure, and perhaps the rage, of much of the world— certainly one-fifth of the world's population which is Muslim, most of whom I will remind you are not Arab, is upon us. Look today at the fourteen people killed last night in several explosions in Casablanca. And this rage, in a world where almost fifty per cent of the planet struggles on less than two dollars a day, will see us targeted. Terrorism will become a way of life. *(Someone in the crowd shouts, 'No!')* And when we are attacked, we will, like our allies Putin and Sharon, lash out with greater fury.

The circle of violence is a death spiral; no one escapes. We are spinning at a speed that we may not be able to halt. As we revel in our military prowess—the sophistication of our military hardware and technology, for this is what most of the press coverage consisted of in Iraq—we lose sight of the fact that just because we have the capacity to wage war it does not give us the right to wage war. This capacity has doomed empires in the past.

'Modern western civilization may perish,' the theologian Reinhold

Niebuhr warned, 'because it falsely worshipped technology as a final good.'

The real injustices—the Israeli occupation of Palestinian land, the brutal and corrupt dictatorships we fund in the Middle East—will mean that we will not rid the extremists who hate us with bombs. Indeed, we will swell their ranks. *(Whistles.)* Once you master people by force you depend on force for control. In your isolation you begin to make mistakes. *('Where were you on September 11?')*

Fear engenders cruelty; cruelty…fear, insanity, and then paralysis. *(Hoots. 'Who wants to listen to this jerk?')* In the centre of Dante's circle the damned remained motionless. *(Horns.)* We have blundered into a nation we know little about and are caught between bitter rivalries and competing ethnic groups and leaders we do not understand.

We are trying to transplant a modern system of politics invented in Europe characterized, among other things, by the division of earth into independent secular states based on national citizenship in a land where the belief in a secular civil government is an alien creed. Iraq was a cesspool for the British when they occupied it in 1917. It will be a cesspool for us, as well. *('God bless America,' a woman yells.)* The curfews, the armed clashes with angry crowds that leave scores of Iraqi dead, the military governor, the Christian Evangelical groups who are being allowed to follow on the heels of our occupying troops to try and teach Muslims about Jesus, the occupation of the oilfields.

(At this point, the microphone gets unplugged. When it is fixed, Rockford College President Paul C. Pribbenow addresses the audience: 'My friends, one of the wonders of a liberal arts college is its ability and its deeply held commitment to academic freedom and the decision to listen to each other's opinions. If you wish to protest the speaker's remarks, I ask that you do it in silence, as some of you are doing in the back. That is perfectly appropriate, but he has the right to offer his opinion here, and we would like him to continue his remarks.' People blow horns and boo and some applaud.)

The occupation of the oilfields. *(More boos. A woman says, 'We're not going to listen. We've listened enough. You've already ruined our graduation. Don't ruin it any more, sir.')* The notion that the Kurds and the Shiites will listen to the demands of a centralized government in Baghdad (the same Kurds and Shiites who died by the tens of thousands in defiance of Saddam Hussein, a man who happily butchered all of those who challenged him, and this ethnic rivalry has not gone away). The looting of Baghdad, or let me say the looting of Baghdad with the exception of the oil ministry and the interior ministry—the only two ministries we bothered protecting—is self-immolation. *(More boos.)*

As someone who knows Iraq, speaks Arabic, and spent seven years in the Middle East, if the Iraqis believe rightly or wrongly that we come only for oil and occupation, they will begin a long, bloody war of attrition. It is how they drove the British out. And remember that, when the Israelis invaded southern Lebanon in 1982, they were greeted by the dispossessed Shiites as liberators, but within a few months, when the Shiites saw that the Israelis had come not as liberators but as occupiers, they began to kill them. It was Israel who created Hezbollah, and it was Hezbollah that pushed Israel out of southern Lebanon.

As William Butler Yeats wrote in 'Meditations in Time of Civil War', 'We had fed the heart on fantasies/The heart's grown brutal from the fare.' *(Horns. 'I never would have come if I knew I had to listen to this,' a woman yells.)*

This is a war of liberation in Iraq, but it is a war now of liberation by Iraqis from American occupation. And if you watch closely what is happening in Iraq, if you can see it through the abysmal coverage, you can see it in the lashing out of the terrorist death squads, the murder of Shiite leaders in mosques, and the assassination of our young soldiers in the streets. It is one that will soon be joined by Islamic radicals and we are far less secure today than we were before we bumbled into Iraq. *('USA, USA,' some in the crowd chant.)*

We will pay for this, but what saddens me most is that those who will, by and large, pay the highest price are poor kids from Mississippi or Alabama or Texas who could not get a decent job or health insurance and joined the army because it was all we offered them. For war in the end is always about betrayal, betrayal of the young by the old, of soldiers by politicians, and of idealists by cynics. Read *Antigone*, when the king imposes his will without listening to those he rules, or Thucydides' history. *(Heckling.)* Read how Athens' expanding empire saw it become a tyrant abroad and then a tyrant at home, how the tyranny the Athenian leadership imposed on others it finally imposed on itself.

This, Thucydides wrote, is what doomed Athenian democracy; Athens destroyed itself. For the instrument of empire is war, and war is a poison, a poison which at times we must ingest just as a cancer patient must ingest a poison to survive. But if we do not understand the poison of war—if we do not understand how deadly that poison is—it can kill us just as surely as the disease. *('It's enough, it's enough, it's enough,' a woman says.)*

We have lost touch with the essence of war. Following our defeat in Vietnam we became a better nation. We were humbled, even humiliated. We asked questions about ourselves we had not asked before.

We were forced to see ourselves as others saw us, and the sight was not always a pretty one. We were forced to confront our own capacity for atrocity—for evil—and in this we understood not only war but more about ourselves. But that humility is gone.

War, we have come to believe, is a spectator sport. The military and the press—remember in wartime the press is always part of the problem—have turned war into a vast video arcade game. Its very essence—death—is hidden from public view.

There was no more candour in the Persian Gulf War or the war in Afghanistan or the war in Iraq than there was in Vietnam. *(Horns.)* But in the age of live feeds and satellite television, the state and the military have perfected the appearance of candour. *(Heckling.)*

Because we no longer understand war, we no longer understand that it can all go horribly wrong. We no longer understand that war begins by calling for the annihilation of others but ends, if we do not know when to make or maintain peace, with self-annihilation. We flirt, given the potency of modern weapons, with our own destruction. *('That's not true!')*

The seduction of war is insidious because so much of what we are told about it is true: it does create a feeling of comradeship, which obliterates our alienation and makes us, for perhaps the only time of our life, feel we belong.

War allows us to rise above our small stations in life. We find nobility in a cause and feelings of selflessness and even bliss. And at a time of soaring deficits and financial scandals and the very deterioration of our domestic fabric, war is a fine diversion. War, for those who enter into combat, has a dark beauty, filled with the monstrous and the grotesque. The Bible calls it the lust of the eye and warns believers against it. War gives us a distorted sense of self; it gives us meaning. *(Shouts of 'Go home!' Then a man in the audience climbs to the stage and says, 'Can I say a few words here?' Hedges responds, 'When I finish—yeah, when I finish.')*

Once in war, the conflict obliterates the past and the future all is one heady intoxicating present. You feel every heartbeat in war, colours are brighter, your mind races ahead of itself.

(Boos, and the microphone is unplugged momentarily again. 'Should I keep going?' Hedges asks President Pribbenow, who responds, 'It's up to you.' Hedges asks, 'Do you want me to stop?' Pribbenow says, 'How close are you? Why don't you bring it to a close?' More shouts of 'Go home!' One person says, 'It's not your graduation.')

We feel in wartime comradeship. *(Many loud boos.)* We confuse this with friendship, with love. There are those who will insist that the comradeship of war is love. The exotic glow that makes us in war feel as one people, one entity, is real, but this is part of war's intoxication. *(More boos.)*

Think back on the days after the attacks on 9/11. Suddenly we no longer felt alone; we connected with strangers, even with people we did not like. We felt we belonged, that we were somehow wrapped in the embrace of the nation, the community. In short, we no longer felt alienated. *('Go home!')*

As this feeling dissipated in the weeks after the attack, there was a kind of nostalgia for its warm glow. And wartime always brings with it this comradeship, which is the opposite of friendship. Friends, as J. Glenn Gray points out, are predetermined; friendship takes place between men and women who possess an intellectual and emotional affinity for each other. But comradeship—that ecstatic bliss that comes with belonging to the crowd in wartime—is within our reach. We can all have comrades.

The danger of the external threat that comes when we have an enemy does not create friendship; it creates comradeship. And those in wartime are deceived about what they are undergoing. And this is why once the threat is over, once war ends, comrades again become strangers to us. This is why, after war, we fall into despair. *('Atheist stranger!')*

In friendship there is a deepening of our sense of self. We become, through the friend, more aware of who we are and what we are about; we find ourselves in the eyes of the friend. Friends probe and question and challenge each other to make each of us more complete. In comradeship, the kind that comes to us in patriotic fervour, there is a suppression of self-awareness, self-knowledge and self-possession. *(Heckling.)* Comrades lose their identities in wartime for the collective rush of a common cause—a common purpose. In comradeship there are no demands on the self. This is part of its appeal and one of the reasons we miss it and seek to recreate it. *('Go home! Go home!')* Comradeship allows us to escape the demands on the self that is part of friendship.

In wartime when we feel threatened, we no longer face death alone but as a group, and this makes death easier to bear. We ennoble self-sacrifice for the other, for the comrade. *(Boos.)* In short we begin to worship death. And this is what the god of war demands of us.

Think finally of what it means to die for a friend. It is deliberate and painful; there is no ecstasy. For friends, dying is hard and bitter. The dialogue they have and cherish will perhaps never be recreated. Friends do not, the way comrades do, love death and sacrifice. To friends, the prospect of death is frightening. And this is why friendship—or, let me say love—is the most potent enemy of war. Thank you.

(Loud boos, whistles, horns, a little applause. A man says, 'This is the most destructive thing you've ever done to this college, Dr Pribbenow. You should never have allowed him to speak.')

Adam Hochschild
b. 1942, New York, New York

My first real encounter with the world outside the United States came in 1962, when I spent several months working for an anti-government newspaper in South Africa. Some of the people I came to know had spent time in jail; some would spend a good deal more, and one was later hanged. The battle against apartheid was my first exposure to serious politics, and to a nineteen-year-old, as I was then, it was overwhelming. Part of the experience was realizing that the USA was on the wrong side. Fine speeches at the United Nations were one thing, but the directory board in the lobby of the American Embassy in

Pretoria, with its long list of military attachés, told a different story. A local CIA man, hearing I was working for the newspaper, tried to find out from me all he could about what this particular band of anti-apartheid activists were doing. (I ran into him again forty years later, now retired and looking a little shrivelled, working as a 'consultant' in Washington.) Learning something of the cooperation between the USA and the white regime in South Africa—a sorry record whose full extent we know much more about today—was my first lesson that America was not always the noble force for freedom I wanted it to be. A few years afterwards, the Vietnam War underlined that lesson, for me and for millions of other Americans of my generation.

Later encounters with the rest of the world have underlined it in different ways. Despite President Bush's cowboy foray into Iraq, the way most nations experience American might these days is not military, but economic. Time abroad is always an education. I had not thought much about globalization until my wife and I lived for six months in India in the late 1990s. To read even India's mainstream newspapers was a revelation. Indians were outraged by American corporate attempts to patent basmati rice and a medicinal extract of the neem tree, products that Indians had been using for centuries. The local press abundantly covered an agreement then being signed, urged on the rest of the world by the United States and Europe, regarding free trade in 'financial services'. Under it, American banks, insurance companies, investment firms and the like can now get access to customers in countries like India, while their Indian counterparts, of course, can in theory have equal access to the American market. Guess which country's companies have the capital and infrastructure to come out ahead? The Indian papers quoted despairing and angry finance officials from Third World countries, even those which are usually compliant American allies. The accord went almost unreported by the US media.

To travel anywhere these days with open eyes is to see a world dominated by an increasingly arrogant superpower. When it comes to a different kind of international agreement, those of which the human race has reason to be proud, the United States has refused to sign almost all of them: the treaty establishing the International Criminal Court, the ban on landmines, the Kyoto accords on global warming and many, many others. Probably this is no greater arrogance than was shown by superpowers of the past, from the Roman Empire to the British to the Soviets when they shared that status with us, but today we live in a world where the stakes are higher. For America to defy even the universal scientific warnings about climate change, for example, is to defy Nature itself. It recalls the arrogance of the Persian emperor Xerxes, hindered by a storm in crossing the Dardanelles to invade Greece in 480 BC, ordering his soldiers to whip the sea.

And yet, another type of image appears in the mirror the world holds up to Americans. The children of a neighbour of ours in India, a high official in the Communist-led government of the state where we lived, had chosen to live in the United States. It was not money which had lured them, for the family was well off. Rather, the die had been cast, my neighbour thought, many years before, when, spending a year in the USA, he had sent his son to an American high school. To be treated as an individual, in a school unlike the regimented ones he had known previously, was staggering; the boy came home the first day saying, 'This place is for me.'

From the classes I've taught and experienced abroad, I've come to understand why hundreds of thousands of people from all over the world scrape together the money to study in the United States. In Indian universities, I was expected to hold forth from a raised platform, while the men sat on one side of the room and the women on the other. My first act was always to ignore the platform and rearrange chairs in a circle, but even so it was like pulling teeth to introduce the idea of no-holds-barred discussion. I can still recall my triumphant joy when finally a student summoned up the courage to disagree with me.

At a workshop for newspaper editors in Zambia, I tried to put students at ease by saying, American-style, 'I've never done anything exactly like this before, so I'm hoping to learn as much from this as you.' The workshop seemed successful, despite an unexpected visit by the Information Minister, who had once jailed one of the participants. But at the end of it, one of the editors wrote on his evaluation form, 'Instructor was very competent and the material covered was very useful. But he said he had never taught such a course before. Was he properly qualified?'

And in Russia, I sat through a history class in one of the most elite high schools which consisted of one student after another, when called on by the teacher, standing up to nervously summarize a portion of the textbook.

Sure, many come to the United States simply for an American degree, which is often a ticket to a good job. But education systems always reflect the larger society, and if the arrogance of American military and economic power reflects the worst about us, our schools and colleges, at their best, reflect something more hopeful. What that is, I think, is more than just the tradition of free speech—something Americans did not invent, after all, and which, happily, we have no monopoly on. Rather it is a marked indifference to rank and hierarchy. If the American language had a second person familiar form, we'd use it with everybody, just the way Americans assume the right to call strangers by their first names. Paradoxically, this American informality coexists with a far more unequal distribution of income than one finds in Europe and in many other countries. We may not be economically equal, but we assume a kind of social equality with others, and it is this, I think, which lies at the bottom of much of what I love about American life, from the liveliness of its classrooms to the inventiveness that continues to shape the Internet, to the thousands of civic organizations whose progenitors caught the eye of Alexis de Tocqueville more than a century and a half ago.

American democracy is at risk today from many sides: from media ownership concentration, from the power of money in politics, from the red scare atmosphere of our nebulous war on terror and Islamic fundamentalism, and from an administration that has a touch of fundamentalism of its own. But even an American society that has suffered the depredations of George W. Bush and John Ashcroft holds more hope as a model than one shaped by the caste system of India, the lockstep vision of al-Qaida and its supporters, the ethnic rivalries of the Balkans, or the strongman politics of most of Africa, Central Asia and the Arab world.

This, to me, is the paradox: that what is, at home, perhaps the most vibrant civil society on earth is, abroad, a trigger-happy superpower of terrifying arrogance. If there is a single hope I have for my country it is that the great promise of the one can begin to rescue us from the great dangers of the other.

A. M. Homes
b. 1961, Washington DC

In 1970 my school class was invited to the White House for Richard Nixon's welcoming of the new French president, Georges Pompidou. I played in the grass at the far edge of the south lawn while Nixon's speech echoed, only stopping to listen when Pompidou responded in French. My grandfather was French. I took French class in the mornings before school and Hebrew class after it and before long I combined the two into a language of my own. My classmates made so much fun of me that I later dropped both languages. But at that moment, Georges Pompidou sounded like a good person to be friends with, someone who would be friends with the other George— Curious George, someone who would have interesting people, like Babar, over for dinner. In my nine-year-old mind, Babar the elephant was also a person and in many ways, Babar and his family of elephants were my first exposure to the world outside my own: they travelled around the world, went on adventures, wore nice custom-made suits—and the books were written by a Frenchman.

My sense of the world outside America (which I inherited from my parents) was that it was better, more cultured, sophisticated. But I also had my own, youthful, deeply American fear of anything old— things that had previously belonged to anyone were dirty, grotesque, scary and overwhelming. History was hard to handle.

First there was the strangeness of my growing up; I am a native of a city that belongs to no state—Washington DC. In my neighbourhood, the CIA and FBI went door to door collecting information like little old ladies collecting for charity. They wanted to know if we'd noticed anything suspicious at the neighbours' house—people coming and going at odd hours, people from other places, or did they say *races*? Men in unmarked sedans would cruise the streets. We would see the Nixon girls perpetually shopping for shoes in Saks Fifth Avenue; our bicycles would be stolen by children who could not be held responsible because they had diplomatic immunity. It was a company town where the company kept changing. Friends and neighbours turned over every four years as the political tides shifted. Instead of selling Girl Scout cookies we went door to door hawking political memorabilia—Hubert Horatio Humphrey key-chains and ashtrays that we made in someone's basement. My friends' fathers were spies, not like peeping Toms, but men whose professions were entirely unknown. 'What does your dad do?' I would ask. 'Dunno, I'm not supposed to ask,' my friends would say.

When I was a teenager practising the fine art of rock and roll in the afternoons after school, blasting my guitar and screaming into a microphone, the East German Ambassador moved into the house just behind ours. At a party he asked, 'Who is the black man singing punk rock at that house up the hill?' and someone told him, 'The Homes girl.' When this scene was relayed to me it was the greatest compliment I'd ever received—akin to Mick Jagger being told he sang like a Negro. Not only did I sound black but I sounded like a man.

I was eleven when my family went to Europe. London was everything it should be: a tourist fantasy land, the pomp and circumstance of the Changing of the Guard, the notion that the Queen herself might step out and say hello, the food hall at Harrods, tea in the afternoons, the discovery of room service and most importantly, *orange squash*. I wanted to bring bottles of the concentrate home but my parents lied, saying it was illegal to take it out of the country. I fell asleep at an Athol Fugard play and woke up to see a naked man pulling up his pants on stage. I had an ice cream at intermission.

London was classy, civilized, and a little sad; as though tea for the average Englishman was less Fortnum & Mason and more a cracked pot with a crocheted cosy. My parents spoke about problems of class, the complications of a monarchy, the troubles in Northern Ireland. There were tanks at the airports and soldiers on balconies. The Tower of London—where a bomb had recently exploded and taken off someone's foot—was closed. There was a sign at the Victoria and Albert Museum announcing that there was a bomb threat and that we were viewing at our own risk.

And then we went to Paris where I was fascinated by filterless cigarettes and darting tongues spitting out bits of tobacco. When no one was looking I bought a pack of Gauloise and later, at home, lit one. I nearly passed out from the intensity. Paris was *pain-au-chocolat*, cafes, tiny cars, motorbikes, *joie de vivre* and cobblestones. We went to the building on the Rue Vielle du Temple where my grandfather had lived as a boy. His family had had a small apartment on the inside of a courtyard—they had all moved away long ago but their name was still on the bell. My mother and grandmother stood in front of this old building—my grandfather had died the year before. They told the story of how my grandfather's little sister had died in a fire; their parents weren't home and my grandfather and his brothers tried to put out the flames. Every time I am in Paris I visit this building and look up at the windows, trying to imagine how painful it must have been for my grandfather to watch his little sister go up in flames. I think of how that building and all of the buildings around it will always be there. They won't be knocked down by someone who wants to build a bigger building, or disappear like the Massachusetts dairy farm where my grandmother grew up which is now an ugly housing development.

We visited our cousins in their new house in a suburban neighbourhood just outside of Paris—he worked for El Al airlines and she was a radiological technician; together they had three boys and were so pleased with their beautiful one hundred per cent modern house in their entirely new town. They served steak. They served steak so rare it was dripping in blood—*bleu*, they called it. I kept asking could they cook it more; by the time it was barely rare they were convinced I was crazy and that the meat was ruined. The old white-haired, whiskered ladies of the family looked at me and clucked in French.

I grew up in a generation where everything was clean and modern and sanitized—wrapped like a hotel drinking glass. We prided ourselves on putting cold, clear ice in our drinks and there was a whole industry devoted to making soft toilet paper and paper towels that would absorb anything. Like every country we wanted to believe that we were better than everyone else. America was all about convenience, progress and building a nation of consumers.

We find the rest of the world terrifying; we fear Europe—the judging parent we escaped—and we have taken a vow to liberate (i.e. make like us) any other country we can get our hands on. There is Europe and then there is the rest of the world which, we believe, needs our help, economically, politically, philosophically. We are willing to lose our sons and daughters ensuring for others (who have perhaps not even asked for our help) what we cannot guarantee for ourselves. It feels confusing to be an American now. We are a powerful country yet the American people feel increasingly powerless as they lose jobs, health care coverage and retirement savings. The American-Dream prospect of a house, two kids, two cars, two weeks of vacation, success and prosperity, which at some point became more of an entitlement than an aspiration, is no longer guaranteed. We are in need of inspiration.

'I should like to be able to love my country and still love justice,' is a quotation from an essay by Camus which the artist Sister Mary Corita Kent turned into an anti-Vietnam War poster. The red, white and blue poster which used to hang in my parents' bathroom in the 1960s now hangs in my kitchen. On September 11, 2001, I was at home in New York City. I got a phone call which told me to go to my window. I looked out and saw the second plane bearing down. I watched the towers burn and fall and watched New Yorkers, Americans, walking home covered in corporate and human ash. I breathed the smoke, the fumes of burning buildings and burning bodies for days and knew that while we were forever changed, we were still not smart enough.

The disdain for America is complex. It has to do with our arrogance, but at the same time, everywhere you go there are American brands in the shopping malls, American food in the grocery stores, American movies in the theatres, and Gap stores on every corner. The only remaining Woolworth's five-and-ten stores are outside the United States.

It is a difficult time to travel, there are long lines at the airport where people search our sneakers and scan our baby carriage to see if it converts into something else. Like what—a *tank*? When I leave the United States, I try to hide my American identity—it feels unsafe to announce my nationality.

I was recently in Europe—introducing my infant daughter to London, to Paris, and to her family in France. At six months old, she has just had her first international adventure. She loved it; she knew that each of the places we visited was different but she went without fear, with only curiosity.

Before we left Paris, my cousin came to me with something in her hand. 'I never knew who to give it to, it doesn't have any value, but I thought you, if anyone, might appreciate this.' Her hand was still closed. 'It was during the war, we had no food,' she said almost apologetically. She opened her hand. It was the innards of a pocket watch. 'This was your great-grandfather's watch,' she said. 'The gold case is missing. We had no food,' she said again, still apologizing. 'We sold the gold to feed ourselves. It has no value.'

It has enormous value, it is both heartbreaking and heartwarming. It is the passing down of experience, proof of the power of memory. This watch is still in the war, it is still 1942, it is still six o'clock.

In the airport I was stopped by the customs inspector. 'Have you anything to declare?'

'No.'

'What's this?' he said, poking at the watch carefully wrapped in my bag.

I took it out and slowly unwrapped it. 'The skeleton of a watch.'

'Insignificant,' he said, passing me through.

Chalmers Johnson
b. 1931, Buckeye, Arizona

Like most male Americans who came of age in the early 1950s, my introduction to the greater world came thanks to the government. Conscription was in effect, and I did my military service as a US Naval Reserve officer. My ship, a rust bucket in the Pacific Fleet (USS *LST-883*), spent most of its time in Japanese and Korean waters hauling Marines around for training exercises. But my encounter with Japan cracked my parochial American gestalt—both culturally and linguistically—and shaped my subsequent life. I was fascinated by Japan, its people, artistic heritage, architecture, literature, and modern history. I started studying Japanese at the naval base at Yokosuka whenever my ship was in port. This ultimately led to a lifelong commitment to academic research and teaching on the countries of East Asia and to long periods of residence in Japan and Hong Kong.

In 1955, I returned to the university at Berkeley and did a PhD in Chinese and Japanese politics. I was in the right spot at the right time but also clever in a university-careerist sort of way. Berkeley hired me, gave me tenure three years later, and promoted me to full professor in 1968. I was chairman of the Center for Chinese Studies during the height of the protests against the Vietnam War. I wrote extensively on Chinese Communism, the Sino–Soviet dispute, the Cultural Revolution, Japan's economic 'miracle'—and my own country's increasingly militaristic responses to the way the world was unfolding.

Meanwhile, some other influences were helping turn me into a 'rootless cosmopolitan'. Many of my professors at Berkeley in the late 1950s were exiles from Nazi Europe, and we graduate students spent lots of time discussing with them when they had made the decision to get out, particularly since so many came from fully assimilated (or so they thought) Jewish professional families within German society. During these years I also met and married my wife of forty-six years, a Dutch woman who had lived through the Nazi occupation and remembered it vividly. Her very elderly mother still lives in The Hague, kept alive by Dutch socialism, gin and herring, while bitching about the North Sea weather.

Language study certainly contributed to my changing perspective. I spent my entire adult life studying Chinese and Japanese, while my wife took on French and Spanish and made a brave but unsuccessful attempt to conquer Russian. We travelled quite a lot—two trips to Indonesia, a one and only visit to Saigon (in 1962), shorter sojourns in Mexico, India, Italy, Scandinavia, Israel and China, as well as the Galapagos Islands. In 1978, I made my only trip to Brezhnev's Russia, travelling from Moscow through the trans-Caucasus states of Azerbaijan, Armenia, and Georgia. For a decade my wife and I spent every year's end in Japan, primarily to escape the increasingly gaudy American celebration of Christmas.

My growing intellectual detachment from the United States was abetted by the difficult choices surrounding the Vietnam War. My own ambivalence still perplexes me. I was opposed to the war but also opposed to the protesters against the war, rationalizing that having entered it, we could not afford to 'lose'. At the same time, I was viscerally disgusted by the American world of discrimination against African-Americans and have never even contemplated travelling to places like Mississippi and Alabama. I was proud of the progress made by the civil rights movement and this was the main reason I supported Lyndon Johnson.

My main break with academic conformity—registered Democrat, reader of the *New York Review of Books*, but willing to take all the establishment perks that came my way—came as a result of the end of the Cold War. When the Soviet Union disappeared, instead of demobilizing as we had done after all previous wars, our leaders and the Pentagon did everything in their power to find replacement 'enemies' and to shore up our Cold War empire of military bases around the world. This unexpected development seemed to cry out for analysis: had the Cold War been only a cover for an underlying

American imperialism? Were the forces of militarism and the interests of the military-industrial complex so entrenched that republican government itself was threatened? What was military service like now that it was no longer an obligation of citizenship but instead a career choice?

This led me to a new research project, which resulted in a book that was more important to me than many I had written as a professor. (I had retired from the University of California and no longer needed to prove anything to bean-counting deans.) The book, *Blowback: The Costs and Consequences of American Empire*, was written as an explicit warning to my fellow American about the kinds of retaliation they should expect because of the crucial American decision to maintain a cold war posture in a post-cold war world. Prior to the September 11 attacks my book was largely ignored in the United States but it then became a best-seller. I am cheered by the book's reception and seeming impact, and the worldwide anti-globalization and anti-war movements that grew up after the November 1999 demonstrations in Seattle offer some further grounds for optimism. It should not be too difficult to send George W. Bush packing since he has already largely discredited himself. But I fear that even if we get new leaders, it is unlikely they can prevail against the Pentagon, or the secrecy of the intelligence agencies (making legislative oversight impossible), or the massive entrenched interests of the munitions industry.

Of course I hope I'm wrong. Mistaken pessimism is easily forgiven because people are so pleased you were wrong, whereas mistaken optimism is long remembered. I am an old man and will probably stay and ride things out, but younger Americans should probably start thinking seriously about moving to Canada, Germany, Italy, Mexico, New Zealand, Brazil or wherever. For my part, I would probably choose Spain because it's one of the few countries that will take a cat without a long quarantine, and I have a geriatric Russian Blue as one of my closest companions.

Murad Kalam
b. 1973, Seattle, Washington

During the six months leading up to the Iraq war, I was living in Cairo.

I was a relatively new convert to Islam; I was brought up a Baptist but lapsed into atheism as I grew older. But, in college, when I stumbled across the Qur'an in translation I was so struck by the force of its message and its literary power that I gave up drinking and carousing and changed my name.

As a Muslim in Amercia I was already used to being treated with ignorance and suspicion and now I was increasingly sickened by the prospect of a reckless but inevitable war in Iraq. Of course, I was impossibly naive: the Middle East existed for me, like all things Islamic, in a sort of exotic orientalist ether of veiled women, the Ka'ba and the Virgins of Paradise. I set off for Egypt convinced that, unlike America, there was no corruption and hypocrisy in the Arab Muslim world and that it bore no responsibility for its own appalling condition. People told me that Egypt was, like its Muslim neighbours, a ruthless dictatorship, but until I lived there I refused to admit this to myself. I wanted only to be an expatriate novelist, a dissident, and to enjoy the celebrity of being a convert in a Muslim country.

For a week I managed to persist in the happy belief that I was not living in a brutal police state. As I took a wild, honking Peugeot taxi along the Nile my driver would laugh and curse at the campaign posters of the Egyptian president, displayed at every block, which bore the absurd slogan MUBARAK: YES! YES! I took no notice as I stared wide-eyed through my window at a horizon of needle-shaped minarets suspended in the Cairo smog.

Everyone I met, street sweeper, professor, doctor, tea boy, *bowab* seemed so cheery, even in the squalor of Cairo. On this slight evidence, I decided that the American pundits who criticized the Middle East for its all-pervading despotism, had it all wrong: the Muslim world did not want democracy, only to be left alone.

The next week, I was introduced to a progressive thirty-year-old Egyptian judge who'd studied human rights in France. In a posh Cairo restaurant, he whispered, 'Do not confuse the happiness of Egyptians with what they want. It is our culture to be happy. There are gross human rights abuses and torture. If the wrong person overheard us talking now, they would report me to the government.'

My mood began to shift. On the Internet I followed the case of Dr Saad Eddin Ibrahim, a prominent Egyptian advocate of democracy, who was locked away in a dusty Cairo prison for criticizing the government. I began to notice at every street corner the groups of scowling Egyptian soldiers in black berets, shouldering worn Kalashnikovs.

Across the street from my flat in downtown Cairo, I smoked shisha and drank coffee every day with all my new Egyptian friends at the Café Riche; it was famous as an old haunt of Saddam Hussein during his days as a student at Cairo University. My Egyptian friends refused to believe me when I told them the war would come early next year. The French or the UN would stop the war, they promised, even when this seemed hopeless. But my friends who were mostly tour operators—self-described street hustlers who modelled themselves after American rappers—seemed not to care about the problems which seemed so obvious to me: the coming war, the declining Egyptian pound, the crowded, overpopulated streets, the incompetence of the government at everything but putting down dissent. The war would come or it would not. Only Allah knew. The police were brutal, the ministers stole the people's money, everyone, doctor, lawyer, *bowab*, imam, bureaucrat would rob you the moment you turned your back. Of course, nothing in Cairo quite worked. But what could they do?

Whenever I mentioned democracy to them, they would always talk of sex, asking me if it was true that all American girls were the nymphos they appeared to be in the imported subtitled action movies my friends adored. Still, most subjects with my otherwise garrulous friends, anything of civic importance, were off limits: the president, the government, any topic except for the Jews whom my friends blamed for everything including the catastrophic state of the Egyptian economy. I wondered what my poor friends would do if the Palestinians ever got their state, and they no longer had the Jews to blame.

I went to Saudi Arabia to perform the hajj. When I tried to confirm my ticket to Mecca, the fully veiled Egyptian woman at the Egypt Air counter charged me a non-existent 'confirmation tax'—her attempt to swindle me occurring just moments after the noon call to prayer. I wondered why she bothered to wear a headscarf at all.

In Mecca, I found the same mixture of confusion, oppression and apathy I thought I had left behind in Egypt. But as in Egypt, nothing worked, even at the blessed hajj, for we were visitors not to an Islamic state but to yet another cynical Arab kleptocracy which only pretended to adhere to the true ideals of Islam.

The Saudis couldn't even organize the hajj safely. Each day, as I performed the rituals of the hajj, I was part of massed crowds of Muslims from all over the world: Turks and Pakistanis, Nigerians, Malaysians, Arabs. We would shamble forward without order or seeming direction, endangering lives as we knocked over women, the lame and the elderly in our hurry to get from one ritual to the next. Once, in a street so filled with pilgrims that I could not take one step forward, I was forced to jump into the back of a truck to avoid being killed in a stampede.

At night, I would wander through the pilgrim camps, disgusted by the sight of the mud-faced pilgrims who were only too happy to sleep on the filthy streets. In the morning, the streets would be clogged again, and veiled women who had trouble walking because they'd so rarely been let out of their homes would waddle slowly before me. At the stoning ritual, I watched little girls fall under the crowds of pilgrims: Turks shoving Arabs, Africans shoving Indians until each day a few more pilgrims were trampled to death. The next day I would read of the incident in the *Saudi Times* (FOURTEEN PILGRIMS KILLED IN STAMPEDE) which would quote a hajj official who never took any responsibility for the deaths. He would only say that since the pilgrims had died on hajj they would 'surely enter Paradise'. There was never any promise to cut the number of hajjis or control the outsized crowds to prevent these needless deaths.

The *mutawan*, the dreaded Saudi religious police who enforce the rigid observance of Wahhabi Islam, patrolled the streets, beating or arresting anyone they caught missing a prayer; it was impossible ever to know if the native Meccans prayed out of genuine piety or to avoid a whipping.

I returned from prayer in the Grand Mosque one morning to find my sandals stolen from the shoe racks.

I went back to Cairo in February; by then even the Egyptians, who will try to forget anything that is not pleasant, realized the war was coming. I witnessed fist fights at the street cafes and for the first time I drew stares when I ordered bread and instant coffee at my local street shop in my American-accented Arabic.

I was riding a train home from a short trip with friends to Assuit in Upper Egypt when the war in Iraq began. Our Egyptian guide told us the bombing had started the night before and that we should no longer speak English on the shuddering train or venture out of our apartments when we got back to Cairo. I locked myself in my flat and waited for word from the American Embassy. The next Friday from my balcony I watched a quarter of a million Egyptians rioting in the streets below, men and young boys chanting, smashing windows, pelting soldiers with stones and carting banners. A giant tank rushed down my street, its water cannons hosing the crowds while the soldiers drove back the protesters with batons.

I fled home the next week, leaving all my illusions of the Arab world in my Cairo flat. I couldn't wait to be in America again. On the long flight home, I promised myself I would never accept anything less than full democracy for my fellow Muslims in the Arab world or apologize for the tyranny that now masquerades as Islam.

Yet, for all the hypocrisy and suffering I witnessed during my time in Egypt, it was impossible to ignore the sincerity of the poor and righteous and the depth of the belief of Muslims and Copts alike. I studied Islam with a village sheikh from Giza; I watched shop owners feed strangers during the nights of Ramadan; the local beggars, men who should have lost all hope, prayed each day without fail on tattered sheets of cardboard. It is only because of these expressions of true spirituality that I never lost my faith.

Even now, I can remember the dread in the faces of my Egyptian friends at what would become of their lives. Could it be, that the fascism which once bubbled up in Europe has now invaded the Middle East and that in our time, all hope for the true Islamic values of freedom, modernity and equality in the Muslim world lies not in the East, but in the West?

J. Robert Lennon
b. 1970, Easton, Pennsylvania

Okay, think of the world as a family: a big, dysfunctional family with a mother, and a father, and lots of sons and daughters and cousins and nephews and nieces. The father is America—he is big and strong, and wants to protect the family. And the mother—the mother is out of town. Or dead. No—the mother is Great Britain, except technically she's the grandmother, because she gave birth to America. So now America is totally huge, and married to his tiny little mother.

Bear with me here.

One day the father (America) notices that the lawn, which is Iraq, is looking a little shaggy, and there's some crabgrass, and something that looks like it might be poison ivy, so he asks a few of his teenage sons—France, Germany, Russia, etc.—to help him take care of the problem. Except they think the lawn doesn't look so bad, really, and that's not poison ivy, that's regular ivy, and didn't we just cut the grass like ten years ago? So the father gets all huffy and says, 'Fine, I'll do it all myself,' though in the end he gets some of the little baby kids, like Poland and Eritrea, to help out by making lemonade or something. Except the baby kids are actually older than the father, so they're like really old little kids. Like tiny little old people.

Anyway, Dad really goes at that lawn. He cuts it right down to the dirt and hacks away at the crabgrass, and rips out all the ivy, which turns out to be just regular ivy after all. Except now that the grass is gone, actual poison ivy starts growing in, and Dad is beginning to get itchy. So he's like, 'Hey, Germany! Hey, France! Come and help me clean up here, do you want your old man to be itchy for the next five years, and you might get itchy too,' and the teenagers, who are actually quite old, in fact some of the oldest people in the whole family, are like, 'Go and buy some cortisone, jerk,' and even the little kids are mad, because Dad never thanked them for the lemonade. So—

Scratch that.

The world is really more like a zoo. America is the zookeeper, and there are lots of assistant zookeepers, like Great Britain and Germany and France and Russia, who have various duties at the zoo. Except they also have outside interests, for instance Russia likes kite-flying, and France likes stamp-collecting. Kite-flying being space exploration, and stamp-collecting being wine. But at the zoo, America is the head zookeeper.

There are a lot of animals in the zoo, and some of them are allowed to walk around the zoo outside their cages, but others, like the lion (Iraq) are locked up. Anyway, a while ago, the old zookeeper, who was the father of the current zookeeper, got in a fight with the lion, but didn't finish him off. (America is his own father here, but you know what I mean.) So the current zookeeper hates the lion because the lion humiliated his father. And one day he looks into the lion's cage with binoculars, and he thinks he sees chemical, biological and nuclear weapons. So he sends some monkeys in there to check it out. They don't find anything, but the zookeeper attacks the lion anyway, and he kicks the lion's ass, and it turns out the monkeys (UNSCOM) were right, and now the lion has fleas. Diseased fleas. So America has to get a flea collar.

No.

The world is an orchestra. America is the conductor. And Europe is the strings, with Germany and Britain as first viola and violin, respectively. And Asia is the woodwinds, and Africa is percussion, etc., etc. And everything sounds pretty okay, when suddenly there's this terrible squawk from the brass section (the Middle East)—it's Iraq, on the French horn, and he isn't playing the right notes. In fact, these are tyrannical notes he's playing, and they're destroying the hearing of the rest of the brass section.

Let's make Iraq a trumpet, Iraq can't be French.

Also, the brass section was already in trouble, because the trombone (Israel) and the tuba (Palestine) keep spitting at one another. No—Palestine is too small to be a tuba. So it's…a tiny tuba. A tiny tuba that's been taken apart, so the pieces are all over the place.

Never mind.

The world is an anthill, and each country is an ant, and the ants are very busy, doing their various ant-jobs. Some of the ants are black, and some are white, and there are Muslim ants and Jewish ants, and ants who talk in funny accents. But America is the top ant, he's like a regular ant but approximately forty-seven times larger.

The world is a computer, and America is the screen. No, the operating system, and there are lots of programs (countries) that run on it until the user, who is nobody in particular, looks at pornography (France) on the Internet (international trade), and gets a virus (Iraq). Which is not to say that Iraq comes from France. That's wrong.

The world is a pie, except that every slice is a different kind of pie. And some of the slices are actually cake, or hamburgers.

No, wait.

The world is a planet. Yes: a planet, hurtling through space, maintaining the optimum temperature, atmosphere, chemical composition and ocean-to-landmass ratio to support a vast, teeming variety of life. This life is dominated by a single species, itself governed by rules of infinite and ever-evolving complexity. Indeed, no other species in the history of this planet that is the world has ever exhibited such a dazzling array of contradictory behaviours.

And let us assume that the dominant group of the dominant species of this planet has a leader, and that leader was elected in a free and fair election, even if technically he wasn't, but this is all a for-instance, so just let me finish here. And this leader takes a long look at this planet that is the world, and he looks back on its long, complex history (or rather his aides brief him on it, although he gets a faraway look in his eye whenever they do), and he clears his throat, and he adjusts his necktie, and he says, simply, 'Bring it on.'

And all the denizens of the planet say, 'Bring it on?'

'Bring it on,' repeats the leader and the denizens reply, 'But—'

'No buts,' says the leader.

'Yeah, but—'

'I said no buts,' the leader says.

'Okay. However—'

'No howevers, either.'

'No howevers?'

'No buts, howevers, in facts, actuallys, or you-sees,' says the leader, through an interpreter. 'No wait-a-minutes, no can't-we-discuss-thises, no hold-on-a-moments. No heys. No stop-its. No aren't-you-listenings. No comparisons, metaphors, allegories, or similes. No what-ifs, how-abouts, or just-supposes. No nos. Just...bring it on.'

And so, the denizens get together and confer over this new state of things, and they are forced to decide whether to bring it on, or not to bring it on. It's a hard decision—it keeps them up all night. But really, there never was a choice. Ultimately, unfortunately, unavoidably, it must be brought on.

And so it is.

Jacki Lyden
b. 1959, Milwaukee, Wisconsin

Two months after the September 11 attacks, I was hailing a cab at Bagram Air Base in Kabul, Afghanistan. I'd spent much of the past dozen years reporting for National Public Radio from a dozen Middle Eastern and Central Asian countries, places often synonymous with war. But Kabul was the most destroyed place I had ever seen. I was alone and NPR's translator was nowhere in sight.

Every word I've gathered depends on someone who speaks my

language and guides my perceptions. I had one name from our correspondent Anne Garrels, of a guy called Zalmai, but she had never met the man who 'might turn up'. And then he did.

Zalmai Yawar was twenty-six. He had twice contemplated suicide in Afghanistan, 'since I knew I was dying every day the Taliban were in power'. His sister had had a mental breakdown. He had gone to Peshawar, over the border in Pakistan, with the idea of fleeing to Australia. But he'd been robbed there and had to return to Kabul and to his family. He had watched television in his seedy hotel in Peshawar as the other guests exulted over the destruction of the World Trade Centre towers. He was horrified, he said. He hoped the Americans would now attack Osama Bin Laden.

We met at the Hotel Intercontinental in Kabul, and he agreed to work for me, though 'work' doesn't quite define the exchange that began—the long journeys around Afghanistan, and endless waiting for interviews, the conversations out of which grow friendship. Why did he alone not cheer the screen in the Peshawar hotel that night? One evening, when he and our other two helpers missed their 8 p.m. curfew, I said they should have a 'slumber party' at the house we'd set up together. I was about to explain this American concept when Zalmai said, 'A slumber party! Then I shall recite from "The Fall of the House of Usher" and "The Cask of Amontillado"!'

Zalmai had learned his English from movies as a teenager and refined it in the ransacked libraries of Kabul. When the Taliban destroyed the libraries, books were sold by the kilo on the streets. English-language books had their covers ripped off and buyers were invited to place the soles of the feet—a Muslim insult—on the book, to have the soles of the feet traced and the book covers made into sandals. The words of Edgar Allan Poe became the dirt beneath the feet of many Taliban. But Zalmai took the books home, and read them. Zalmai always thought for himself; he chose to learn English as a matter of cultural passport, he did naturally what we so pride ourselves on in the West: he questioned authority. He became a human being with more than one world inside him.

On September 11, 2003 I drove Zalmai Yawar to Amherst College, which had generously given him a scholarship. A State Department contact of mine helped him obtain a visa. I picked him up at JFK airport, and we were sightseers for a day: the Brooklyn

Bridge, Ground Zero, St Paul's Church, the Staten Island Ferry. 'I want to see the Statue of Liberty,' Zalmai said. He didn't exclaim over everything he saw: the cash machines, the merchandise, the break dancers on the street. He mostly said, 'I am so glad I am here, and I will never forget the kindness shown me.'

Not every translator is a worthy fellow traveller; but every worthy one is more than a translator, and the best ones—the ones who are your teachers—are a kind of cultural talisman. These are the people on whom we all depend.

Todd McEwen
b. 1953, Orange, California

My thinking about the world began, as it must have for many, on the carpet. The living room carpet, stretching as far as I could see, like an ocean I couldn't have named. On the horizon of the book shelf sat one of those creepy globes on which the seas are black. Occasionally it would be handed down to me. There was a dial on top of it which demarcated the time zones—I used to spin that when I tired of spinning the globe, and wondered if I were causing night and day to flash nauseatingly on and off for some unfortunate pink nation. Later I was given an 'Erector' set with a motor. I made the globe spin very fast by holding the motor against its belly. This had the effect of ripping up the paper equator and for some months I was banned from handling the world.

There was a European city made of wood. It lived in a hexagonal carton and came with a green cloth which represented parks and streets, with a blue river printed on it. But I preferred to design my own haphazard town. There were small semicircular wooden cars, but no people.

I was devoted to some picture books which featured a black Scottie called Angus. My mother told me that was a Scottish name, and I began to fashion a Scotland in my head, made up of our surname and a few others, the blue-black coat of Angus, and the curious upholstered furniture under which he often hid. I, too, was known to hide, to exist, behind our sofa (I was pleased to discover Robert Louis Stevenson exulted in the same thrill). When I finally encountered a person named Angus, it seemed shocking and even perverse.

I was still at the stage of playing on the carpet, thinking it huge, when Mr Mali started visiting our house. He was a Czech who had come, or more precisely fled, to America and worked in the same laboratory as my father. Mr Mali was very tall, all smiles, and had thick straw-coloured hair which he brushed straight back—before Elvis, an unusual thing to do—and from my carpet I marked him as an exotic straight away. He wore sharp suits in unanticipated colours and shoes with decorations on them, and seemed always to be in a flowing topcoat, also outré for southern California in the Fifties. Now they'd probably kick him to death.

I was aware of the word 'Europe' but had no clear idea what it meant. It was a place where things were recognizable, such as the houses in the box, but quite different. My materials for thinking about Europe: Mr Mali's hair, smile and topcoat; odd airline-advertisement representations of the globe as a cruelly flattened ovoid; pastel-and-ink drawings of Paris and the Eiffel Tower which somehow seeped into everyone's consciousness, many of them by Ludwig Bemelmans and Jean de Brunhoff. I amused myself by naming this amalgamation of sharp images and hazy ideas 'the BENELUX feeling'. Hardly anyone refers to the Benelux nations any more, but we had to learn about them in school and I daydreamed about what life was like there. I imagined that queer, flattened globe was always hanging on sky blue walls in Benelux homes. Thanks to my depopulous wooden city, I had no idea what the people might be like.

My father once brought home a Swedish man who was visiting the laboratory. He too had brushed-back yellow hair and smiled a lot. My sister and I gaped, GAPED when during coffee at our colonial-style dinner table he drew out a tin of 'Café Crème' cigars and offered one to our mother.

A cousin astonished the family entirely by marrying 'a European'. No further information ever came about his name or where exactly he was from. I think they must still be living in 'Europe' somewhere, that pastel, Benelux Europe of the crushed globe.

I got the Benelux feeling whenever I saw cartoons or *New Yorker* covers by Jean-Michel Folon. His cityscapes of humane buildings and slightly timid traffic lights contained the little men who had been missing from my wooden Benelux on the carpet. Hatted and hunched into topcoats, they scurried humbly through their grey-and-blue streets between gentle, perfectly spaced raindrops.

Later, I enjoyed a revival of the Benelux feeling when I came across Bemelmans' wonderful book about travelling as a tourist across postwar Europe, *The Best of Times*. On showing it to my friend Fred, educated in a French school, I found he too had always been amused by the word Benelux. I can still make him splutter by picking up the phone and saying merely 'Benelux'.

But it was the picture puzzle of Scotland in my head which pre-occupied me. Sometimes I cut out pictures of Edinburgh or deer from magazines. I would imitate the few Scottish accents I heard at the movies. This kind of thing leads only to useless and cack-handed romanticism, which wasn't helped by my obsessive devotion to Alfred Hitchcock's version of *The Thirty-Nine Steps*.

I travelled by train to Edinburgh, for the first time, on an Easter Monday holiday, fantastically excited—'overstimulated' would have been the judgement of the family—*a young man without a thought for Paris*. The task I had set myself on arriving in Scotland was to find the village of 'Alt-na-Shellach', where Hitchcock's Richard Hannay has some of his adventures. (I would have to content myself with *Ach*-Na-Shellach, in Wester Ross—Hitchcock's wife glued *Alt*-Na-Shellach on to an empty space in the map of Perthshire.)

When I left the station, Edinburgh seemed deserted. It was five on a grey afternoon, with no taxis, buses or cars to be seen. I struggled up to the bridge with my lurid American backpack and goggled at the Castle, the gardens, the Bank of Scotland, the huge, heavy city with no one in sight. *God*, I said out loud, *they were right in London—no one lives in this country AT ALL.*

I schlepped my junk to a hotel and fell asleep dreaming of crofters' wives. The next morning, I opened my window and was both relieved and astonished to find the capital full of motor vehicles, and, scurrying humbly about their business, thousands of little men in topcoats.

Darryl Pinckney
b. 1953, Indianapolis, Indiana

A journey doesn't always begin with a suitcase. Sometimes it starts with the wrong book. I was a student. I faced a failing grade if I did not finish that term's paper, but my mind was wintering elsewhere. Expatriate solitude, seemingly graceful expatriate poverty; fellow feeling among sinners; outrageous licence; beautiful people in a state of doom—*The Berlin Stories* by Christopher Isherwood was a book I never got over.

I dreamed of living in Berlin. Then I misplaced the dream, to find it some years later when I spent a few summers in the city: West Berlin, as it was then. What time do you close? I asked a woman behind a bar in Potsdamer Strasse. Here we are never closed, she said, and let her head fall on the cash register. Berlin was not Germany, just as New York was not America. The Kreuzberg district, with its anarchists and Turks, had been hailed as an outpost of cool. Be careful, I hear that there are a lot of blacks and drugs in Berlin, my mother said. The illicit and the dreadful sundry of the world were part of its necrophiliac atmosphere—the kitsch, the nostalgia for Weimar. Self-renewal seemed possible in that place where history was over. Finally, on New Year's Eve of 1987, I took the last of my bags to JFK and went to live there.

In those days, Berlin was still a barracks town, but also a small town with a big past. You could crawl into the disfigured city as into a shell. You could write your own ticket, regard the city as a theatrical setting, and appropriate the citizens as extras for your modest daily dramas or your tremendous inner opera buffa. The late Berlin air cast a spell. You were going to walk out the door and reinvent yourself. You were going to turn a corner and there in the neon haze would be the agent of your conversion. Or you could go around in a nervous silence for days, as if the city had been depopulated, leaving only an architecture of signs, layer upon layer, and a dialogue between vanished buildings and their usurpers. The fragment of the Anhalter Bahnhof shot up from its memorial dust to scream at a circa 1970s tower dumb as the Himalayas.

Paradise is locked and bolted; we will have to make the journey around the world to see if it is open at the back, Kleist said. Berlin hid its historical face, until you slipped over there, into East Berlin, into the Wilhelmine immensity of Unter den Linden, neoclassical baroque and the ineptitude of Karl-Marx-Platz. I almost forgave myself for liking the dereliction, the forgotten pockets of buildings so scarred I would not have been surprised had Dietrich emerged from a doorway to sing 'Black Market'. Overdressed in the moral superiority of my compassion, laden with a socialist currency about as serious as Monopoly money, the usual racial situation for me, a black, was reversed: these white people who spoke low like inhabitants of a ghost town were the primitives, the needy tribesmen I couldn't take back with me.

Back in louder West Berlin, the Wall was an apotheosis of found art, an explosion of graffiti, like an American high school yearbook. I was told that a man was sometimes lowered in a cage from the featureless earth of no man's land to wash away the scrawl of slogans and hearts. I didn't believe it, though none of the graffiti went back very far, certainly not as far back as the crosses behind the Reichstag in memory of those who were killed trying to escape. But the Wall made the lucky part of Berlin an island, held its grumbling, caustic population in the jealous embrace of privilege. It was a poor city, West Berlin, and also a subsidized city. Germans willing to live in West Berlin received tax breaks and exemption from national service. The real estate was worth nothing and there was no industry. The only business was culture.

The students, artists and intellectuals were the aristocracy, and a foreigner, an intruder, never had to make sense. Tall black American ex-GIs and their hennaed German wives; a black American model and her Israeli pianist boyfriend; a Chilean historian ready to remind you that America was not the only country in the Americas; engineers from Ghana, Palestinian doctors—some of us were camp followers of the US army, but most were genuine refugees. Many had flown to East Berlin and then been allowed through the border. Meanwhile, seasons came and went as I avoided adult life. The scent of summer water in the Schlachtensee was followed by the smell of damp wool in the argumentative coffee shops. And then, on November 9, 1989, the fortress island was overrun and its past seemingly overcome in the celebrations of freedom. It was a miracle, people said, as if the cobblestones had, indeed, yielded oysters and a rain of gentle lemon juice fallen, just as in Heine's poem. In a mood of sublime impudence, we ran along the slippery surface of the Wall at the Brandenburg Gate. Something like Rhine wine did flow in the gutters, amber and emerald beer bottles rolled about pavements. After a while it unsettled me to see so many Germans having a wild time; Berlin at that moment succeeded in making me feel what I had never, as a black man, felt before—like an American. I stood on a ledge at Invalidenstrasse on November 9, watching strangers talk like best friends. Their tears said the Allies could go home. The moon rose higher in the night, and turned from alpine white to Prussian yellow. Many West Berliners had gone about their lives as if the conscience of Germany were over there, on deposit, though sentimentality about the Good Germany could scarcely cope with the revelations about what it had really been like. Resentment arrived, as West Germans condescended mercilessly to East Germans in a way that must have reflected how West Germans felt about the authority of the Allies for all those decades. Open hostility to foreigners also came, especially loathing of the obviously foreign-born, though American clothes, even on a black man or a black woman, seemed to intimidate East German thugs. The Poles had nothing, but at least they were Poles, whereas the East Germans had been made to feel second-class. East German youths attacked Turkish youths behind West Berlin's main train station the very night the Wall fell. Later, asylum centres were stormed. Anyone brown, whether from the Punjab, Iran, or Brazil, was vulnerable to attack on the U-Bahns. A Vietnamese woman made sure her children left the house well-dressed so that the Germans might take them for Japanese. Guest workers and trainees from Angola and Mozambique living in the small East German towns near Berlin were attacked, sometimes murdered. What flared up in East Germany spoke to dormant emotions in West Germany. Perhaps xenophobia is an inevitable by-product of national reconciliation, like the rise of the Ku Klux Klan after the defeat of Reconstruction down in Dixie. Nationalism brought much attention to the formerly neglected. In Berlin the sound of following footsteps had never bothered me as I walked home at night; I never bothered to turn around. But there came a late night in 1991 when that sound behind me on a bright street made me sweat.

In 1992, I gave up my illegal sublet. I could no longer pretend I was young. I go back sometimes. Unemployment is high, but, considering what could have gone wrong, unification has been a success. Unified Berlin ignored the coffee-shop dwellers' terror of change. The politicians and businessmen are back. It is once again the German Chicago, as Twain saw it, a town in a state of becoming, furious with secrets, deals, smugglers, contractors, conventions. I once stood looking into the leafy dark of the Schoneberger Ufer with the actress Marianne Hoppe. That Berlin air, she sighed as she took a deep breath and recalled her Berlin in the wonderful days—the Weimar, Isherwood days—before she *had* to go to Hitler's Bunker to watch those awful films.

Eric Schlosser
b. 1959, New York, New York

When Ronald Reagan was President, I spent a few years studying British imperial history, trying to comprehend why empires rise and fall. I was particularly interested in the period between 1898 and 1902, when the British Empire began to stumble, America's empire was born, and a 'special relationship' between the two nations was secretly formed amid colonial wars in South Africa and the Philippines. The end of the century marked a historic turning point, a convergence of imperial paths that soon transformed the world. Long-standing attitudes changed, and traditional roles were reversed. At the beginning of the 1890s, Americans still embraced a revolutionary foreign policy: friendship with all nations, entangling alliances with none. The United States was the world's leading industrial power, but did not possess a single battleship and had only 25,000 men in its army. Great Britain was the world's dominant financial and military power. Its banks supplied capital to Wall Street, and its navy maintained eleven bases and thirty-three coaling stations in the seas around the United States, ensuring those loans would be repaid. Although wealthy members of the East Coast establishment admired the British Empire and sought entry to its upper class, most Americans despised both.

In 1898 the Spanish–American War provided the United States with an opportunity to emulate British imperial policies. The war was initially justified, however, as an anti-imperial crusade to liberate the Cuban people from tyrannical Spanish rule. American newspapers, especially those owned by William Randolph Hearst, stressed the necessity of extending American freedom and democracy overseas. Doing nothing might lead to disaster. 'Within a few days,' one New York paper warned, 'Spain will have it within her power to lay waste and ravage this city as the volcano of Vesuvius ravaged Herculaneum.' The sinking of an American battleship, the USS *Maine*, supplied the requisite *casus belli*. The US Navy claimed that the ship had been sunk by a mine in Havana harbour, an outrageous act of terrorism; historians later concluded that this was misinformation. The powerful explosion aboard the *Maine* was most likely the result of an accident. Just five days after being declared, the noble war to liberate Cuba was somehow transmuted into a campaign to secure coaling stations and port facilities in the Far East. The United States soon annexed Hawaii, Guam, Wake Island and the Philippines.

Many Filipinos were unhappy to find themselves being traded from one imperial power to another. The American occupation sparked guerrilla warfare and a popular uprising that lasted for years. The conquest of the Philippines provoked an angry debate in the United States about imperialism. William Jennings Bryan, the Democratic candidate for President in 1900, argued that the most important question of the campaign was: 'Republic or Empire?' Bryan was soundly defeated by Wall Street's candidate, William McKinley, but popular distrust of militarism and imperialism endured in the United States for another fifty years.

In retrospect, the same fundamental issue was at stake during the presidential elections of 1900 and of 2000: republic or empire? Imperial power has once again become fashionable. In London and Washington DC, you hear suggestions that perhaps the British Empire wasn't such a bad idea after all—and that an American empire, properly administered, might do a lot of good. Such arguments have been well received in today's political climate. For some reason, celebrations of the British Empire are not welcomed the same way in India, Pakistan, Kenya or South Africa. The whole notion of selfless conquest, of a 'White Man's Burden', was always a lie. Outside of Rudyard Kipling's poem (written in 1899 to persuade Americans to keep the Philippines), the real burden was borne by the colonized, not the colonizer. Although British rule may have conferred some lasting benefits, altruism was hardly the guiding force of that empire—or of any other. 'Destiny' can also be ruled out as a plausible explanation, despite the many attempts throughout history to claim it as one. President McKinley described America's acquisition of the Philippines as 'a gift from the gods', failing to mention that the undersecretary of the navy, Theodore Roosevelt (a great man, yes, but not divine), had secretly ordered the American fleet to Manila. As the historian A. K. Weinberg once observed, 'destiny' tends to be invoked in the very circumstances which, upon further analysis, seem to give it least justification.

In November 2000, only months before becoming the director of policy planning at the State Department, Richard N. Haas gave a speech entitled 'Imperial America'. Haas argued that the United States should assume a world role similar to that of Great Britain in the nineteenth century, exerting control through both informal and formal means. 'America's destiny is to police the world,' says another prominent supporter of President George W. Bush's foreign policy. Although members of the Bush administration have strongly denied that they are seeking to create a new American empire, their current plans for administering Iraq seem vaguely familiar. 'We come, not as invaders or conquerors,' President McKinley told the Filipino people, 'but as friends, to protect the natives in their homes, in their employments, and in their personal and religious rights.' McKinley called his policy 'benevolent assimilation'. An estimated 200,000 civilians died between 1899 and 1902, as the United States benevolently assimilated the Philippines.

A century ago those who questioned America's god-given right to rule the world were often accused of treason, an accusation frequently made today. Mark Twain is now considered the quintessential American novelist, yet he too was called a traitor for opposing the annexation of the Philippines. Twain was thought un-American. 'Shall we?' he asked, attacking McKinley's foreign policy. 'Shall we go on conferring our Civilization upon the peoples that sit in darkness, or shall we give those poor things a rest? Shall we bang right ahead in our old-time, loud, pious way, and commit the new century to the game; or shall we sober up and sit down and think it over first?' Twain suggested a new flag for America's imperial conquest: the American flag, with the white stripes painted black, and the stars replaced by a skull and crossbones.

Gary Shteyngart
b. 1972, Leningrad, USSR

When I leave America, people try to kill me.

In Baku, Azerbaijan, two police officers in the metro throw me to the ground, mistaking me for an Iranian terrorist. 'I'm just a dark-looking Soviet-born Jew,' I explain, showing them my stuffed wallet by way of explanation. 'Jew,' they whisper in awe, thumbing through my money.

In Berlin, a group of angry young pub-meisters mistake me for an Indian computer programmer. They follow me around the bar shouting *'Kinder statt Inder,'* ('Children instead of Indians,') as if I were an immigrant from the subcontinent out to scam the generous German welfare system. Perhaps I should take out my Jewish wallet to placate them.

In a small Czech town, at a disco named, appropriately enough, 'The White Rose', I am mistaken for an 'Arabian' by a gang of local skinheads who casually prepare to disembowel me until I take out my American Express card, proving that I am indeed American and not some kind of mega-Turk.

Wherever I go outside the United States, people see me as a repository for their greatest fears, and soon enough they try to inflict bodily harm upon me. I have olive skin which fluctuates in its oliveness depending on the time of year, an anger-inspiring goatee as black as the night sky above Montana (or the Serengeti), and dark, suspicious eyes that flit about inquisitively. In many northern parts of the world, I am too swarthy; south of Sicily, I am not nearly swarthy enough.

And so America, or New York, to be perfectly precise, has always meant for me safety through heterogeneity. I am ecstatic, almost teary when the plane dips its wings on its approach to Kennedy airport because I know that soon I will be walking the streets without fear, my eyes on the beautiful young citizens around me, instead of darting about in search of my next assailant.

Only two years ago, I remember being chased through the streets of a certain foreign capital by a madman who wished to carve me up with a machete. Oh, how I longed for the shelter of the East Village as I ran past lanes of honking traffic to save myself from a brutal carve-up. *Safe at last,* I thought when, back in New York, the taxi pulled up to my downtown tenement. And yet, only a month later I found myself standing on my rooftop, watching the World Trade Centre disintegrate some twenty blocks away. Two days later a patron at a Manhattan bar wondered aloud if I were a member of al-Qaida (no) and wanted to blow him up (yes). 'I don't like you,' he said. 'You're funny-looking.' So much for safety through heterogeneity.

Despite the events of September 11, I am still less despised in America than elsewhere. It may be a cliché, to say that America's diversity is its greatest asset. New York and Los Angeles, hugely imperfect as they may be, are the world's true multicultural cities, while burgs like Berlin or Rome, seem, well, German and Italian, respectively. Don't get me wrong: I leave America whenever I can (in fact, I am writing this from the relative safety of a fourteenth-century signal tower in the Tuscan hills). The messianic mission of America's fundamentalist government, the fundamentalist nature of our messianic populace, the stealthy fusion of church and state, leaves little room for an agnostic thinking person outside of several East Coast and West Coast area codes. Multiculturalism aside, I prefer Joschka Fischer to Colin Powell. But when my feet hit foreign ground, when the man at immigration wants so desperately to spit into my eyes, when the continental sun grills my skin a touch too olive, I worry.

I want to live.

Studs Terkel
b. 1912, New York, New York

My first trip overseas was to France in 1962, when I was fifty. I felt immediately at home in my down-at-heel hotel off the Left Bank. I'd been raised in a similar lodging, a Chicago working-men's hotel run by my mother, where all were made welcome, including the wayward lovers who couldn't afford a smarter rendezvous. The Paris hotel had the added grace of a coffee-and-croissant breakfast on the house—then a rare feature.

As I came down the stairs from my bedroom on the second morning of my first visit to a foreign land, I felt remarkably French. With a cigarette stuck to my lip, I was Jean Gabin as Pépé le Moko. A timid British couple at the desk addressed me as 'M'sieur' and wondered if I could translate their request to have tea rather than coffee with their croissant. This was gratifying. I shrugged Gabinesquely and using the very few French words I knew successfully conveyed the idea to the desk clerk. I still remember her name: Françoise.

Unfortunately, it doesn't appear to be that easy for American tourists with more than a few bucks—or for those we call diplomats—to know the names of those who serve. James Baldwin made that clear in his memoir, *Nobody Knows My Name*. The context may be different, but the substance of his complaint is the same. Being the wealthiest, the most powerful, the most generous people on earth, we Americans have no need to become acquainted with shadows. As well as their names, their customs and manners of worship are of small consequence. Two wide oceans separate us from the rest of the world. As a result, there is an innocence of the patterns and troubles of other societies, especially those of colour.

The people who have taught me most about this innocence or ignorance have been the cab-drivers of my own city, Chicago. Many come from what we know as the Third World. With the slightest encouragement, they'll talk about their astonishment at how little their passengers—my respectable and friendly fellow Chicagoans—know about the world beyond the United States. And yet, as a Nigerian cabbie told me, 'your wars have always been fought elsewhere': in this unknown world. His words echoed those of Admiral Gene LaRoque, an American officer who had taken part in several such adventures and whom I interviewed for my book, *Hope Dies Last*: 'In the name of national security, we've been attacking different countries around the world, small ones. Many that Americans don't even remember: Grenada, Libya, Panama. All this without any remonstrance from the American public. We always find an excuse to do it. We attacked five Muslim countries—Lebanon, Libya, Iraq, Afghanistan and Sudan— in twenty years. Is it any wonder some people don't like us?'

The horrendous events of September 11 brought home to us the looniness that was afoot in the world. To compound the obscene, our appointed chieftain showed his utter disdain for the United Nations and ordered a 'pre-emptive' invasion of Iraq. Though millions protested, outside and inside America, our leader had the unswerving support of Prime Minister Blair. I think of them as a strange version of that famous pair from P. G. Wodehouse: Bush as Bertie Wooster, Blair as his consummate British butler, Jeeves. How wonderful it would be—how necessary it is—to change both regimes.

Paul Theroux
b. 1941, Medford, Massachusetts

This took place forty years ago in Africa, and still I ponder it—the opportunity, the self-deception, the sex, the power, the fear, the confrontation, the foolishness, all the wrongness. The incident has informed one of my early novels and several short stories. It was something like First Contact, the classic encounter between the wanderer and the hidden indigenous person, the meeting of people who are such utter strangers to each other that one side sees a ghost and the other side suspects an opportunity. It won't leave my mind.

I had gone from America to Africa and had been there for almost a year: Nyasaland. Independence came and with it a new name, Malawi. I was a teacher in a small school. I spoke the language, Chichewa. I had a house and even a cook, a Yao Muslim named Jika. My cook had a cook of his own, a young boy, Ismail. We were content in the bush, a corner of the southern highlands, red dust, bad roads, ragged people. Apart from the clammy cold season, June to August, none of this seemed strange. I had been expecting this Africa and I liked it. I used to say: I'll get culture shock when I go back home.

With Christmas approaching I went via a roundabout route to Zambia and on Christmas Eve was sitting in an almost empty and rather dirty bar outside Lusaka, talking to the only other drinkers, a man and woman.

'This is for you,' I said, giving the man a bottle of beer. 'And this is for your wife. Happy Christmas.'

'Happy Christmas to you,' the man said. 'But she is not my wife. She is my sister. And she likes you very much.'

At closing time they invited me to their house. This involved a long taxi ride into the bush. 'Happy Christmas. You give him money.' I paid. They led me to a hut. I was shown a small room, the woman followed me in. I stepped on a sleeping child—there was a squawk—and the woman woke him and shooed him from his blanket into the next room. Then she sat me down, and she undressed me, and we made love on the warm patch on the blanket where the child had been lying.

That was pleasant. I had had a year of women in Malawi, the casual okay, the smiles, the fooling, Jika's bantering, Ismail's leers. But, in the morning, when I said I had to leave, to go to my hotel in Lusaka, the woman—Nina—said, 'No. It is Christmas,' and made a fuss.

The brother—George—overhearing, came into the room and said that it was time to go to the bar. It was hardly eight in the morning; yet we went, and drank all day, and whenever beer was ordered, they said, '*Mzungu*'—the white man is paying, and I paid. We were all drunk by mid-afternoon. The woman was taunted for being with a white man. She answered back, drunkenly. The brother stopped several angry men from hitting her. Loud, drunken fights began in the bar.

We went back to the village hut and I lay half-sick in the stinking room. Nina undressed me and sat on me and laughed, and jeered at me.

I was dressing in the morning when she asked me where I was going. Once again, I said I had to leave.

'No. It is Boxing Day.' And she summoned her brother.

'We go,' George said and tapped my shoulder and smiled. His smile meant: You do what I tell you to do. We spent Boxing Day as we had done Christmas: the bar, beer, fights, abuse, and finally that dizzy nauseating feeling of mid-afternoon drunkenness. Another night, Nina's laughter in her orgasm and in the morning the reminder that I was trapped. 'You stay!'

In her refusal to let me go was not just nastiness but a hint of threat. And her brother backed her up, sometimes accusing me of not respecting them. 'You don't like us!'

When I protested that of course I did, they smiled and we ate boiled eggs or cold peeled cassava roots or a whitish porridge, and then off we went to the bar, to get drunk again in the filthy place. And as she grew drunker she pawed me and promised me sex—now an almost frightening thought. Another day passed and I realized I did not know these people at all. The food was disgusting. The hut was horrible. The village was unfriendly, the bar was outright hostile. The beer drinking was making me ill. I was the only *mzungu* in the place—as far as I knew, the only one for miles around. The language that I knew—Chichewa—was not their language, though they spoke it. Their own language—Bemba, I think—was incomprehensible to me, and I knew they were plotting against me when they spoke it—quickly, muttering, so that I wouldn't know what they were saying. I belonged to them, like a valuable animal they had poached. Whenever they wanted money for beer, for snacks, for presents, for whatever reason, they demanded it from me. When I handed it over they were excessively friendly, the woman kissing me, licking my face, pretending to be submissive; her brother and the hangers-on praising me, praising America, saying Britain was bloody shit and asking me to let them wear my sunglasses.

That first night I had been wearing a light-coloured suit. The suit was now rumpled and stained; my shirt was a sweaty mess. They were the only clothes I had.

They said what a great friend I was, but I knew better: I was a captive. They were out of money. My weakness and arrogance had sent me straying into their world from my own world. And I represented something to them—money, certainly; prestige, perhaps; style, maybe. After the first night we never had a sober conversation. I was a colour, a white man, a *mzungu*. I had been captured and they wanted to keep me: I was useful. When they said, as they often did, 'You no go!' I was afraid, because they spoke with such irrational loudness and threat. The boldness in Nina that had attracted me I now feared as wildness. Drinking deafened her and made her a bully as cruel as her brother. George peered at me with odd brown-spotted eyes, as though at an enemy. Sometimes at night I was wakened by the human stinks in the hut.

I think it was the fourth day. My terror was so great and the days so similar I lost track of time. We went to the bar in the morning and at noon they were still drinking—I had lost my taste for it, as I had lost my libido; I just stood there and paid with my diminishing wad of kwacha notes. I said, 'I'm going to the *chimbudzi*.'

'Go with him,' Nina said to one of the tough boys hovering near. I protested.

'He will not come back,' she said, and I realized how shrewd she was. She had read my mind, another suggestion of her malevolence. I took off my suit jacket and folded it on the bar.

'Here's my jacket, here's some money. Buy me a beer, get some for yourselves, and hand over the jacket when I get back.' The *chimbudzi* was outside the bar, a roofless shed behind the tin-roofed building, upright bamboos and poles. Maggots squirmed in the shallow bog hole. I stood there and was too disgusted even to unzip, and then I stepped outside, looked around, and seeing no one, I ran—at first cautiously, then really hard until I got to the road and flagged down a car. Of course the man stopped. He was African, I was white, it was Christmas, he needed money for petrol. He took me to my hotel: I had not slept even one night there. I asked him to wait, I paid my bill and got in again and when the driver said where, I said, 'Just keep going.' He drove me twenty miles outside town and dropped me at a roadhouse, where I spent a sleepless night.

What a fool I had been to trespass. The time I spent had not helped me to understand them. Apart from my initial sexual desire, my curiosity, my recklessness, there was no common ground, other than mutual exploitation. I was reminded of who I really was, a presumptuous American. In spite of my politics and my teaching in the bush school, I was little more than a tourist, taking advantage. To me they were desperate Africans, seizing their chance to possess me. It was Tarzan turned inside out, and redefining itself. I saw nothing more. I had simply feared them and I wanted to get out of there. Later the incident kept resonating, telling me who I was. Much more dangerous things happened to me in Africa—serious fights, deportations, gunplay—was there anything more upsetting than being held at gunpoint? But this was my first true experience of captivity and difference, memorable for being horribly satirical. It had shocked me and made me feel American.

Joel Turnipseed
b. 1968, Duluth, Minnesota

I can still remember the awe of seeing the lights of Alexandria, Egypt as our C-5 cargo transport plane flew over on its way to Saudi Arabia in 1991. We had passed beyond the shimmering and unreal blue halo of CNN on the hangar televisions in Torrejon, Spain. We were going to war. I was standing in the cockpit, talking with the pilot, co-pilot and navigator. They were giving me a hard time about the seabag full of books I'd brought with me. Plato's *Republic*, Thoreau's *Walden*, T. E. Lawrence's *Seven Pillars of Wisdom*—a founding mythology of self-invention.

Like Lawrence, I was a little bastard. I was born in 1968 in Duluth, Minnesota—at that time a gateway for Vietnam draft deserters on their way to Canada. My father stopped on the way to meet my mother, just long enough to get caught by the Feds and spend the rest of my gestation in jail. Violent and desperate separations became a kind of template for my life, none more than when I took a Greyhound bus out of Duluth in 1983, leaving for my long-divorced mother's place in Minneapolis. I watched the rust- and soot-stained houses of West Duluth slip away, the homes of its iron miners and steel and paper-mill workers—my neighbourhood, a neighbourhood of more than twenty per cent unemployment and angry, drunk fathers. It was June, but the vast horizon of Lake Superior was still choppy and grey, as cold and unforgiving as when it froze and cracked off islands of ice whose breaking pounded the ears like artillery shells.

When I graduated from high school a couple of years later I joined the Marine Corps. I loved the hot sun of Marine Corps Recruit Depot, San Diego. I loved the hardness of the Corps: the slap of hands against rifles, the ringing of iron on the weight bench, the clean smell of night in the desert hills of Camp Pendleton on our long forced marches. The Cold War was still on, and our only success since the disaster of Vietnam had been the rescue of medical students in Grenada—a small affair compared to humiliation of the Beirut barracks bombing and the hostage-rescue debacle in Iran. During our close-order drill, we sang the romance of power and victory as our combat boots shook the streets.

By the time Saddam Hussein invaded Kuwait in 1990, that romance had faded for me and I was an AWOL Marine Reservist hanging out on the edges of the University of Minnesota, petitioning to be readmitted after flunking out. In five years the world had changed in so many ways: the Berlin Wall had fallen, double-digit unemployment and interest rates had been forgotten, Reagan's 'Morning in America' had become a mere cocktail hour. I wanted out of the Marine Corps, out of the everyday altogether—I craved a blank slate.

And so it was that what I saw and did in Saudi Arabia had nothing to do with the Wahhabis and the oil and the Shi'a who would soon be sacrificed while we went about packing our gear. I did not arrive on camelback, whistling beneath the high desert sun, but came storming down the ramp of a C-5 military transport full of Marines, landing at night in confusion and clouds of swirling dust.

Much of America was waiting for me in the desert: KFC, Pizza Hut, and 7-Eleven had their franchises in Al Jubayl, where I was stationed. The stores sold Camels and Marlboros and Coca-Cola and the highway signs were in English. When trucking up the road between Al Jubayl and Al Mishab, I could have been cruising through California on I-15 between Twentynine Palms and Barstow. Unlike Lawrence, I had no Auda or Prince Faisal to join me in my war: only conscripted drivers from Somalia and Ethiopia, Cambodia and the Philippines. I learned from Yusef, the one Saudi Arabian driver with whom I drove, that times had become hard and many of the former middle classes had to work. His leisurely past betrayed itself on our rests: his elegant manner of drinking tea and smoking cigarettes while sitting cross-legged on a Persian rug laid out next to his truck. My closest encounter with nobility came in the person of one of the younger Khameini Brothers, whose outfit had been contracted to supply us with civilian tractor-trailers. He had taken leave from his finance degree at Northwestern University to come home to Saudi Arabia, where every day I saw him reading the *International Herald Tribune*, smoking English cigarettes and sipping tea from a styrofoam cup. Profiteering never looked so refined.

The old romance of power and victory was forever eviscerated on the day I spent carrying Iraqi POWs. In four days, we took in 100,000 of them. Broken, bloodied, grinning like embarrassed schoolchildren. We'd bombed them for six weeks—some were still showing blood in their ears from the concussion, and now they were grateful for our presence. Beyond the POW camps were the thousands of their comrades who didn't survive: charred in tanks or lying in the desert, their blood drained into the sand. Later we learned that we had gunned down thousands of retreating Iraqi soldiers on the 'Highway of Death' between Kuwait City and Basra. The scene was so gruesome it prompted a near riot in our tent as we heard it described on the camp radio, and the chairman of the joint chiefs of staff, Colin Powell, was so disturbed that he asked President Bush to end the war. He did so within the hour.

I had come to Saudi Arabia as America's worst export—wearing full body armour and carrying an M16, with a head full of obscene idealisms and an insane lack of regard for other people's lives. I left in a kind of daze, not yet understanding that, amid the wreckage of metal and corpses, beneath the skies filled with smoke and fire, I had traded abstract truth for the messy world of real people.   ☐

June 6, 1944

ROBERT CAPA/MAGNUM

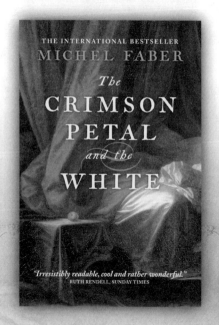

BEDTIME.
READ?

THE INTERNATIONAL BESTSELLER
MICHEL FABER

The
CRIMSON
PETAL
and the
WHITE

"Irresistibly readable, cool and rather wonderful."
RUTH RENDELL, SUNDAY TIMES

"Even better than sex"
TIMES MAGAZINE

www.canongate.net

GRANTA

THIS IS
CENTERVILLE

James Buchan

DAN EHL

In the imagination of strangers there is a small town in America which represents not just itself but the whole country. It will have a strip mall and a high school band and a Pancake Day in the fall. It will be known on its Chamber of Commerce website as America's Hometown.

On a map of the United States, the town of Centerville, Iowa 'America's Hometown'—looks promising. It stands midway between the Missouri river and the Mississippi, perhaps a hundred miles from Des Moines and 200 from Kansas City and about as far from the ocean as it is possible to be. In the Midwest's simple geography, with its tiers of counties stacked like supermarket boxes and highways straight as section lines, Centerville appears to be as ordinary as ordinary.

As Highway 5 runs south from Des Moines airport, the prairie flats begin to roll and break into wooded valleys. The prehistoric ice sheets that flattened northern and central Iowa and ground it up into six or seven feet of the deepest, blackest, richest agricultural soil on earth, here melted and gouged out bluffs and valleys. Monotonous fields of Monsanto corn and soybeans—fields flogged by agriculture as if they had done something unspeakably wicked—give way to black cattle sheltering under oaks, hog sheds, overgrown creeks, rough pasture, hunting ground for turkey, quail and white-tailed deer, see-through towns.

Centerville, the only place of any size in Appanoose County, arrives in a stately procession of chain stores: Wal-Mart, McDonald's, Sonic, Subway, a shuttered mall, one-room insurance brokers, a John Deere dealership, a Hy-Vee supermarket. From the highway, you can see down to a big old-fashioned courthouse square, where at fifty-yard intervals between the cast-iron lamp standards there is an American flag to tell you in which jurisdiction you find yourself.

Around the square, each side of it a double-block long, are lunch-rooms, a J. C. Penney, bank buildings, five-and-dimes you thought had vanished before the Second World War, clothing stores, chiropractors, doctors, a pair of pharmacists, optometrists, furniture stores. On the brick facades are the faded symbols of small-town fraternities—Masons, Shriners, the Independent Order of Oddfellows, Rotary—from the epoch before television. You wonder why nobody bothered to knock the place down. A couple of blocks north, east, south and west, the streets run out past one-storey houses cluttered with swingseats, wind chimes and bank mortgages worth $20,000 on a good day, some in a kind of everlasting yard sale—till they lose themselves in weedy oak and hickory woods or cornfields.

Centerville has twenty-two churches, some of Baptist subsects evidently invented just for articles such as this one, two motels with rooms for cleaning game, two banks, the neo-Romanesque courthouse with its stopped clock, and half a dozen saloons. Its factories make plastic yard furniture and sheds, sterile packaging for food, automotive spare parts, steel wire and mesh and muzzle-loading rifles. It has a high school and community college, a cattle auction, one jail with eighteen inmates, a museum, a movie palace, an old folks' home, a broadband service run by the water company, a National Guard (militia) transportation unit now in Iraq and about 800 family farms. It also has the largest per-capita use of home-made metamphetamine in the state of Iowa.

The 6,000 Americans of Centerville live on beef, pork and potatoes, eat dinner exactly at noon and supper exactly at six. For all the prejudice of Europeans, they are not noticeably overweight. In ten days I saw nobody read a book, eat an apple, use a cellphone (but once) or drink anything stronger than beer (except Jim Milani, a lawyer and rancher, and that was only by way of hospitality). Few men wear neckties even to church or lock their vehicles. The farmers and their wives drive early-model pickups round the courthouse square at fifteen miles an hour as if they were in horse-drawn buggies. More than twenty per cent of the population is over sixty-five, and at the factories middle-aged farmers put in a shift for benefits and health insurance and then go back to their rowcrops. There is at least one Puerto Rican and one African-American. Apart from a young Albanian woman just arrived in town, the nearest Muslim is a doctor in Unionville, ten miles away. People talked of this person as they would an indigo bunting in the woods.

Yet the bland, flat, American surface of Centerville, Iowa is full of depths. In the parking lot of Hy-Vee there is a depression where (according to Gary Craver, who lost his job as a police dispatcher and now investigates the town's history) the ceiling of a longwall mine collapsed. Out to the west on Highway 2, just behind the Pale Moon supper club, there is a grassed-over slag pit where the Sunshine Coal Company ('For Economical Heat, Always Good') once undermined nearly 300 acres and employed 150 men and boys. The ground under Centerville becomes a dimension, like its history.

Certain institutions appear grossly oversized in a town of just 5,924 in the decennial census of 2000: a sixty-bed charity hospital with a CT scanner, the *Daily Iowegian* newspaper, a fifth-generation hometown bank with $100 million in deposits, and the city's very own freight railroad with two dozen miles of track, two diesel locomotives and a ballast car. Imagine such things in a British market town of the size, say, of Selkirk in Lanark or Wallingford, Berkshire. You sense that the town must have been quite rich once.

In reality, Centerville is poised in the balance between boom and failure and always has been. With not many more people than at the time of the War Between the States—11,931 in 1860, 13,721 in 2000—Appanoose County has risen and fallen and fallen and risen on convulsions of commerce or politics.

First there were natives, then pioneers and Mormons, coal, railroads and cattle, then Union Carbide and the Corps of Engineers, then Newell Rubbermaid. In a small town 1,000 miles from the Atlantic, hundreds of Croats, Slovaks, Italians, Germans, Austrians and Jews became good Americans. Just as the people of Centerville know where they are by the compass, and can direct a stranger twelve blocks north or eight to the east, and say which side of the square you can eat French toast and pancakes, they know where they stand in history. That is: that Dad raised a family on 120 acres and I can't make much of a living on 2,000, and I milked two cows before school each day and I delivered coal on Saturdays to the houses in Moravia.

Jeff Young is the fifth member of the Bradley-Young family to run the town bank, Iowa Trust and Savings, and can tell how his great-great-grandfather took the business through the crash of 1873, and his grandfather through the Depression 'though he was not an educated man' and his father and Dave Taylor through the farm crisis of the 1980s without initiating a single farm foreclosure. To hear the phrase 'great-great-grandfather' in modern America is a surprise. Rich or poor, the people of Centerville know they are actors in a colossal economic drama which started before them and will see them out and extends far beyond American borders to places they have never seen even in the Service: Canada, Mexico, Brazil, Europe, China, the Middle East.

Iowa was always prolific of soldiers. In the courthouse square, called in Centerville but nowhere else The Largest Square in the World, young men marched off behind the flags and pipes to fight and die at Vicksburg and Marks Mill, Arkansas; Cuba; France; Belgium and Germany; the Pacific. The day the Bloomington newspaper came into the Post Office with the news of the capture of the Confederate fortress at Vicksburg, the blacksmiths and farriers in the lanes behind the square that now carry the transmission lines rang and rang their anvils and the copperheads pulled down their blinds. When the Iowa National Guard 2133rd Transportation Company set off for Kuwait earlier this year, the highway north to Albia was lined for twenty-five miles by men, women and children waving flags. The National Guard armoury out by the industrial park is now deserted, but for a single woman sergeant, back home on family discharge to look after a teenage son with special needs. Iraq does not come naturally into conversation. Once introduced, it casts a shadow. In this small town in the centre of a powerful country, a disaster in the making reverberates like a telephone two rooms away that rings and rings and rings.

Once known as Chaldea, then as Senterville (which was taken to be a misspelling at the State offices in Iowa City), the town of Centerville was surveyed or 'platted' in 1847. The first log-cabin courthouse was built that summer, and within ten years there was the Bradley bank, grocers, blacksmiths, general stores, three hotels and an insurance agent. In 1857, the first bituminous coal mine was worked at the outcropping of the seam at Mystic in Walnut Township to the north west.

With the coming of the rails from the 1870s, there was a ready market for the coal to fire locomotives. Two railroads came into Centerville, the Chicago, Rock Island and Pacific from Unionville and the Missouri, Iowa and Northern from Keokuk, and crossed at a place about a mile south of the courthouse square called The Levee, and still a place of bars and saloons: after Pancake Day on the last Saturday of September, Sheriff Gary Anderson gets in his vehicle and drives real slow 'so they finish their fighting before I get there'.

By 1906, the mines were bringing up more than a million tons of coal a year. They attracted miners and their families from central and eastern Europe, whose names, somewhat Americanized, make a sort of layer above the old legal and merchant aristocracy of Bradleys, Youngs and Woodens. Jim Milani, whose forebears kept an ice cream parlour on the north side of the square, pronounced his family name Mullaney till he learned better on a visit to North Italy. By then, it would have been an affectation to change. There is not much affectation in Centerville, Iowa.

Because the coal seam was never more than twenty-eight inches deep, the miners dug it out by hand on their knees, sides or bellies. Shetland ponies drew the coal cars up to daylight. Some spent all winter down the mine and lost their sight. The slag hauled out and heaped was fired and then used to surface the gravel back roads. It is hard to imagine that the endless grey roads between the farms were once a brilliant red.

The last brick building on the square, now the Dannco sporting goods store on the east side, went up in 1912. In 1917, seventy-four mines produced a peak tonnage of 1,663,454 tons of coal. That year the railroads began to switch to diesel to fuel their locomotives, and the town entered a decline that lasted until the 1960s. The banks survived by lending not to local people but to Uncle Sam, taking in the public's deposits to buy risk-free Treasury bills. There was no money to build or knock anything down. Centerville was becalmed.

Coalmining lingered on, even if was sometimes just a man and his sons working what was called a dog mine. Dean Kaster, county supervisor, whose father operated the Kaster Coal Company in the Chariton river valley which closed in 1952, as a boy used to unload two mine-trucks after school and on Saturdays took coal to the houses in Moravia to the north. A large fan blew fresh air into the mine which on cold days condensed into a fog at the mine entry. 'When it steamed, that's when you knew it was safe from the blackdamp to go in,' he said. The last mine in Centerville, located just behind the commercial strip on Highway 5, closed in 1966. In the Appanoose County Historical Society Museum, which was set up in the old US Mail building east of the courthouse square, there is a film of the last shifts at the New Gladstone mine, to the west of town, which was the last to shut, in 1971. The men trudging down the slope with their carbide lamps and lunch pails look like grandfathers and probably were. 'In later years,' said Bill Heusinkveld, a local historian who showed me round, 'young men didn't want to go into the mines so we ended up with nothing but older men who had worked in that mine all their lives.' Rollie Reznicek, proprietor of the Owl Pharmacy on the east side of the square and a former mayor of Centerville, said, 'The end of the mines persuaded people in the town they had to work together.'

The Sixties brought a revival in the town's fortunes. In 1962, Union Carbide, a chemicals company with headquarters in the east, chose Centerville for a factory to make shrink packaging for meat from high-density polyethylene pellets delivered from the oil companies by railroad car. The plant employed 400 people. Two years later, the United States Army Corps of Engineers began building the two-mile-long Rathbun Dam to control flooding in the Chariton valley just to the north.

But in the early 1980s, Centerville was down again. In 1980, the bankrupt Rock Island line was shut down and the CBQ Burlington Northern, which had inherited the other track into town, announced that it would close its spur to Centerville in March 1982. To keep Carbide in town, Centerville had to find more than $2 million to buy the track and right of way to a Norfolk and Western junction at Moulton, ten miles to the east. Led by Dave Taylor, who had been brought in by the Youngs to manage Iowa Trust and Savings, and Bob Beck, then publisher of the Daily Iowegian, the people of Centerville subscribed part of the money and raised the rest from state and federal grants. In 1993, when the railroad now known as Norfolk Southern abandoned part of its line, the Appanoose County Community Railroad bought twenty-six more miles of track to connect to the interstate network at Albia to the north. Carbide stayed, though the plant now operates under the name of Curwood. In 1985, Rubbermaid Corp., a consumer products company based in Freeport, Illinois, took over an abandoned factory next door to make outdoor storage bins and sheds, wheelbarrows and cattle drinkers from the same polyethylene that supplied Union Carbide. After three expansions, the factory now employs 500 people at rates of $10.60 an hour, which is not bad for the rural Midwest. A third company, Relco Locomotives, will next year open a works to recondition old locomotives and test them on the lightly used track. 'Without these industries,' said Jim Senior, manager of the Appanoose County Community Railroad, 'Centerville would be a ghost town.'

Mr Senior employs seven grizzled old railwaymen and two fifty-year-old locomotives that haul about 500 cars a year and unload directly into silos at the back of the industrial park. Out on the track are two open-sided cars, used once a year for a town excursion that seems to belong to some golden age of jollification before the invention of liability insurance.

The same people who saved the railroad are now restoring the courthouse square, with the help of a local benefactor. Morgan Cline grew up in Centerville, studied pharmacology at Drake University in Des Moines, practised for a while in the town before moving to New York where he went into pharmaceutical advertising. His practice, Cline, Davis & Mann, has $500 million in customer billings, including the account of the largest pharmaceutical company in the world, Pfizer Inc. Mr Cline is credited with persuading the former Senate majority leader, Bob Dole, to advertise Viagra. Mr Cline began with the restoration of the best building on the square, the Continental Hotel of 1893, which had become a flophouse. According to Bill Burch, who handles Mr Cline's business in Centerville, he has spent some $15 million in the district, and it shows. On every side of the square, the aluminium siding is coming down. 'He's the one,' said Linda Howard, who is active in civic affairs, 'who's shown us we can save these beautiful old buildings. We were more worried about having a strip mall, maybe because that's what the people saw when they went to Kansas City—a mall. Morgan helped us turn that corner.' The city now wants to convert an old movie house in the Spanish colonial style into a concert hall and do up the town's bandshell and a library built by General Francis M. Drake, who was wounded at Marks Mill in 1864 and went on to be Governor of Iowa. A group of white men in their seventies are restoring by hand the Baptist church that was used by the African-Americans in town. Thus a tonic for male impotence revives a fatigued old town in the Midwest.

To see what Centerville could have been and might still be, travel east along Highway 2 to Sunshine Corner then turn north to the old coal-mining town of Mystic. Mystic, named by a railway engineer for his hometown in Connecticut, is a place where the transformation from boom town to ghost town so evident across Appanoose County is not quite complete. On the railroad is an old water tower for the steam locomotives, and the sort of gas station Bonnie Parker and Clyde Barrow might have robbed and driven away laughing. Under the brilliant starlit nights, the long freights wail and the coyotes yip.

On what was once Nob Hill, where the mine owners and their lawyers lived, there are trailers among broken-down palaces. The mud roads and vanished subdivisions are overwhelmed with second-growth timber, where, walking in the rain, I came on a Mountain Dew bottle stopped with duct tape with a long, clear tube coming out the top.

Sheriff Anderson sent two officers to pick it up the next day. It was the remains of a home-made lab to make the speed known as metamphetamine or more generally 'crank'. Farm-country crack, it is, say the police and hospital people, just as savage, antisocial and habit-forming as its counterpart in the ghetto. Its active pharmaceutical is the decongestant ephedrine. Users buy Sudafed from the Fareway or Hy-Vee, then cook it up into rock or paste with a mixture of anhydrous ammonia from off the farm, acetone, hydrochloric acid, alkaline battery fluid and lye. Every now and then, according to Sheriff Anderson, a shed or garage out in the woods goes up to high heaven. Originally an overtime drug of factory workers and long-distance truckers, it has colonized the underclasses of the rural Midwest. 'I guess the meth epidemic is rather like the crack epidemic a few years back, except it is out in the rural parts of Iowa, Missouri, Indiana, out in the chicken coops, so it doesn't stand out,' said Dr Paul Novak, a senior doctor in the emergency room at Mercy Medical Center on Highway 5. Its most lurid symptom, it seems, is the delusion among users that insects have got under their skin. Dennis Sturms, ambulance manager, said, 'Unless you're with the police or medical services, you wouldn't know it was going on. But go into Wal-Mart, and look for people with scabs on their arms.' Mary Lou Sales, manager of the emergency room clinic, said that children were at risk from fumes or spillages, or where chemicals had seeped into the walls of microwave ovens, from lye stored in pop bottles, and from the violent and unpredictable behaviour of users.

Mystic's Main Street is paved with brick, but only a few solid buildings survive like teeth among the weeds: the American Legion or the Coalminers Inn where a young man tried to pick a fight with me in the gloom, but did not know enough about Britain to find a cause. Up the street, beyond a chain-link fence, was a scuffed park and playground and a civilian notice: NO FIGHTING. NO PROFANITY. NO ALCOHOL.

On a vacant lot opposite, a small crowd had gathered in the rain for an auction of domestic furnishings out of the back of a truck.

'Dollar-bill-dollar-bill-half-dollar-half-dollar-dollar-bill-two-dollar-dollar-bill.'

The auctioneer, his long straight hair held by a baseball cap, called for a cigarette. A man in the truck, as sunburned and worn out as a Confederate infantryman at Appomatox Courthouse, manhandled an exercise treadmill from the truck. Jim Buban, the chief automobile dealer in Centerville, stalked round the crowd till greeted by me, when he jumped.

'Treadmill. Works,' he said. 'Dollar-bill-two-dollar-two-dollar. Nobody want it. Put it back.'

Each item brought down or taken up again—golf clubs, a grade-school desk, mechanical drill, a metal table, two snowboards (eight dollars)—carried traces of foreclosure or some other domestic failure. For this was the end of the road. Here, in Mystic and places like Mystic, the surplus objects of a society in surplus had come to rest, discharging their last vestige of value in commerce—the final half-dollar—into the wet American air.

'Dollar-bill-dollar-bill-half-dollar-half-dollar. Nobody want it. Put it back.'

In the modern suburbs of, say, Atlanta, Georgia, Americans do much of their business by hand signals from vehicles or formulaic conversations across store counters. Centerville, in contrast, is a partly pedestrian civilization. People walk, on their legs, along the sidewalks of the courthouse square or stop to view its little dramas: Sheriff Anderson bringing in two cuffed and orange-jumpsuited prisoners for arraignment and, a little later, Judge Dan Wilson stepping out in his suit and tie for his dinner. Everybody knows far too much about everybody else's business and that, for example, Tom Johnson, one of two optometrists in town, was late for his 9.30 Friday because he took that British writer to watch ospreys at the lake and came in still in his rubber boots. At night, teenagers lounge

Centerville Hometown committee

by their trucks as late as nine o'clock. Centerville is a town where people still make their own amusements, in church suppers, band suppers, drive-through dinners. It is not the fragmented and isolated American suburbs of Robert D. Putnam's *Bowling Alone*.

Beside the courthouse, the third on the site after No. 2 burned down in the Fourth of July fireworks of 1881, you might at any time see a man in a Hawaiian shirt and drooping moustache, carrying a digital camera. He looks like Dennis Hopper in *Apocalypse Now*, minus the shakes, and indeed the man once served in Vietnam and Germany as a military photographer. His hair is long and lank, for which he was once fined a dollar at Rotary. This is Dan Ehl, current managing editor of the *Daily Iowegian*. A liberal Democrat, a passionate opponent of the war in Iraq, pro-UN, pro-France even, Mr Ehl likes to write editorials in favour of such causes as legalizing marijuana. For a while, the cops used to flag down his truck and examine his tongue for something or other, but now Sheriff Anderson has come round to him. In reality, Mr Ehl is the life and soul of Centerville, a symbol of its tolerance and self-absorption, and of the ability of small-town America to convert rebellion into light comedy or corn pone. Mr Ehl recently hitch-hiked from Des Moines just to show it could still be done as in the days when America was young.

Centerville was not always a political backwater. In the 1860s it found itself just thirty miles from the border of a slave state, and every cellar step and peeling outhouse, it now seems, was a station on the underground railroad to Canada for runaway slaves from Missouri. In the depressed conditions of the 1920s, the Ku Klux Klan set up on 12th Street and for a few years tried to make a political programme out of anti-Semitism and a ban on immigration. The Republican hold on the state of Iowa established at the Civil War broke down in the mid-twentieth century, and in the presidential election of 2000, Appanoose County voted by only 432 votes for George W. Bush and Al Gore took the state's votes in the electoral college. As this January's Iowa Caucuses swung into view, and one by one the Democratic challengers to Mr Bush broke cover, Centerville found a party-political language in which to talk about America's place in the world and the Middle East.

It was as if the tremendous shock of September 11 still

reverberated. 'I would say we in the Midwest are pretty patriotic people,' said Bill Belden, local manager of the Iowa Farm Bureau and an active Republican. 'I would say at this point we don't want to see terrorism in our shores again.' Democrats, in contrast, saw the Iraq invasion as only making matters worse, and impugned Mr Bush's motives. 'It just all felt so powerless,' Ms Howard said. 'He [Mr Bush] was going to do it [invade Iraq], it didn't matter what anybody said. And he just did it, playing cowboy. And now we have the burden of helping those people [Iraqis] recreate their country and we don't know how to do that.' Ms Howard, who has spent most of her life outside Centerville and has just returned, paused: 'But you know 9/11 upset us. It was so frightening and so unpredictable. It was like all the rules were gone. Any Joe Blow on a plane...'

At Bruce Dickerson's US History class at Indian Hills Community College, a majority of students did not believe that Iraq had any hand in the assault on the USA on September 11, 2001. A small majority, and not just those from army and National Guard families, believed that the United States and the United Kingdom should stay in Iraq to install an American-style democracy. Nobody seemed very proud of what had occurred. 'I guess we were on a roll after Afghanistan and already wound up,' a young woman said. 'We're a pretty aggressive country, I think.' The students were shy, for Americans, and reluctant to express an opinion.

What unites both parties in town is lip service to the safety and welfare of the Iowans in Iraq. The unit had its first fatality when David M. Kirchhoff died on August 14 as a result of heatstroke in Kuwait. The National Guard unit is now stationed a hundred miles west of Baghdad, backing up operations in the insurrectionary Sunni towns and villages of central Iraq, ferrying back front-line personnel for leave or to call home by satphone, transporting prisoners.

Attending the Moravia Fall Festival in her Humvee and fatigues, Sergeant Robin Page of the National Guard said, 'One thing that Dan [Mr Ehl] and I can agree on is that we must support our people over in Iraq.' This common loyalty keeps the peace in a small town and allows people to sit down together at the Farm Bureau steak supper. In truth, people are deeply shocked by the cost in lives and money of the expedition. They try not to think too much about it.

At the First Presbyterian Church on North Main Street, the

minister, Dr Beverley Leonard prayed for rain for the crops but not for Iraq. She said it slipped her mind. Older people have their own anxieties. Pat Clark, a former athlete and Navy rating, said in a saloon one night, 'One here, one there. Two here, two there. Pff.' He sighted down an imaginary sniper's rifle and squeezed the trigger. 'There's one word that explains it all. V-I-E-T-N-A-M.'

The word 'powerless', once uttered, seemed to describe many aspects of life in Centerville. In the dog days of coal mining in the 1940s and 1950s, labour unions gained a hold in Centerville but the modern factories are ununionized. At Rubbermaid, the work is hard, heavy and noisy. To cut the flash off the stamped plastic panels, the workers use hunting knives, as if they were cutting meat or field-dressing a deer, and there is a constant danger of injury. 'It's probably the most physical of our plants,' said Kevin Wiskus, plant manager.

What attracts employers such as Newell Rubbermaid and Curwood to Centerville is a tradition of hard physical labour from the farms. Phyllis More, a packer of 7ft x 7ft tool sheds at Rubbermaid, laughed at the exertion: 'This is no harder than dairy farming.' Yet Centerville must compete with similar hard-working small towns in Oklahoma, Texas, Alabama, Mississippi. Centerville knows that its muscle is a mere American commodity, and, that should labour unions ever gain a hold in town, the industrial employers would leave and take with them 1,800 ten-dollar-an-hour jobs.

The farmers have no more control over their lives than the men and women stacking pallets of flat-pack storage bins at Rubbermaid. According to Bill Belden, Iowa farmers get to keep about eight cents of each dollar spent on food at the supermarket. Prices of beef were at all-time highs this autumn, but none of the cattle ranchers seemed to know why and many had sold forward at lower prices. Corn and beans looked good on the Fourth of July, but a scalding August without rain meant both crops would be short.

Pretty well all the large farmers in Appanoose County grow Roundup Ready crops: that is, corn and soybeans genetically modified by Monsanto of St Louis so they can be treated safely with the Monsanto glyphosate herbicide Roundup. It keeps the weeds down, they say, but not as much as it used to and they must buy seed anew each season and pay Monsanto a royalty on the seed, known as a tech fee. If they hold back seed from their own harvest to sow themselves, Monsanto will prosecute them. At harvest, they sell the corn to colossal merchant-processors such as Cargill Corp. of Minneapolis, Minnesota, and Archer Daniels Midland of Decatur, Illinois. The farmers complain they are squeezed on price at both ends. 'Cargill and Monsanto own the country,' says Tom Teno, who farms 2,000 acres of rowcrops and cattle just across the county line in Monroe County.

Mr Teno is a handsome man, who talks like John Wayne (born at Winterset, Iowa some forty years before Mr Teno). The night before, he had broken a metacarpal in his right hand vaccinating his cows, and it pained him, though that didn't stop him talking or preparing the combine to harvest his corn.

Mr Teno is by all accounts one of the very best farmers in southern Iowa but even he finds the going tough. 'Crop prices are the same now as when my Dad raised five kids on one hundred and twenty acres,' he said. 'In 1952, Dad bought a tractor and all the train for eighteen hundred dollars. Now you have to spend hundreds of thousands on machinery and farm half the county to make any sort of living. It's one hell of a battle. Yet if I die tonight, people round here would be fighting for the land I cash-rent before I was cold. We should all refuse to sell crops at these prices, but it will never happen.' As well as cutting one another's throats, the farmers are conservative to the point of obstinacy. Mr Teno was once asked to grow just forty acres of artichokes. He refused unless the seedsman guaranteed to take the crop. Even now, he pronounces the word artichoke as if it somehow did not belong in the English language. There is almost no conception in Centerville that there might be some other way to farm other than selling manipulated commodity foods into a fast-food culture, drawing subsidies that beggar other nations and seeking evanescent savings from genetic modification. Iowa farmers have had more than $10 billion in farm subsidies since 1996, more than those of any state in the Union. They latch on to any new use—ethanol, bio-diesel—that Cargill discovers for corn and beans. When a visitor says that in England families pay premiums for a species of uncooked ham from Parma, Italy, and red wine from Bordeaux, France, they say, Well, I'll be damned. And so it goes round: corn, beans, cattle, hogs, as God or

Cargill has ordained until the greatest agricultural province on earth goes to hell or is displaced by Brazil.

Across in Highland Township of Wapello County, Larry Kinsinger takes a while to reveal just how down he is on his luck. A lean, bright man in his fifties, Mr Kinsinger quit farrowing 500 sows in February. In July his wife said she wanted to leave him. By December, he will have sold the last of his fat hogs, and be working at a job in the town of Ottumwa, probably at the meat-packer, Excel Corp., which is owned by Cargill. For the moment, Mr Kinsinger still has 1,200 hogs to fatten on contract. The hogs (Yorks, Large Whites, and lots in between) are packed tight on concrete slats in a long barn, about eight square feet or less per animal, fed wholly on concentrated feed from silos ranged along the barn. The hogs have their tails cut to discourage cannibalism and that is largely successful. Such 'hog confinements' are unpopular in Iowa, less for the hyper-intensive husbandry than for the stink. The smell of pigshit clings to clothes and rental cars for days on end. It is not a soft heart that brought Mr Kinsinger to grief.

After a spell as an army pharmacist, Mr Kinsinger took over from his father in 1975. In 1994, against his father's advice, he borrowed a couple of hundred thousand dollars to build the hog barn and to buy two neighbouring farms. In 1998, the hog market all but collapsed, with prices falling for a time under ten dollars a hundredweight. Mr Kinsinger sold the two farms and will have soon sold everything else except the barn. He hopes a neighbour might work it for him, such as Dwight Lowenberg, whose 4,000-head sheds gleam brutally white on the horizon.

It is hard to fail when your neighbours succeed. It is hard to work at a meat-packer that treats farmers like employees, specifies breed, genetics and feed and won't buy from independent farmers. It is hard to have your money in pork, when your wife has her money in the stock market. It'll be harder still this winter in town to watch the cattlemen driving round in their new-model trucks. It is hardest of all not to take your sons with you. 'Our house was three-quarters of a mile from the farm,' Mr Kinsinger said, 'and my sons would see me go off in the truck, but they'd stay and maybe help my wife around the house. They might have been living in a city. I remember back when Tom broke his arm at football, he was waiting around in the doctor's office and the nurses said what are you going to do

when you're grown. He said, "Somebody'll have to work the farm."
I said, "Nobody *has* to work the farm, Tom."' Tom Kinsinger is now
a freshman at Iowa State.

The truck passed a couple of cornbins, lopsided in the weeds,
where a farm had been, and failed, like this one. Mr Kinsinger turned
to his visitor. 'I didn't fail, the farm failed. I've been reading about
George Washington and Abraham Lincoln. You can lose and lose,
but it's the last battle that matters; only the last.'

Centerville is a town the American founding fathers might have
dreamed of building on the prairie: civic, self-reliant and law-
abiding. Yet those very virtues have their shadow existences as
arrogance, overconfidence and naivety. A sojourn in a British small
town would turn up a different composition of virtue and vice. And
both towns would have contributed to the catastrophe in Iraq.

There was one more visit to pay. This was to the Vanderlinden
place, south of Centerville towards the Missouri state line. The
long gravel road that is 600th Street was deserted, except for
mourning doves on the wires and turkey vultures quartering the corn.
A cloud of dust ahead resolved itself into an Amish sulky returning
from school, a boy driving in his straw hat, his two sisters in their
blue bonnets behind. The Amish are moving into Appanoose County,
paying top dollar for land, and paying in cash. Their aloofness makes
them unpopular. Out on the gravel roads, they look no more exotic
than the drifts of monarch butterflies.

Kirk Vanderlinden is a large, tow-haired man with big spectacles
that slide down his nose, fattening 300 cattle (mostly Angus) in a
long trough on a muddy feed-lot behind his father's farmstead. He
buys the cattle at the Ballanger auction in Centerville. He has 200
acres under corn, 200 under beans, and the rest under sown grasses.
His grandfather bought the farm off an insurance company in 1948,
and not a whole lot has changed since then, but a new steel silo
($7,500) and cutter for the cattle feed ($7,000). His wife, Debbie,
teaches elementary school, which brings in $30,000 a year plus
health benefits. They have a son, Evan, who is nine. Last spring, to
the astonishment of every single person in Centerville, Kirk and
Debbie Vanderlinden travelled to St Petersburg, Russia and adopted
four children out of a state orphanage. 'Actually,' Marilyn

Vanderlinden, his mother, said at church, 'we thought Kirk had gone mad.' The youngest of the Russian children, a little girl named Roselana, raced ahead into the machinery barn, crying 'Kombin! Kombin!' at the harvester.

Kirk Vanderlinden worked in fibre optics in North Carolina before taking over three quarters of the farm in 1990. With the price of cattle up at nearly one hundred cents per pound, he had done very well. (He would have done better, he said with a smile, if he hadn't sold some forward at seventy-four cents and vowed in future not to spend so long at his computer.) 'I wouldn't recommend this life to anybody. I have five hundred thousand dollars' worth of capital, another seven hundred and fifty thousand in land, maybe a hundred thousand in machinery, that's one point five million dollars in assets that if you're lucky makes a return of thirty thousand dollars. It's just the lifestyle. My kids enjoy some of the lifestyle I had as a kid. That's all you can ask.'

Roselana cried out. Beyond the yard and the house, beneath an immense elm tree, a yellow school bus was drawing gently to a stop. Roselana bolted and Mr Vanderlinden and his visitor ran after her. Their muddy boots slowed them down. As the bus started up and pulled away, four children were standing on the grass, a pretty girl of about seventeen and three sturdy boys. They stood with their lunch boxes and satchels, looking at Mr Vanderlinden with the most intense yearning. Mr Vanderlinden looked back. 'How was school?'

'Good,' said Liza.

'Good,' said Ivan.

'Fine,' said Ilya.

'Good,' said Evan.

Roselana chattered away.

Something about the children was altering beyond all restitution. In the yellow Midwestern light, under the colossal elm tree, I could see that they were ceasing to be what they had been and that they were becoming something else. They were becoming Americans. □

GRANTA

MAPPING AMERICA
Martin Rowson

Mapping America
by Martin Rowson

1. **A**ll attempts hitherto to produce a *definitive* map of the United States of America entirely accurate in all regards have been *woefully* constrained by the limitations of *conventional* cartography with its outmoded insistence on the primacy of *purely territorial* factors (fig.1)

Fig.1

ALASKA

Pacific Ocean

CANADIA

UNIDED STADES of AMERIKA

Atlantic Ocean

HAWAII

Mercator's Projection

MEHICO

Gulf of Mehico

COOBA etc.

2. In the first instance United States allowing A more accurate TERR

U

Washington Stat

Orego

S

Alaska

Nevada

California

Hawaii

Pacific Ocean

A

World T

approach necessarily compromises the territorial integrity of
ely *physical features* (oceans, Canada, *etc.*) to get in the way.
RIAL MAP is shown in Fig. 2

Dakota Sea

Rowson/Mercator's Projection
(with several of the States
rearranged for Tidiness's sake)

However, even this is so *ultimately inaccurate*
n so many levels as to be practically USELESS.
An entirely new and radical cartography is
erefore required.

©Martin Rowson '03

3. This new cartography is predicated on factors *in addition* to mere acreage, including *social & economic determinates, geopolitics, aspiration, religion, New Age philosophy, shoe size,* etc., etc. By calculating AREA in this way (which is *very hard* but ultimately rewarding) a far more representative MAP (or *series* of maps) is now possible.

For example, to take the historical *long view,* we can calculate the AREA of the infant United States at the time of the *Constitutional Congress* using the following SIMPLE SUM

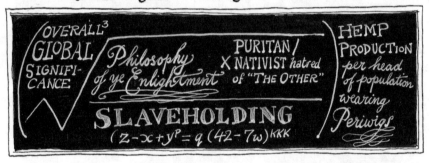

OVERALL[3] GLOBAL SIGNIFICANCE / *Philosophy of ye Enlightment* / X PURITAN / NATIVIST *hatred* of "THE OTHER" / HEMP PRODUCTION *per head of population wearing Periwigs*

SLAVEHOLDING

$$(z - x + y^p) = q (42 - 7w)^{KKK}$$

Which produces the COMPLETELY ACCURATE MAP below (Fig.3)

UNITED STATES of AMERICA

Hanover

Romanof

Hapsburg

Bourbon

Empire

NB. European area calculated according to Killane's Projection as a sub-factor of 12 to the power of Monarchy

4. Using these *simple rules*, the FOLLOWING MAPS can now be produced:

Fig. 4: UNITED STATES of AMERICA showing $\dfrac{\text{OBESITY} \times \substack{\text{WATCHING} \\ \text{JERRY SPRINGER}}}{\text{CHURCH ATTENDANCE}}$

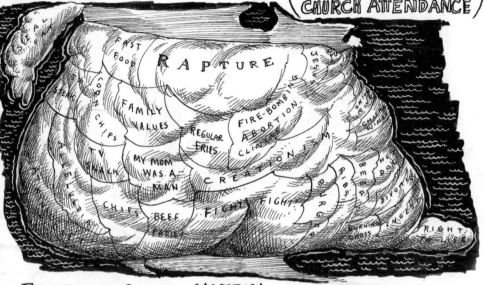

Fig. 5: UNITED STATES of AMERICA

showing $\left(\dfrac{\text{GUN ownership*} \times \text{Former Membership of The Weather Underground†}}{\text{"DAUGHTERS of the REVOLUTION" having had 3 or more HUSBANDS£}}\right)$

Arctic Circle

Loft on W 83rd St. Manhattan

2nd Hand Bookshop in OAKLAND, Ca.

MEXICO

*Where font is constant
if variant, typified thus:

$\left(\dfrac{\text{N.R.A.}}{\substack{\text{Symbionese Liberation} \\ \text{Army}}}\right)^{\text{Sex}}$

to the power of 8 recurring

† Where font is *Copperplate*,
assume Ivy League as a multiple
of (FUCK YOU DAD)^{23·8} × Drugs −18

£ Where $\left(\dfrac{\text{SUBURBAN ALCOHOLISM}}{\text{SOCCER MOM}}\right)$
is divisable by 27.

5. A further refinement of the process can be achieved by using this absurdly straightforward 8 dimensional graph:

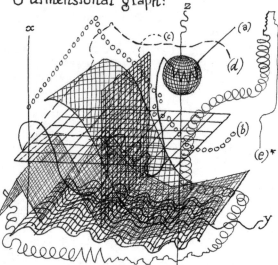

* where (e) equals the amount of vomit produced hourly at DISNEYLAND in imperial gallons set against number of ENRON shares owned per redundant employee as a factor in the War against Drugs. Source: *American Journal of Bowk*.

6. A yet furth
TOPOGR
where *nort*

Fig. 7:

Thus this map of U.S. Ethnic Tension (fig. 6)

MELTING POT

PRISON
(Blacks & Hispanics)*

* Formerly Jews, Italians, Norwegians, Irish, Apaches, Poles, Unitarians, etc.

Key to LITERARY RESPON
to THE AMERICAN DREA

① FLIGHT ② EXILE ③ DRUG
④ DRINK ⑤ VISCERAL DISGU

Melville/Hawthorne
Poe   Henry James
Zane Grey   Pound/Eliot
Fitzgerald/Hemingway
Kerouac/Ginsberg
Burroughs
Heller/Roth/Mailer etc
Gore Vidal
Brett Easton Ellis, etc
Grisham/Crichton/Leon
Uris, etc $

7. Although space forbids me from showing all the maps of AMERICA *The New CARTOGRAPHY* makes possible, here's three more...

Fig. 8: UNITED STATES of AMERICA showing

((PATRIOTISM × PURITANISM) Political Cohesion) $elf-Intere$ted OPPORTUNI$M

COMPLETE LACK of any INTERAL or EXTERNAL THREAT, REAL or IMAGINARY

HEY! WHERE HAVE THE YANKS GONE?

'OO CARES? 'AVE ANUZZER CROISSANT!

N.B. Most of the Atlantic Ocean has drained away into the new void

Fig. 9: UNITED STATES of AMERICA shown as

POLITICAL CORRUPTION × Enterprise

The following unprintable joke:
Q: What's the difference between a NEO-CONSERVATIVE and a traditional RIGHT-WING REPUBLICAN?
A: The NEO-CONS let jews into their golf clubs.

YEHARRR!!

TEXAS

Washington D.C.

FLORIDA

WORLD PEACE

Fig. 10: THE UNITED STATES of AMERICA shown as

DEMOCRACY CAPITALISM × (Manifest Destiny) Complete BAFFLEMENT*

* In this 2 dimensional projection, the Earth is naturally assumed to be FLAT.

THE AST EST OPE

FOR CHRIST'S SAKE QUIT MOANIN', YA UNGRATEFUL SONS OF BITCHES!

GRANTA

MAN WALKS INTO A BAR

James Kelman

I had been living abroad for twelve years and I was gaun hame, maybe forever, maybe a month. Once there it would sort itself out. In the meantime I fancied seeing my faimly again; my mother was still alive, and I had a sister and brother. The plane out of here was scheduled for one o'clock tomorrow afternoon. I was in a room at an Away Inn, out in the middle of nowhere, miles from the airport and miles from downtown, but it was cheap as fuck so there we are and there I was. The woman on reception gied me a look when I asked if there was a bar within crawling distance. Then she thought a moment and told me if I walked a mile or so there was a place. She had a twinkle in her eye at the idea of the mile or so walk. Then she said she never used the place herself but reckoned they might do some food.

I hadnay asked about food in the first place so how come she threw that in? I think I know why. I just cannay put it into words. But it turned my slow move to the door into a bolt for freedom. I had the anorak zipped right to the top, pulled the cap down low on my heid. Outside a freezing wind was blowing. Ye were expecting tumbleweed to appear but when it did it would be in the form of a gigantic snowball. While I walked I wondered why I was walking and why outside. Why the hell could I no just have stayed in the room, strolled up and down the motel corridor if I felt energetic. Better still, I could have read a book. Or even allowed myself to watch some television. Who could grumble about that; I was entitled to relax. Yet still I left the place and walked a mile in subArctic conditions. Mine was a compulsive, obsessive, addictive personality, the usual—plus I felt like a beer and the company of human beings; human beings, not tubes in a box or words on a page, and masturbation enters into that. In other words I was sick of myself and scunnered with my company, physically and mentally. And why was I gaun hame! I didnay even want to go hame. Yes I did.

No I didnay.

Yes I did.

No I didnay. No I fucking didnay. It was an obligation. Bonné Skallin man it can only be an obligation. The faimly were there and one had to say hullo now and again. Posterity demands it of us. Once I am deid the descendants will be discussing departed ancestors: Who was that auld shite that lived in the States? Which one? Him that didnay come hame to visit his poor auld maw! Aw that bastard!

This is the obligation I am talking about.

Jesus christ.

But the reality was that my mother wasnay keeping too well. Let us put an end to the frivolity: if I wantit to see her again this seemed the time. I spoke to my brother on the phone. What an arsehole. Never mind, the point was taken, I had bought le billet with return scheduled a month from now and here I was. Yeh, the wind, and polar bears on the street. I like polar bears. And I like this part of the world. The auld ears, nevertheless, were being nipped at by icy spears. I settled into a catatonic march. Blocks of low-level factories and warehouses were on baith sides of the road, disused, some derelict. Maybe a cab would pass. I should have phoned one from the motel, I know that. But I didnay. Okay?

The wind whistled between buildings, rattling the roofs. Can the wind rattle the roofs? It did sound like that. This land was good land. But these capitalist fuckers and their money-grabbing politico sidekicks had turned it into a horror. I had an urge to write down my thoughts but where was my notebook? In my room at the Inn. And so what if it had been with me, in this gale it would have blown away or else my fingers would have froze and fell aff. I bought the notebook yesterday in a decent wee bookshop no too far from the bus station. It was a real surprise. But that can happen, ye enter a town in the middle of nowhere and discover some enthusiast has opened a bookshop. In this case a middle-aged couple who had grabbed their dough and skipped out of Denver or somewhere. So they opened a pure nirvana of a place. These folks were good folks. Although no doubt they were millionaires and the shop was a hobby. If their bookshop was in the vicinity and open I would have gone. I am convinced of that. But now it was evening and it surely would have been closed and how far away was I from the bus station? I had seen the day where I might have thought fuck it and tried to hitch a ride but buddy, no just now.

The cheery neon sign blinking a welcome to weary travellers had nothing whatsoever to do with my decision. I saw it ahead, its fissures of light streaming upwards to the moon. Jeremiah Brown, grunted the sign—for such was my name—rest ye here oh weary one.

Sure, I replied. Show me yer fine food, yer fine beer, yer wine, yer spirits; and what about an Isla malt at an affordable price?

Walk straight ahead oh venerable one oh wise one, the gravelly voice intoned.

I was either hallucinating or a god had collared me for his ayn.

The place was huge and empty, built for stagecoachloads of customers who never arrived. There was something about it, like it had been abstracted from a 1940s movie, made for hot dogs and hamburgers and all kinds of similar fastfood sustenance. It was like it wasnay a bar at all it was really something else, a fucking what do you call it, a restaurant.

A restaurant! It wasnay a bar at all, it was a goddam restaurant. There was a little bar right enough, set into a corner in the style of a rock and roll obsessed backwoodsman's den, Jim Bridger goes electric. You entered the den you entered the bar. There were ossified wee creatures and paintings of such; toads, squirrels, foxes and beavers, mink, a huge bear, game-birds and big fucking brown trout and carp; fishing rods and single barrel shotguns. Some interesting auld signs; one read, PIKE'S PEAK OR BUST and another CALAMITY JANE'S ROCK N ROLL. Stuck alongside on the wall were 78 rpm records with sleeves, and LP and EP covers showing Little Richard, Jerry Lee Lewis, Fats Domino, Elvis Presley, Chuck Berry, Buddy Holly, Franco Corelli and Eddie Cochrane. The bar was done in the image of a redwood tree trunk and the bar stools looked like sawn-off portions of thinner trunks. Naybody here. I was about to vamoose but a guy had spotted me, poked his head out from behind a door and was across immediately. Yes sir how are you sir?

I'm fine, how's yerself in this here jungle?

Okay okay. He attempted a smile, it became a question.

I didnay bother explaining. Just a lite beer, I said, I dont care which brand, nor its state, nor yet its country of origin.

The guy attempted another smile. I rubbed my hands together. It's damn cauld tonight.

Yeh, gonna be snow later, maybe sooner.

Aye, it's in the air. Time for Santa Claus eh!

Yes sir.

That bottle of beer later I skedaddled. To leave a bar on one such item isnay exactly typical. Maybe I had turned over a new leaf. If so naybody had telt me. Naybody never tells me fucking nothing but so that is okay. If they did one might prepare.

I was gauny call a fare-thee-well to the bartender but he was out of sight, no doubt blethering to a lassie in the kitchen, if he was lucky enough to have a lassie in the kitchen. I worked in bars much of the time and I never had nay lassie in nay kitchen. It was just the usual sentimental fucking shite man it came pouring out my brains. The reality is the guy in this bar was living a boring nightmare. What chance did he have? What life lay ahead? What
fuck.

Right, on we go. And so did I, out the door. In the lobby I phoned a cab which is what I should have considered back in the Away Inn. Never mind. Ten minutes later I was in the back seat of an elderly Lincoln, just about my favourite jalopy, that yin with the unEuropean lines, which is what I liked about it, it was just so fucking unEuropean. Times have changed for the better when the taxis are elderly Lincolns. Yes sir. There was a large sign pinned to the rear window.

'S YORE RIGHT TO SMOKE IN HERE,
'S MA RIGHT TO SHOOT YA.

I must not smoke I must not smoke I must not smoke. The guy himself wasnay smoking although his side window was a quarter way open. He had a woollen hat on his napper and a thick scarf wound round his neck. All the heaters were blowing warm and his music playing softly, a solo clarinet. Yeh, it was snug. Where was his flask of coffee and the nip of brandy? At certain periods ye could envy taxi drivers. I called to him, It's a miserable cauld night outside but warm in here!

Yes, very cold, the snow is coming.

What time do you finish?

I saw his eyes in the rear-view mirror, studying me. There was a chance he was a writer. I finish at four, he said, maybe five.

He was from Africa but from what part. You from Ghana originally?

Ghana...

Yer accent is familiar.

He nodded, but noncommittally; was I right or wrong, who could say. His nod was to my idea about the accent and how I had arrived at the 'Ghana' deduction, no about whether the guess was accurate which was irrelevant. He kept his eyes on the road. To hell with it, I leaned forwards and called: Nowadays we do not ask people personal questions. But once upon a time that was okay, that was civilized behaviour. I would have tried my guess out on ye without a moment's consideration but nowadays that is asking for trouble and the likelihood is you think I am some nefarious undercover Security agent from the anti-unPatriotic Front, masquerading as whatever, a down-at-heel Skatchman. I'm no, I'm just an ordinary guy, I'm just an immigrant. I shrugged.

I didnay say 'an immigrant like you' or 'unlike you I am an immigrant' or 'I am not an immigrant, like yourself, or unlike yourself.' Nayn of that stuff. I didnay say fucking nothing. Ah but conversations are fraught, deadly dangerous. Then too the poor guy, the driver, just out for his 12 or 14 hour shift trying to earn a dollar and he gets hit by me.

The chat was now at an end.

The feller no longer watched me in his mirror, only drove to the appropriate area, one with a choice of bars. Okay. And the district we were in now, it had that familiarity about it, like I had been through this way in the past. It was funny how ye got these sensations. I was gauny mention it to the driver but naw, I had blown it, and when I got out the cab he avoided looking at me. I hoped he had grasped that I wasnay a right-wing racist bastard and I wasnay an undercover member of some counter-insurgency agency whose speciality lay in perceiving the alien threat. I tipped him a typical sum and said, Have a good night.

There was a sign for the local community college and I saw a little river, and there were some no bad looking bars, and farther on there was a leisure place, tenpin bowling. Neat. As burgs go it was a small yin but here it had its ayn wee downtown area and all kinds of people should have been out walking, all kinds of people. Nayn of them was so walking, no tonight. It was just too cauld.

But at least there was nay snaw. I checked the first bar; busy enough and a young crowd; and the music, though dull and boring, was very loud and rhythmic. Could I cope, that was the question. There were a couple of beautiful girls; the boys with them seemed too young to buy a drink never mind act as escorts. I was inside the lobby and about to push open the door and saunter in but my arm locked and I was unable to fulfil the operation. But my legs were fine and they did a march on the spot while my upper body conducted a reverse manoeuvre. Next thing I know I am out the door thank god. When in doubt trust yer physicality.

Next along was a joint called the *Shooters and Horses Sports Bar*. This was the last place I should have gone, should ever have gone.

Thank you for the warning fates, now it was up to me.

In the bright interior I could see baseball on a few large screens, yep, Corey Parker. He was everywhere ye went. It was reaching the end of the season and everything had stopped to see if the new boy wonder could set an all-time record. I didnay think he could and would have taken bets all day. I reckoned it was down to his name. If the feller had been christened some less macho moniker—e.g. Herbert Summerbottom III—he would have remained in obscurity. Mind you the auld timers were saying the guy was special.

Never trust an auld timer but, no when ye want to lay down yer dough. Ever met a rich auld timer? There are a few rich ones but you will never meet them. The ones ye meet for daily communion are either skint or else do not gie a fuck about the dollar, almighty or no.

But I wasnay gaun to no fucking bar to sit and stare at the tube. There were five of them thar screens in this here joint, probably they even had one in the pisshouse. What a dive. But my feet led the way, I pushed open the door. It got worse. In this bar a man could hit the Oregon Trail without leaving his stool. Not only was Corey Parker a feature so too were the ladies, and a large poster screamed to lascivious boozers that come midnite adult entertainment was scheduled, sit back and relax: here come the Wicked Women from the Wild West. Then I saw the poster was dated 1872.

One feller was seated on a stool at the bar, he was doing a crossword puzzle. Six others were sitting below the main screens, their occasional comments no doubt concerning the league of all-time bat-swinging immortals. Fine, what is wrang with that? Nothing at all except I had to leave, leave, right at that moment man I couldnay fucking stand it. Stay!

Go!

Stay!

Go!

Fuck. How come I aye insisted on tempting the fates? It isnay as if I had never been warned. Once upon a time I wound up with a knife in the gut. Of course that was in fucking Glasgow, coming out a chip shop.

The bartender frowned. Had I paused by the exit just to annoy him? How come I had done that? Or was I wondering what to drink? What else could it be? Surely I couldnay have paused there just to annoy him? Really? Yeh. Fuck him. Needless to say I returned, stepped to the bar and ordered a beer in blasé fashion, tethering my anorak to a nearby stool. The bartender nodded like what else. He was an aulder guy and I sensed he was a frustrated intellectual. No matter the deviant politics here was a feller that enjoyed whatever mentally stimulating data life tossed at him. I caught him examining me, gauging what I was, who I was, why the hell I had come to his bar. I resisted winking when he knew I had caught him in the act. Make that a lite beer, I said.

A lite beer?

Yeh.

You bet, he said. His brow had furrowed then frowned; now relaxed, now frowned again and yeh, I knew he was placing bets with himself: 8 to 5 this guy with the funny voice is a conman, evens he is on the run, 4s an unfrocked priest. But I warnt no christian never mind no catholic christian. And if he read my mind I would get accused of blasphemy and he would fill me full of holes and be awarded the congressional medal for services to the almighty while I would be buried at the crossroads, a lonesome coyote growling.

Now he nodded to himself. It was okay, it was just I was an unintegratit furnir, a member of the alienigenae, all was explained.

Why the fuck had I left the goddam motel room? why could I not have been satisfied with a relaxing night in front of el tele, instead of the baseball I could have bought into the porn and chastised myself mightily.

I should have known the evening would go wrang from the first pub I entered. This was the kind of town where the barstaff are aye depressed out their skulls, where the customers are forced to stay on for an extra couple of hours just to cheer them up. This is done no by overtipping but by getting them to tell ye about their life to date and dreams for the future. This guy was one of them, I knew the signs. And he looked about fifty years of age unfortunately, so was gauny need a week to tell it all. I sighed but the drink was set down in front of me, I squared the shoodirs and reached out my right haun,

111

accepting the challenge. But my god it was damn tasty. It was just lite beer but what a flavour what a flavour. Nice beer, I said.

The bartender nodded, wondering if I was being sarcastic. He was hovering by me. I was obviously mair interesting than Corey Parker, ergo he wasnay a baseball fan, ergo he was on the outlook for displaced persons.

Of course he had that cigarette smouldering in the adjacent ashtray. The first time he left to serve another customer I was gauny steal a puff, a lungful of blue air is what I needit. I had gien up smoking six months previously. It was proving the biggest mistake of my short but doleful existence. I wished I was the psalmist. Only the psalmist ever spoke for me. One day I would speak on my ayn behalf. Until then no sir, it was best to leave. Immediately.

But I have never been good at extricating myself from awkward situations. Usually I just resign myself, unable to make the decisive move that might allow my liberation. If I did make a decision it was guaranteed the wrang yin. Often I made such a decision on purpose. I enjoyed testing myself. Was my resolve steely? 12 gets you 5 I would fall by the wayside

Strange how the lite beer was so enjoyable. At this rate I would be here all night. Still the bartender hovered. I thought I would craïc a joke. It was like he read my mind. He grabbed a quick drag on his smoke and settled himself to listen. If ye dont mind, I said, I would like to tell ye a joke. A sort of a joke, it is predicated on a knowledge of international politics, reinforced by a punchline that assumes a radical audience.

Oh yeh.

Tricky to declaim in an ordinary bar.

The bartender stared at me, no with outright hostility, just quizzically. He already knew I wasnay from these parts but now suspected the difference was planetary. Or else I was having some fun at his expense. Dangerous. But he rose to the challenge. This aint no ordinary bar, he said, then he winked. And you aint from Colorado.

Where ye from yerself? I said.

Me? He inhaled on his cigarette.

Forget it, I said, I dont really care where ye're from. See it from my point of view.

Pardon me?

This next part of the conversation is aye tricky for somebody of my status. How to say I am no from this part of the world at all. I am no even an Uhmerkin and then have to go on from there. It is difficult.

Just tell the truth son.

Okay, I aint an Uhmerkin. But the faimly of one of my ancestors was. My great-great-great-granddaddy. He passed along this way once, a long time ago. He was a fairly conscientious auld feller; he startit out as a prospector but soon hit the harder stuff. I'm called eftir him. So it's possible I've got roots that arenay too far from here, and maybe long lost cousins. Aint that something?

He nodded, stubbed out the cigarette, pointed to a notice on the wall. It was that federal one with the blue borders advising customers they were required to display appropriate ID on request, in the case of visitors from abroad this meant displaying their alien status. I held up my hands in a gesture of surrender. I got it here, I said, patting my chest and keeping my hands in view at all times, lest he brought out the shotgun from beneath the counter. Do ye want to see it? I said.

I surely do, nothing personal.

Yeh it's personal.

Not for me, he said, it aint personal for me.

I sighed and brought out my wallet to show him. It's always personal for me, I said.

Oh you got a Red Card? He pretended no to look too closely. Who did he think he was kidding. He reached for his cigarette pack while squinting again at my photograph. He called to the guy doing the crossword puzzle: Hey Barney, this guy's got a Red Card.

Aye, I said, no just any auld alien.

Right... The bartender smiled, still squinting at it. You an atheist and a socialist?

Yeh, well, mair an anarchist I suppose, I'm opposed to authority on principle. Mind you, I'll negotiate on particulars. They aint deportit me yet.

Right... He grinned, studying my fizzog. Hey you've aged a bit since this was taken? He squinted at it again. What's that, Jeremiah?

Jeremiah, yeh.

Nice name. Bible name, he said returning me the ID.

Correct, I said. I stuck the wallet back into my hip pocket then drank some beer and gestured with the bottle. Could I have another?

Sure you can. He reached below, opened one and placed it before me. You a Swede?

Naw.

German?

Nope.

Dutch?

No.

Irish?

Nah.

English?

Not at all, I'm Skarrisch.

Skarrisch? Neat. Ever since I was a kid my dream is to go to your country, I mean from childhood.

What like to emigrate?

Huh?

To go and live there?

To go and live there, no sir.

Aw ye mean as a tourist?

Naah, like the kids do, backpacking.

You talking about rambling across the country, the islands and the highlands, gaun where ye like and doing what ye like? That kind of thing?

Yeh.

Mm.

Something wrong in that?

Naw. The whole world's yer oyster.

The bartender glanced to the side where the blokes were gawping up at the screens. It occurred to me he had been speaking quietly. Maybe he didnay want them to eavesdrop the conversation. It would have embarrassed him. He was discussing a childish fancy and wantit it kept secret. It so happened the crossword-puzzle guy *was* eavesdropping so he was right to be cautious. Listen, I said, your dream is shared by thousands of people, tens of thousands of people.

Yeh?

Bet money on it. What essentially it is: ye all want to go to the motherland in the offchance ye bump into one of yer ancestor's descendants, a long lost cousin. What ye hope to discover is if ye are related to a clan chieftain, if ye are descended from royal blood and maybe own a mountain or something, if ye have any cheap servants at yer disposal, with luck they'll be wearing a kilt and sing praise songs for yer wife and faimly; bodies like me, we'll call ye sir, hump yer suitcases and dedicate pibroch airs and fiddle tunes to this race of which you are a leading member if not the central progenitor.

The bartender sniffed and stared at my forehead, then he smiled.

The chieftain of a clan is like a king, I said, although no too much like a king because in the auld days the clans practised a form of democracy.

I read history.

Aw right, okay, yeh, anyway, it was a communal experience, that is what I am saying.

I heard that, yeh.

Like an early form of communism, I whispered, sshh, keep it quiet.

He smiled, shook his heid, reached for his cigarette.

I expected ye to go pale there at the very use of the word.

How long you been in my country?

Twelve years.

Not long enough.

I know. What was I saying—like the clan chieftain was mair of a big brother kind of figure, paternal, ye might say presidential. Of course in the latter days he wound up stealing the clan property, just like the yoorpeen aristocracies, whatever, like the mafeeeaa.

Oh yeh?

Yeh, I said, loudly and clearly, the mafeeeaa.

He chuckled. I got you figured: you can discuss the mafia in public places, speak out loud with your voice, right? But you cant discuss politics? The words like 'communist', you got to say them in a quiet voice, you got to whisper, yeh?

Now I chuckled. This guy was mair devious than me. I felt like shaking his hand. He took a quick drag on his cigarette, returned it to the ashtray. He crossed to the other end of the bar where the crossword guy was seated on the stool, murmured to him.

Smoke from the cigarette drifted towards me, it smelled good. The guy had got up from his stool, was returning with him, but left his money and the crossword at his place. We exchanged nods.

This is Barney.

Hi.

Hi, I said.

Barney aint a big baseball fan.

Okay.

So what about your kings and queens? are they the same? like you were saying there, you spoke about the mafia.

Yeh.

You want to say it to him... The bartender nodded at Barney then went off to get an order for one the baseball customers. He called back: Keep on talking.

Kings and queens, I said, basically what they did was they stole the wealth held in trust for their faimly, they transformed it all into assets, their assets. Just like governments do, they steal the people's wealth and make assets out of it, then they fucking sell it off to their sidekicks and get themselves whatever, penthouse suites in Manhattan, luxurious trappings in benign climates, acres of land in Calabria and Montana, Guerrero, Andalucia or back in Skallin they purchase the purple mountains, the beautiful wee islands and the deep mysterious lochs, the shebang—all of that belonged to the clan chieftains, who were the big brothers and the fathers, first in the male line, and they selt it to the highest bidder.

Barney pursed his lips, took a sip of beer. Then he said, So that reminds you of—what did you say, the mafia?

I closed my mouth to resist replying, noting the bottle of beer in my hand and the other on the table. Baith were empty. How else could I speak such shite. And if I was carrying on like that the now, how was it gauny be once I stepped onto the plane tomorrow, or once I got into Glasgow Airport and then hame. The booze had gone right to my heid. Unless maybe there was an oxygen deficiency somewhere.

Hey, did I say 'hame' there? Yeh. My faimly was my faimly and that land was my birthplace. This was undeniable. Being away for so long it just went out my mind. How long had it been since I considered the word 'hame' in regard to myself? Other exiles think about hame much of the time, they get together and talk about the guid auld days and all that stuff. I could chat about the dear auld motherland as well but it was aye with an uncommon sense of relief at no being there. I pretended otherwise to my mother whom I phoned every blue moon to apologize for the lengthy gap in communication.

I never spoke to my brother or sister unless they happened to be in my mother's house. Me apologizing, that was about all that went on in these conversations. Baith were a few years aulder than me and we didnay have too much in common, no that I could figure.

I noticed Barney still standing there, probably wondering if I was gauny continue talking or if he should return to the crossword puzzle. But how come he didnay talk to me? How come the social onus lies with the stranger! Twas ever thus. Hey Barney, I said, ye're no Irish are ye?

No.

It's an Irish name. See what I've noticed, Skarrisch folk I meet in various places, English folk, they go to bars and reminisce. But Irish folk I meet, they dont bother reminiscing, they want to sit there in the company of one another but they dont talk, they just like to be there and every now and then they turn around and nod their head and maybe later on they sing a song.

Yeh?

But if they do talk they talk about the here and now, what is the actual material substance, baseball and horses, boxing and football, the weather, what's on the tube.

About the mafia? You want to know about the mafia? You a newspaper reporter?

Pardon me?

You want to know about the mafia?

No.

You dont want to know about the mafia?

I dont, naw.

I thought you did.

Naw

Italian people?

What about Italian people?

I guess you dont like them?

Yeh I like them, what ye talking about?

Italian people aint the mafia.

I know that.

No sir, said Barney. You think that but they aint, you got too much propaganda nowadays, this is the problem, this is why things go so bad for people. He sniffed then returned to his beer and his newspaper. The bartender was now wiping the counter close to where I was propped. What happened to the conversation? he said, glancing at Barney as well as myself.

What d'ye mean like highlands and islands?

You guys were talking, now you aint.

Barney said, The guy has ideas about Italian people.

Naw I dont, I said, the world's just full of misunderstandings.

Barney gied a wry smile. We watched the bartender lift a solid looking, spotlessly clean ashtray from close by my empty beer bottle. He winked at us and flipped the ashtray into the air. I had to appreciate the way he got it to ground by a form of sleight of hand like he had performed a telekinetic feat or something. Barney made a show of applauding. I grinned and said to Barney, I would be wary of playing cards with him.

Oh you play cards? said the bartender.

Now where had that come from? I stared at him. Barney was smiling. But I didnay smile in response. My real opinion was that the bartender would have made a fine pickpocket. But in furin parts the sense of humour is a fragile entity and I didnay risk saying it aloud. Maybe he was a genuine villain, and this bar stuff was a diversion; during the night he crept stealthily off to rob banks but was always hame in time for breakfast and naybody was any the wiser. Unless he had retired to here, following his life of crime. He had got fed up with grumpy victims and the constant hassle with the cops, used the last of his ill-gotten gains to invest in this wee sports bar. It was either that or a bookshop. Maybe he spun a coin. If it had been me I would have opened a betting parlour.

One of these days...

The bartender had gien the ashtray a wipe, it glistened. Dont worry about it, I said, I stopped smoking ages ago. This is my sixth month down the lonesome trail and the coyotes are wailing. Getting worse by the hour but, I have to confess.

Yeh? The bartender nodded and reached for his cigarette pack. This set Barney off, he went into his pocket and came out with a fresh ceegar.

I stared about the pub. At the other end the baseball fellers were angry about something, gesticulating at the screens. One was onto his feet and swallowing the dregs of his beer, lifting his change from the counter and muttering to himself as he headed for the door. When he got to abreast of myself he paused then threw a mean look in my direction, raised his eyebrows; he strode on. When I frowned at the bartender he said, Having a good time?

Yeh, thanks.

You like our country?

I've been here twelve years.

Some people dont like it, they been here all their life.

No me.

Tomorrow you're flying home? called Barney.

Yeh, I said, it's too long to walk.

Barney looked at the bartender who was reaching for a bottle of beer. And I was thinking fuck it, what a stupit thing to say, let us get back to the motel immediately, watch a movie or something. Then the beer arrived in front of me. The bartender nodded, but less a positive gesture than a tricky self-consciousness. I gied a smile. Thanks, I said. But my smile was one of surprise. I hadnay ordered the beer, no that I could remember. So it was on the house. But I didnay see any fresh bottle in front of Barney, nor in front of the baseball fans. It was just me getting the present. I didnay like that. If I saw somebody getting free beer I would definitely wonder what was gaun on, especially a stranger. How come I was being excluded, that was what I would want to know. Now it was surely time to leave.

I had nay option. In situations like this I just cannay trust myself; life is too short. Also I was hungry. I had noticed an all-night convenience store and they would have a sandwich of some description. Grub grub, I needit grub.

I would drink the beer before leaving.

But there is a time when everything becomes significant. That is the time to watch yerself, in particular yer back. And drinkers are a strange damn breed anyway, especially solitaries, given that I too fit that description. I wouldnay dispute the label 'strange' if applied to myself but I would dispute that it has to be negative. Strange characters may be mysterious characters, no just people who exhibit unnatural behaviour, no necessarily. Anywey, it depends on what we mean by 'unnatural behaviour'.

Some might argue that a Celtic male with pink skin, fair hair (receding) and blue eyes (watery) should have been empowered to travel the world where ere he chose and didnay need no colour-coded federal authorization never mind the okay from stray true-born persons he met in bars. How can Aryans be Aliens, is what they would argue. It is a contradiction. This feller's physicality and language are passport and visa. And then add to the tally that I was an ex Security operative, how Uhmerkin can ye get! Okay, failed Security operative. No really a failure, I just didnay make a career out it. But add to that failed husband and failed parent, failed father, general no fucking hoper. And now I was gaun hame, gaun hame! I was a failed fucking immigrant!

And tobacco smoke being puffed in my direction.

But once hame, if I got scunnered of the entire country in a matter of moments all would not be lost, I would just come back here, it would be fine, I would just fucking hop a plane.

How many fucking beers had I had? Couldnay be mair than— what? four? three? five!

So, what next? What was gauny happen? The usual, he grinned, sidling towards the exit.

No, only joking, I stood where I was, I was minding my ayn business and I was gauny continue minding my ayn business. No matter the pressure. And what business was I minding, what business did I know anything about. I knew nothing about business, I knew nothing about nothing. The truth is that I was a failure. That was the primary reason it had taken so long to book the flight. Failures do not fucking go fucking hame.

But I wasnay a failure. I was a guy that occasionally did crazy things, one who had lost his wife and daughter.

The bleakness of spirit descendeth, a simple bleakness of spirit. It derives from one's shortcomings. One is hopeless, no just at business matters, at everything that matters. I recently accrued ten thousand dollars. Ten thousand dollars. Imagine it. Then it was gone. Ten grand, fucking blown! I do not understand how that happened. Yes I do, it was just nonsense, the usual. I had just eh

Fuck.

Baith of them were looking at me. Maybe I said 'fuck' out loud or else I sighed heavily; one isnay supposed to sigh heavily. I nodded, pointed at the television screens: What about Corey Parker? Is he as good as they say?

Who gives a shit, said Barney. He took off his glasses and smiled, sat back on his stool.

He was waiting for me to speak, but I wouldnay. There is a veil, one may draw it. The veil is drawn.

So you play cards? said the bartender.

Sometimes, yeh, I've played cards.

You got gambling buddies?

I smiled.

You got gambling buddies?

There is nay such thing as 'gambling buddies', I said, if ye're a gambler ye should know that.

So you're a gambler? said the bartender.

What I'm saying is 'gambling buddy' is a contradiction in terms. These guys slit each other's throat on a regular basis.

You a shooter or a horseman? said the bartender.

What?

He grinned.

I dont know that one, I said.

Barney also grinned, shook his heid, puffed on the bold ceegar. What happened to the ten thou, did you lose it?

Ten thou?

You had ten thou, then it went, what did you blow it on the tables?

On the slots? said the bartender.

Pool.

Pool!

You blew ten grand on pool? said Barney.

Yeh, there was a couple of guys I knew.

Gambling buddies, said the bartender with a wink of his right eye.

Winking right back at ye, I said and did so. Naw, they were nay buddies of mine; they owned a bar I used to visit. At the rear they built on a lounge room and installed two pool tables, good yins, then they organised regular tournaments, private tournaments, eftir hours. I was playing no a bad game at that time. They earned a few bucks off me in side bets. At first they backed me against my opponents, until they realised that although I was a fine and subtle player I was a born loser. Show me the biggest dumpling in the hall and he is guaranteed to take money out my pockets. Ye want to bet me on that? Show me the dough. I shall bet ye my whole fucking wad. I shall bet ye my whole fucking wad that I cannay win one damn bet, not one damn bet. Bang bang fucking bang.

Seven letters ends in x, said Barney.

What?

Bang bang fucking bang, said the bartender.

Yeh, I said and lifted the bottle, paused and raised it to him in a salute. Sláinte, thanks for the beer.

It was Barney bought it.

Aw, aw thanks, thanks eh...

Barney shrugged.

Yeh. I nodded. In some places people dont talk to a stranger never mind buy him a drink, I said. But in other places these wee sparks do so occur. One can hit the skids, all things appear bleak, then along comes an act of human kindness. Never mind the 'human kindness', an act of ordinary humanity. But some such acts are born out of desperation. This here is a bar that dulls the brain and quells all passion. Ye have yer dreams of better conversation but yer real dream is escape.

Close, said Barney, I did escape; I escaped to here. This is where I headed, this is my refuge.

Aye okay, fair enough.

So what about you?

Me? I smiled, then noticed the bartender was staring at me. In fact he was fucking glaring at me. Me, I said, I telt ye about me.

So what did you say?

What?

Barney smiled to the bartender.

I said I was gaun hame tomorrow. I havenay been hame for eight years and only twice in twelve. And just now I'm gaun to the room for gentlemen, the lavatory.

So it's a big deal for you?

Eh?

Your family, your wife and daughter?

What?

It must be a big deal, going home, see your wife and daughter. What did you leave them to come here?

What?

You came here. You ran out on them?

What ye fucking talking about?

Hey! the bartender held up his right hand.

Sorry. Naw, I said. I dont understand what ye're talking about. Tomorrow I'm flying hame and I mean by that back to Skallin. My wife and daughter, ex wife and daughter, they live on the east coast.

Oh they do?

I havenay gied ye any reason to think otherwise.

You left them on the east coast? said Barney.

Naw I didnay leave them on the east coast, fuck sake, I'm getting divorced, she's divorcing me.

Hey I told you now your language is a bit too rich.

Sorry.

The bartender nodded. I shook my heid, stared at the bar. He had another puff on his cigarette. Barney was looking at me. I returned him a look. You aint a gambler, he said.

I didnay say I was a gambler. What I said was I gambled badly.

Oh.

Hang on a minute, I've got to go to the lavatory.

Sure, said the bartender, but why d'you insult my place?

I'm no insulting yer place. What d'you mean?

The bartender reached for his cigarette.

All I says was I was wanting to go to the lavatory. And I'll be back in a minute, carry on the conversation. Excuse me, I said and I backed off a step, still watching them. Then I turned, walked down to the side of the television screens where the fir sign signalled the way.

What was that all about, insulting his place? Ye cannay get gaun for a piss in some companies, even that gets misconstrued. There were mirrors round the side and rear walls and I tried to get a look back to the bar, to see what the other two were doing. Yeh, please dont talk about me when I'm gone. I wouldnay say they were. But at the same time, things change in weird ways, nothing would have surprised me.

It was a wee bit of a quandary though, I have to confess. I aint keen on these bars where ye have to walk miles for a piss and the only escape route is back the way ye came. The signs pointed on down a short corridor then round a bend, where there were arrows pointing ye along to another corner where the toilets were side by

side, and if ye turned the wrang corner ye landed in some godforsaken end staircase or else in a dark and dusty storeroom, and
when ye push open the door there is a group of bodies in white hoods
and robes, armed with fiery crosses. No sir, I aint keen on these kind
of bars. Funny how in tricky situations this is how it works, you
finish in a labyrinth. And a quick exit is the only saviour, if ye can
find one, because it isnay guaranteed. Fucking hell, it was gauny be
one of these nights. I felt like making an escape there and then, except
the anorak, the fucking anorak, it was lying across a barstool.

Yeh, weird, weird how things happen. Inside the men's room there
was a urinal and a wc cubicle. The urinal was overflowing man it
was horrible. I was about to enter the cubicle but that seemed a likely
trap. At times like these I could have done with something; my
Security operative stick for instance, it would have been ideal. But I
wasnay wanting to get my shoes drenched so I chose the cubicle. Then
oh jesus christ I might have known, the outside door opened suddenly
and my back to them. I rushed to finish the piss and managed it just
as the inside door was closing. I zipped the trousers, took time to rinse
my hands and use the drier, shifting side on so any sudden move was
covered, then to the first door and out, and I kept walking, checking
the arrows, making it back along the corridor. The bartender was
down by the television screens, serving one of the baseball fans and
didnay acknowledge me when I passed. Barney had returned to his
former place and kept his head ower the crossword.

I lifted the bottle. I would have preferred to swally down the beer
and just fuck off. Naw. The guy had bought me a drink. Besides,
could I get out alive? Ha ha. But this type of hassle does one's brains
in. One usually associates it with small towns but it happens in major
cities as well: stray into a new district and ye discover it is a
homogenous hotbed of poisonous fuckers all staring at ye because
ye are the wrang 'thing': religion, race, class, nationality, politics; they
know ye as soon as look at ye, boy, you is alien.

Even in places where it isnay obvious and ye think it is okay,
suddenly the atmosphere shifts. It can even be your fault, you say
something out of turn and the fucking roof caves in, ye wake up in
Accident & Emergency with a guy in a grey suit staring at ye and
naw, he isnay a doctor, he is a snooping bastard from the indigenous
aliens' section of the *Federal Bureau of Immigration and Assimilation*.

The subtleties of social behaviour can alter in drastic ways and one never knows what other people are fucking talking about. Maybe that was at the heart of the breakdown of my relationship, just something as basic as that. We were supposed to speak the same language but did we did we fuck. Much of it was my ayn fault and I would never have denied that. I stopped trying to write my private eye story about the same time I stopped trying to be a good father, good husband as well. Coinciding with that was another breakdown, the breakdown of my concentration. Thoughts drifted in and out my mind. Where the fuck did they come from, where did they go, what happened when they lodged there, and was havoc wreaked? Similarly in conversation, I forgot if I was talking, who I was talking to. I came in and out of perception like I was on dope. Yeh, I needit to get hame and see my mother, and the fucking cat of course, it had been a mere kitten when I left, now it was a proud castrated male. If I had been there at the time I wouldnay have allowed it.

But I needit to get back to something. It had nothing to do with homesickness or notions of a motherland. Fuck the motherland, blood and guts and soil and shite, it didnay matter a fuck to me, it was just

Christ almighty I needit to get out right now. Hey, I said to Barney, can I buy ye a drink?

Pardon me?

Hey, I said, can I buy ye a drink? I need to leave. I need to go back to my motel and have some food, a bit of a sleep. Yeh, I have a long day's travelling tomorrow. I lifted my anorak from the stool and pulled it on. Yeh, I said, pointing at the bartender. Him tae, I'd like to buy yez baith a drink afore I go. It was hospitable you buying me one and I'd just like to return it. Well I mean ye buy a guy a beer and he drinks it down then bids ye a swift farewell! I shrugged.

I dont do that, said Barney.

Naw neither do I. It's no what I do either. I'm talking about the opposite. I would like to buy ye one afore I go. I would just like to return the compliment. I'm gauny go back to my motel, grab a sandwich.

Okay.

So: want a beer?

You talking about me? Do I want a beer?

Well I'd like to buy ye one.

Yeh, I'll take a beer.

The bartender was standing at the opposite end of the bar, his back to us, gazing up at the television screens. I walked down to him. When he turned to me he just was not friendly. Could I have a beer, I said, for Barney, whatever he's drinking.

He nodded.

Could I buy you one as well?

Right now I'm working.

Yeh, I know.

He shook his head, then stared at me.

I didnay say Fuck you to the guy: I said, Okay, two beers; whatever Barney's drinking and one for myself.

There had been mair misunderstandings in the past half hour than I had had in the past month. Everything was getting fankled. And the order itself, I had only meant to get Barney a beer originally, nothing for myself, I was just wanting to fuck off. But now I had bought myself another yin. Because of this huffy bartender bastard. So okay, when he brought them to me I would pay the money and leave. I had nothing to say. I wouldnay even drink the fucking beer, I would leave it there for whoever, it didnay matter; him, Barney or whoever, Corey fucking Parker, I just needit to get away.

I was back at my stool when he brought them. I pushed the money across the counter. He lifted it. I dont know why ye thought I insulted ye earlier on, I said, obviously it was a misunderstanding.

Obviously, yeh.

Yeh well it was.

You think this is a boring place, he said, that's your prerogative.

I dont think this is a boring place.

You said it.

I said it? I never said it. I know boring places man this isnay one of them.

He shrugged. That's what you said.

Naw I didnay.

Now he sighed in a vaguely amused way, and he looked me straight in the eye. I aint going to argue with you feller.

Of course for him to look me straight in the eye means I was already looking straight at him. It was all fucking male fucking keech but at the same time I wasnay gauny back down, no unless I had to. Barney had been spectating. Now he said, Hey ah, Jeremiah...

What?

Plenty bars around here, why dont you test them out.

The bartender smiled. He had lifted a bottle of uisghé and a glass and was set to pour, but no for me no for me. Easy boy easy, yeh, and time to leave time to leave. There was a payphone on the wall nearby the exit. I put my hand in my pocket, checked the coins. Then I checked my breathing. I was okay. I left the beer on the counter, strolled towards it. I glanced behind. Baith were watching me. I gied them a wave and continued on through the exit.

There would be a payphone in the convenience store. I could call a cab from there. It was my ayn fault for losing my last cell phone. It had been in a diner. An elderly woman was waiting table, red lipstick and expressionless countenance. Every time I got a new yin I fucking lost the goddam thing, and I wasnay buying nay other, no until my brains settled down.

The couple of beers had been worthwhile. Now I would sleep. And with a sandwich for my room, if I could maybe get a sandwich. And a late night movie on the tube, yeh, I was looking forward to it.

It really was time to disappear. ☐

NOAM CHOMSKY

HEGEMONY OR SURVIVAL
AMERICA'S QUEST FOR GLOBAL DOMINANCE

'CHOMSKY IS ARGUABLY THE MOST IMPORTANT INTELLECTUAL ALIVE' **THE NEW YORK TIMES**

'NOT TO HAVE READ HIM IS TO COURT GENUINE IGNORANCE' **NATION**

OUT NOW FROM HAMISH HAMILTON

www.penguin.co.uk

SAVE OVER 40%!

Each quarterly issue of *Granta* features a rich variety of stories, in fiction, memoir, reportage and photography—often collected under a theme, like those shown overleaf. Each issue is produced as a high-quality paperback book, because writing this good, deserves nothing less. Subscribers get *Granta* delivered to them at home, at a substantial discount. Why not join them. Or give a subscription to a friend, relative or colleague? (Or, given these low prices, do both!)

GRANTA 'ESSENTIAL READING.'

OBSERVER

ORDER FORM

I'D LIKE TO SUBSCRIBE FOR MYSELF FOR:
- ◯ 1 year (4 issues) at just £26.95
- ◯ 2 years (8 issues) at just £50
- ◯ 3 years (12 issues) at just £70

START SUBSCRIPTION WITH ◯ this issue ◯ next issue

I'D LIKE TO GIVE A SUBSCRIPTION FOR:
- ◯ 1 year (4 issues) at just £26.95
- ◯ 2 years (8 issues) at just £50
- ◯ 3 years (12 issues) at just £70

START SUBSCRIPTION WITH ◯ this issue ◯ next issue

MY DETAILS (please supply even if ordering a gift): Mr/Ms/Mrs/Miss_____

_____

_____ Country _____ Postcode _____

GIFT RECIPIENT'S DETAILS (if applicable): Mr/Ms/Mrs/Miss _____

_____

_____ Country _____ Postcode _____

03MBG84

TOTAL* £_____ paid by ◯ £ cheque enclosed (to 'Granta') ◯ Visa/Mastercard/AmEx:

card no: __ __ __ __ __ __ __ __ __ __ __ __ __ __ __ __

expires: __ __ / __ __ signature: _____

* <u>POSTAGE</u>. The prices stated include UK postage. For the rest of Europe, please add £8 (per year). For the rest of the world, please add £15 (per year). <u>DATA PROTECTION</u>. Please tick here if you do not want to receive occasional mailings from compatible publishers. ◯

➡ **POST** ('Freepost' in the UK) to: Granta, 'Freepost', 2/3 Hanover Yard, Noel Road, London N1 8BR. **PHONE/FAX:** In the UK: FreeCall 0500 004 033 (phone & fax); outside the UK: tel 44 (0)20 7704 9776, fax 44 (0)20 7704 0474 **EMAIL:** subs@granta.com

GRANTA

THE HOME FRONT
Anthony Suau

THESE PHOTOGRAPHS WERE TAKEN BETWEEN
JANUARY 15 AND APRIL 25 2003

Ohio, Illinois. The POW-MIA flag signifies local servicemen missing in action.

Wasco, California. Minutes before President Bush gave Saddam Hussein 48 hours to leave Iraq.

Fort Campbell, Kentucky. The 101st Airborne Division leaving for Kuwait.

Elizabeth City, North Carolina. The bombing of Baghdad.

Richmond, Virginia. A pro-war rally.

Peoria, Illinois. Boxes filled by Hines High School students to be sent to US troops in Iraq.

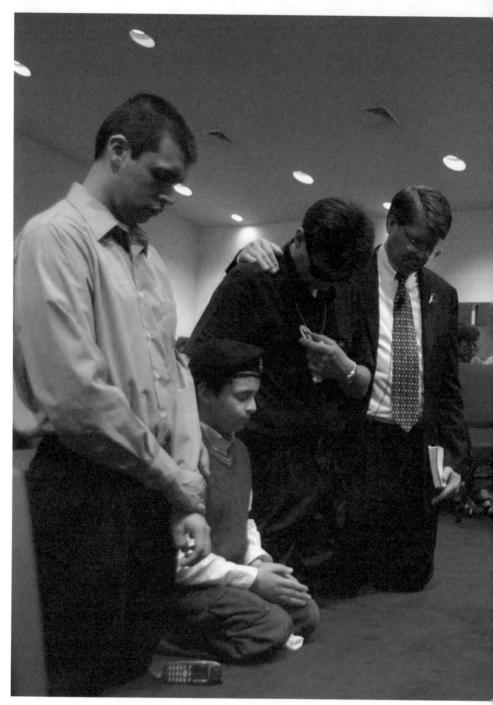

Conyers, Georgia. The memorial service for Diego Fernando Rincon, aged 19, killed in Iraq.
His father, Jorge Rincon, is third from the left.

Peoria, Illinois. Judy Shanahan at home with her children. She claimed she had become addicted to television coverage of the war.

Chicago, Illinois. An anti-war demonstration: (l to r) Vice-president Dick Cheney, Deputy Defense Secretary Paul Wolfowitz, Defense Secretary Donald Rumsfeld, President George W. Bush.

Charlotte, North Carolina.

Lima, Ohio. President George W. Bush at the government-owned Lima Army Tank Plant.

LaHarpe, Illinois. The funeral of Marine Corporal Evan Tyler James, aged 20, killed in Iraq.

Fort Stewart, Georgia. The families of US servicemen based in Iraq at a prayer meeting.

Washington DC. A video at a rally in support of US troops in Iraq.

Canton, Illinois.

OPEN WOUND **BY STANLEY GREENE**

GRANTA

NOTHING BUT GHOSTS
Judith Hermann

TRANSLATED FROM THE GERMAN BY
MARGOT BETTAUER DEMBO

Afterwards Ellen liked to say she had once been to America but couldn't remember it very well. She had driven from the East Coast to the West Coast and back; she had been in California, Utah and Colorado; had seen Iowa, Illinois and Idaho; had gone swimming in the Atlantic and the Pacific, in the Colorado river, the Blue River, and in Lake Tahoe. She had gazed up into the sky over Alabama, Mississippi and Missouri. And she no longer remembered anything.

She says, 'I know I was there because of the receipts from the motel rooms and from the diners, as well as the unsent postcards that fall out of my calendar. I know I was there, but there's nothing I can tell you about it. Sure, I was in San Francisco. In Big Sur and in Redwood National Park. But the only place there's anything to tell about is Austin, Nevada. Austin in Nevada and the Hotel International and Buddy. Buddy is the only one there's anything to tell about.' As though the trip had never taken place, as though she and Felix had not been at all.

They arrived in Austin late in the afternoon. They had left Delta, Utah that morning, intending to cross the desert in one day. They'd checked it on the map—300 miles on Highway 50. And exactly three towns in that desert solitude: Ely, Eureka and Austin. They had three gallons of water in the back of the truck, an extra can of gasoline, a carton of cigarettes, three apples, and a loaf of white bread. The Ford Ranger pickup didn't have air conditioning. They had coffee in Ely sitting on a Hollywood swing in front of the gas station without saying a word. Ellen was perspiring. White light shimmered over the salt lakes, and everything was covered by a layer of sand, her skin and Felix's hair, there was sand in their coffee and sand in her mouth. They sat outside the gas station in silence for half an hour looking at the desert. Ellen doesn't really remember where they were coming from or where they wanted to go. They probably wanted to go to the ocean. They stood up at the same time without saying a word; Ellen threw her empty coffee cup and Felix's full one into the dusty garbage can, and then they drove on.

Austin came up out of nowhere, but presumably everything in the desert comes out of nowhere. Highway 50, in wearisome monotony, had gone past look-alike salt lakes; mountain ranges rose and fell— valley and hill, valley and hill, and always this glittering, searing light.

Now and then Ellen began to doubt that they were actually
driving, moving, making progress. She slept right through Eureka, and
when she woke up nothing had changed. She tried to move as little
as possible, kept drinking water, smoked too much. Sometimes she
looked at Felix's profile, said, 'How can you stand it without
sunglasses?' Then the highway made a sharp turn, descending
unexpectedly and precipitously into a canyon. Ellen looked briefly out
of the window at the steep drop-off on her right. In serpentine turns
the highway took them down into a valley; then houses appeared,
wooden houses, a church, an abandoned gas station, more houses, ten,
maybe fifteen, no human being in sight. Soon the desert spread before
them again, a level stretch and on the horizon the next mountain chain.

But Felix turned the truck to the right, into a parking lot,
stopped, letting the engine idle, and said, 'I think I've had enough.'

The engine rattled softly; the wind blew sand against the
windshield, Ellen gazed out at the parking lot, which seemed to
belong to a hotel, an old western-style hotel with a wide wooden
porch and an openwork railing. The second-storey windows were
boarded up, but a neon Budweiser sign flickered in a dusty window
on the first floor. The neon light seemed incongruous in the daylight.
Above the closed saloon door it said in crooked, weathered wooden
letters HOTEL INTERNATIONAL. Across the street there was a motel,
its vacancy sign swaying on a flagpole in the wind. Ellen said, 'What
do you mean, you've had enough?'

Felix rolled down his window, stuck his arm out to test the air, and
said, 'I can't drive any farther. I just can't drive any more. I'm tired. I
want to take a rest, drive on tomorrow maybe. I'd like to lie down
for an hour.' He pulled his arm back in and rolled up the window.
'Lie down somewhere where it's really cool. Or do you absolutely want
to go on.' He put an audible period at the end of the last sentence.

Ellen said, 'No. I don't know. I don't have to drive on, not
absolutely.'

She sat there like that for a while. Felix said nothing more, and
so she finally got out, leaving the truck door open. She knew it would
annoy him. As she walked across the street to the motel she could
hear the truck door slamming shut behind her. She knew that Felix
had stayed in the truck, leaned across the passenger seat and
furiously pulled the door shut. Ellen could feel the heat of the asphalt

through the soles of her shoes. She spat, feeling the sand crunching between her teeth. She wiped her hands on her pants and looked up and down the street; there was nothing to see. The motel, like all motels, was a low U-shaped building with direct outside access to the rooms; not a single car in any of the parking spaces in front of the doors. On the window of the office a sign warned people not to get into a fight with Annie.

Ellen pushed the door open with her palm; inside it was cool and dim, the venetian blinds were down; it smelled of dust and stale lunch. The door closed automatically behind her, and it took Ellen a moment to make out the thin woman behind the reception desk. She had a towel wrapped around her head and strands of wet hair escaping on both sides; Ellen felt an urgent need to wash her own hair, immediately. The woman was putting on fingernail polish. Ellen cleared her throat and said, 'Are you Annie?' The thin woman screwed the top back on the nail polish bottle, blew on her nails, put a registration form on the counter, a pencil; then she looked at Ellen. Ellen smiled. 'I suppose you can't spend the night at the Hotel International any more?' she asked.

Annie—or whoever she was—said, 'No.'

Ellen began to fill out the form, stopping almost at once when she heard a car drive into the parking lot. She looked through a space between the slats of the venetian blinds that covered the window in the door. The car had parked right in front of the motel. Felix was still sitting in the Ford outside the Hotel International. A very short, very fat woman got out of the car.

Ellen turned back to the desk and carefully wrote her name and Felix's name, in block letters. She had been doing it for weeks. For weeks she had filled out motel registration forms, had been giving their orders to waitresses in diners, dealt with national park rangers in camping areas while Felix simply waited, waited till she had arranged and organized things. It wasn't because he didn't speak English well; it was because he was denying himself to America, denying himself to Ellen.

The short fat woman stepped into the office wheezing, dragging a suitcase and a bulging, very heavy-looking carryall behind her. She was quite out of breath and leaned for support on the reception desk. Ellen moved aside a little. Annie stood up and sleepily took the towel from around her head; the wet hair fell heavy and straight to her shoulders. The fat woman said, 'We spoke on the phone. Here I am.'

And Annie said, 'Yes.' She said everything was ready, and the fat woman asked her something—at first, Ellen wasn't really listening, but then she did listen, dragging out the process of writing the truck's licence plate number on the form.

The fat woman was about fifty years old, yet her face was firm and rosy like that of a young girl; she had small squinty eyes and pale eyelashes; her equally pale, very thick hair was done in a braid at the end of which was a pink bow. She was wearing a flowered summer dress, bright red children's sandals, and she smelled funny, not bad, but strange, maybe of perspiration and a sweetish deodorant. 'Very old ghosts,' she suddenly said to Ellen. 'Gold miners. A bad sort with no manners.' She blushed fleetingly. 'I'm gonna contact them,' she looked at Ellen, remarkably serious, then she turned back to Annie whose face showed neither boredom, nor irritation nor anything else. The fat woman said she was going to photograph the ghosts and would send the photos to anyone who wanted them. She also had a portfolio with photographs of other ghosts. She'd be glad to show them now or later, whichever was more convenient. She looked at Ellen again and smiled. Ellen smiled back, even though it was an effort.

Annie said, 'I'd prefer later.' She was looking vainly for something under the counter, and when she casually remarked that she'd unlock the second floor of the Hotel International toward midnight, the fat woman was beside herself with excitement. She took all kinds of unrecognizable stuff out of her carryall, then a plastic camera, and finally a large old-fashioned and sturdy tape recorder, which she put on the counter, directly in front of Ellen.

Ellen finished filling in the licence plate number of the Ford on the form, gave Annie a fifty dollar bill and received a key from her. The fat woman fiddled with the recording apparatus; it started with a whirring sound and when the whirring changed into another, quite remarkable noise, Ellen said, 'See you later,' and ran across the street to where Felix was sitting in the truck, leaning back with his eyes closed. She opened the door on the driver's side and said, 'Did you see the fat woman?'

Felix opened his eyes, 'Which one?' and Ellen said, 'The fat woman who got out of the Chrysler just now. The one who registered at the

motel the same time I did. She's a ghost hunter,' and Felix said, 'Aha.'
Ellen remembers the ghost hunter. Not the same way she
remembers Buddy. She didn't see her the way she saw Buddy, later,
but she remembers her. She can still see her feet—the skin, milky and
swollen from the heat—stuck into these little children's sandals. She
remembers the colour of Annie's nail polish, a pearly salmon pink,
and she can still recall how the heat in the parking lot in front of
the Hotel International descended on her. Felix had said 'Aha' and
then nothing else; he refused to be impressed, and for a moment Ellen
imagined what it would have been like if—while she was registering
inside the motel—he had simply driven off, down the road and into
the desert again. Imagined how it would have been if he had just
driven off and she had watched him through the space between the
slats of the venetian blind. She would have heard the noise of the
motor fading, getting less and less, and then it would have been quiet
again. He didn't drive off without her, and it's not important, but
Ellen still remembers. She sees sharp bright pictures of it in her mind's
eye, as if everything in Austin, Nevada had had a meaning, but it
wasn't like that, not entirely.

Felix drove the Ford over to the motel parking lot and parked it in
front of Room 14. The ghost hunter's car stood directly in front
of the motel office; the woman herself was not in sight. Ellen unlocked
the door; the room was small and clean—a queen-size bed, a TV set,
an armchair, a bathroom, an air conditioner. It wasn't just cool, it was
ice cold, and Felix switched the air conditioner off. They got their
backpacks out of the pickup; they wouldn't unpack them; they hadn't
really unpacked them even once so far. Still, they got them out of the
truck and set them in a corner of the room. Felix took off his shoes
and stretched out on the bed. He pulled the yellow bedspread over his
legs and said he wanted to sleep for a little while, not long, an hour.
Ellen sat down on the edge of the bed and looked at him, he turned
on his side and closed his eyes. She got up, looked for cigarettes in
her pockets, found a crushed Camel and lit it; then she sat down again
on the edge of the bed. She smoked slowly. Felix lay there motionless;
perhaps he was already asleep, perhaps not. His face wasn't relaxed.
Ellen looked at the freckles around his eyes; the skin on his nose was
peeling. The expression, to love somebody terribly, popped into her

head; she thought it several times in succession, *I love you terribly, I love you terribly*. Then the words lost their meaning. She looked out of the window; the road was empty and silent; the shadows were getting longer and the light was turning bluish. The heat seeped steadily and heavily through the open door. The lights were now on in the first-floor windows of the Hotel International; if she squinted she could see a bar behind the windows, a mirror, and perhaps some bottles, the shadow of a moving figure. She finished smoking the cigarette and carefully put it out in the plastic ashtray on the bedside table. She sat there for a long time, her legs crossed, her head supported in one hand, looking at Felix whose features gradually softened. Or maybe it was just the waning light, turning greyer.

At some point she stood up, undressed, and took a shower. In spite of the heat she showered with hot water, washed her hair twice, and stood under the spray for a long time. Then she showered with cold water. Felix was still asleep when she was done; the room had become dark. Ellen dried her hair with a towel, got dressed and stepped outside. She left the door open and walked down the street; even though it was still hot she felt slightly cold. She tried to imagine what it would be like to get sick here, just a little bit sick, with a temperature of 99.6 degrees. It led her nowhere.

She walked past a closed gas station; in the gas pump there were gaping holes with flaring edges, and out in back, through the skeleton of the little station house she could see wrecked cars piled on top of each other, disappearing in a sand dune. She passed a grocery store, its dirty window covered from the inside with newspaper; two, three houses that were probably inhabited but which she didn't want to see; and after that the town ended. She walked slowly, hands in her pants pockets. Behind the last house the ground, covered with a rampant growth of thorny plants, sloped steeply downward. She followed the road a bit farther until she was definitely in the desert and no longer in Austin. Then she sat down on a rock by the side of the road amidst the spiny plants. The rock was warm. She had just missed the sunset; the sun had gone down moments before. The tips of the telephone poles glowed and the mountains were in silhouette. Austin was no longer visible, and the desert, shimmering blue and cold, swallowed the ribbon of highway long before it rose into the hills.

Ellen recalled that somewhere between Ely and Austin she had told Felix how beautiful she thought the desert was because here she was able not to think anything any more. As always—and this time he was right—he had not answered her.

Far out in the desert two points of light had become detached from the dusk and were growing rapidly larger and brighter. Ellen waited impatiently for the sound of a motor; she was hoping it would be a truck. It was a truck, and as it roared past her she had to make an effort to keep from jumping up. The trucker looked down at her from high up in his cab and blew his horn, dragging the long, plaintive sound all the way into Austin. Ellen thought of Felix in the motel room, on the bed under the yellow bedspread, sleeping so unprotected with the door open. America was the America of the movies, of psychopaths and serial killers, of the most horrible scenes in Stephen King novels; America didn't exist, not really.

She got up and walked on. She didn't go back to Austin, didn't turn back until a pickup truck slowed down behind her, stopped almost next to her, and she could see the driver—a white man wearing a cowboy hat. He made a gesture with his hand that she didn't understand; in any case, he said he'd never allow her to walk around in the desert by herself at night. Really, never. At that instant she turned around and ran back, much too slowly, the way one flees when one is dreaming. She ran along the edge of the road, emptying the pebbles out of her shoes only after she could no longer hear the pickup behind her. In Austin the lights had gone on in two or three houses; otherwise the town was dark, and the road wound its way into nothingness.

Felix was still lying on the bed. The room was now hot and sticky, and Ellen turned the air conditioner back on. She sat down on the edge of the bed and put her hand on Felix's cheek. His face was quite warm and Ellen said, 'Felix. Don't you ever want to get up again?'

He turned away from her, but opened his eyes and said, 'What's the matter?'

'It's late. I'm hungry; I'd like to get a drink,' her voice sounded odd, and she wished that Felix would look at her.

He sat up. 'Where should we go to get a drink?'

Ellen pointed vaguely and almost apologetically out the window to the lights of the Hotel International. Felix brushed the hair out of his face with both hands and sighed deeply. Then he put on his shoes and said he'd like to smoke a cigarette. She gave him a Camel and a light; their eyes met briefly; Ellen had to laugh and he smiled a little.

Buddy came into the Hotel International quite late. As he arrived the fat ghost hunter was just in the process of connecting her old-fashioned recording device to countless mysterious antennae and cables and tuning it. Her movements were either confused or had their own virtuosity. Her face was sweaty; hectic red spots glowed on her cheeks; her fingernails were bitten down to the cuticles. She had spread out all her paraphernalia on the pool table and gradually, as though by accident, the various customers—all of them men— sauntered over, each with a beer in one hand. They never came singly.

When they asked questions it wasn't about ghosts but about the technique. When they tried to touch the apparatus, the ghost hunter clenched her tiny hands into little balls from which her index finger projected like a barb. The men would back off, grin and rub the backs of their necks in surprise. The ghost hunter said coyly and deprecatingly, 'You're thinking of bats. You're probably thinking of bats and the fact that we can't hear their frequencies, but that they can be recorded. However, we're dealing with something else here. Something completely different. Ghosts have their own frequency.'

The ghost hunter had come into the place at about ten o'clock. Felix and Ellen were sitting at the long and massive bar. It was made of dark gleaming wood and went the entire length of the dim room which had filled up quickly. At some point someone lit a fire in the fireplace in spite of the heat; the jukebox was playing. Not all the people seemed to be from Austin; some had come into town from the desert, from the scattered houses that one guessed were behind the mountain ranges, behind the shimmering light. None of them paid any attention to Felix and Ellen. They had parked their cars any which way in front of the hotel, stepped into the saloon, and keeping their baseball caps and cowboy hats on their heads, said hello to Annie who was standing behind the bar—she seemed to be doing a lot of jobs here in Austin—and then sat down at the scratched-up wooden tables or at the bar. If they joined anyone, they acted as if they had only been gone for a little while.

Annie, her hair carelessly done up, greeted Ellen and Felix almost pleasantly but without any sign of recognition. Ellen ordered a cup of coffee, a sandwich and potato chips. Felix ordered a beer; he didn't want to eat anything, stubbornly claiming he wasn't hungry; this annoyed Ellen no end. The fat ghost hunter, determined and self-assured, came in lugging her bulging carryall. She still wore her summer dress but had slipped on a sweater. To Annie, whose face now lit up with curiosity or amusement, she said, 'We can start.' She greeted Ellen warmly, and to her embarrassment, gave her a long hug. She didn't want anything to drink, and immediately began to unpack her bag on the pool table, setting out all her things as if she were going on an expedition.

She paid no attention to the looks the others were giving her; actually she hadn't looked around the room at all, and she didn't seem to notice the silence that fell when Buddy came in. The jukebox had just finished playing. A man got up to press the button for a new number, but sat down again without doing anything when he saw Buddy. Buddy didn't say hello to Annie, or if he did, Ellen didn't notice. Annie put a beer on the counter right next to Ellen. Buddy came up to the bar, took the beer, drank noisily, looked toward the pool table, turned away again, drank some more, and looked back at the pool table—this time for a lot longer. It went on like that for a while. Finally he put the beer glass down and set it out for a refill. Annie softly said his name—Buddy—and then Buddy walked slowly over to the pool table. Ellen assumed that Felix had been sitting next to her not paying attention, but apparently he had been observing Buddy as carefully as she. Now he slid off his stool and said, 'I want to see that up close.'

Ellen got up and reached for his hand. Buddy stepped up to the pool table. He casually touched the fat ghost hunter's wrist and then, using both of his hands, he pushed all her paraphernalia into one pile. He said, 'No ghost stuff on the pool table. Ghost stuff on the pool table is going to ruin every game.' Lifting up all the equipment he pressed it against the fat ghost hunter's chest. It took a while before she raised her arms to hold on to the stuff. She looked at Buddy with her tiny burning eyes, but could not withstand his look. He smiled at her pleasantly; she turned away and carried all her stuff over to the other end of the bar, where she started tinkering all over again. For an unreal moment Ellen had the feeling that they knew each other, that all the people here knew one another, and that the whole thing was a put-up job, a performance, a staged show the meaning of which she didn't understand. And then the group broke up, returning to the bar or to their tables; someone fed the jukebox, and she forgot it again. She looked around for Felix who had gone to the bar and ordered a beer; he was watching Buddy with a new, an interested, somewhat tense expression.

It didn't happen often that Felix looked at other people like that, open, unguarded, overpowered almost. Ellen used to say, 'It happens rarely that Felix reacts.' He reacted to Buddy, and soon Buddy reacted to Felix and then also to Ellen. Afterwards Ellen felt that Buddy understood at once, and yet she couldn't have said exactly what it was he understood. The customers started to talk again. The fat ghost hunter plugged her cables into each other. Buddy returned Felix's look without smiling. Felix turned away and Ellen went over to him.

He paid no attention to her, leaned over the bar and said to Annie, 'Are there really ghosts in the Hotel International?' Ellen had the distinct feeling that he asked because of Buddy, that he asked to show Buddy, who must have heard him, that he could move, could act, could communicate. To attract him? Or to ward him off? He had asked the question seriously without a touch of irony and Annie replied, also without irony, that about a hundred years ago the Hotel International had been moved, beam by beam and piece by piece, from Virginia to Austin, Nevada, to the desert, by a gold miner. The ghosts, startled and torn from their refuges and niches came to Austin with the old hotel, and people were trying to support them a little in their homeless state, that was all, no reason to be afraid of them.

She told the story slowly, and Ellen listened. The fat ghost hunter, who seemed to have finished putting her paraphernalia in order, was listening too, unmoved, almost apathetic. 'Is it creepy up there on the second floor?' Ellen asked, and Annie said, 'No, not really, not really creepy, maybe cosy in a certain way.' And Felix laughed at that, absent-mindedly, a little tipsy.

The fat ghost hunter caught Annie's look, pointed at her wristwatch, cleared her throat and said, 'Well then.' It was eleven-thirty. The little plastic camera hung on a leather strap around her neck. She brushed the hair out of her face with a firm gesture. Annie took a key out of a drawer and slowly came out from behind the bar. It became quiet again—a silence as though someone had struck a glass so that he could say something important.

Out of the corner of one eye Ellen looked over at Buddy who was standing calmly in the shadows behind the pool table. The fat ghost hunter took a headlamp like the ones miners wear out of her bag and buckled it around her head. Then she slung the recording apparatus on which the mysterious antennae were swaying to and fro over one shoulder. Annie went to a door next to the fireplace and unlocked it. The door creaked madly on its hinges, and everyone stared at the ghost hunter who now shook Annie's hand, suddenly looking touchingly serious. She then marched off stiff-legged and disappeared in the darkness on the other side of the doorway. Annie stood there looking after her, then softly closed the door. Turning to the others, without any change in her expression, she took the ghost hunter's carryall behind the bar, and sat down again on her bar stool at the cash register. It remained very quiet, and she raised her eyebrows as though she were warning the others. Someone pushed his chair back; the billiard balls noisily plopped into the pool table pockets. Buddy came out of the shadows.

Ellen ordered a glass of wine. Felix turned toward her, raised his beer and clinked glasses with her, looking politely into her eyes. She wished he would say something to her, say a few words about the ghost hunter who by now must be somewhere above them in the darkness of the second floor. She imagined her in her little children's sandals stealing through the hallways, carrying her absurd equipment, no moonlight falling through the boarded-up windows, and behind the doors, in the corners, or elsewhere, the ghosts—what kind of ghosts, how many? But Felix said nothing, and the others also seemed to have forgotten the ghost hunter. Nobody glanced toward the door next to the fireplace or up at the ceiling. The jukebox music was loud; Annie turned the air conditioner up a notch. Ellen asked for ice cubes for her wine, drank, and watched Buddy, thankful to be able to transfer her tense watchfulness from Felix to someone else. Buddy carefully placed the billiard balls into the triangle, bent over the table, placed the cue against a ball, remained like that, motionless, straightened up again and gave the cue to someone standing behind him.

Buddy talked to a lot of people, dropped money in the jukebox, and pressed a number without looking, tossed off a beer at the bar, and at some point he returned to the pool table. But he didn't play, and Ellen was sorry about that. For some reason she would have liked to see him play. He was still young, maybe thirty, thirty-two years old. He wore a baseball cap; his expression was childlike, straightforward and intelligent. His stomach protruded over his blue jeans, and he looked powerful in a compact way.

Ellen watched him and thought of a conversation she once had with a woman many years ago. Ellen hadn't been much more than a young girl then. She had let herself get involved in a conversation about sexual fantasies and obsessions; not her own sexual fantasies, as far as she could remember there hadn't in fact been any. The woman had told her that sometime she wanted to find out what it would be like to go to bed with a really fat man, the weight of a really fat man, an idea that at the time had made Ellen blush with shame. Now she watched Buddy, and remembered that conversation.

She sensed that Felix was also watching Buddy. He had ordered some mineral water, presumably either afraid he might have to talk to Buddy, or getting ready to. The thing that was attractive about Buddy and to which Felix was reacting—later Ellen had often looked for a word to describe it, finally finding one that she didn't like but that she nevertheless thought fitting—was his dominance. His sureness, something like a visible force and concentration that emanated from him; he was a spokesman, even without saying much. Felix had always reacted to people of this type. Maybe, Ellen thought, because his own dominance was just the opposite, so concealed and restrained.

Buddy, drinking what must have been at least his tenth pint of Budweiser, was staring at the air conditioner. On one of his walks between the bar and the pool table he stopped quite unexpectedly in front of Ellen and Felix. He looked at Ellen, then at Felix, and said, 'How about a game?' Felix shrugged and smiled in that shy and youthful way that made Ellen's heart contract every time.

She leaned forward and said, 'I can't play pool, but Felix can; I'm sure he'll play.' She thought, she shouldn't always be speaking for him, butting in, getting things started, but she couldn't help herself.

Buddy shook hands with Ellen, gave his name. Ellen introduced herself and then Felix, pronouncing both names the American way. *Felix and Ellen, Phoenix in Arizona, and for the salad, Thousand*

Island, please. 'I hate the way you pronounce the name of that salad dressing,' Felix had said to her two days ago, and Ellen had burst into tears. She thought apologetically, there is no other way, Felix. They won't understand it otherwise.

Felix got up and went towards the pool table; Buddy handed him a cue. Ellen could sense how much Felix longed for home, his apartment, his room, his bed, once and for all to be back home and away from here. Years later she would think that this entire time with Felix had at least taught her one thing—that you can't force things, least of all something like love. A ridiculous discovery, still it was consoling.

Buddy put the balls inside the triangle and gave Felix the first shot. Ellen swivelled around on her bar stool so she wouldn't have to watch the game. The tension between her shoulder blades and in her stomach lessened. Buddy was taking care of Felix, now she didn't have to do anything, didn't have to make any more effort, or offer anything, or have to compensate for her presence, the terror of this trip, being imprisoned in America for the three months between the two flights of a non-cancellable return trip airline ticket, for being at each other's mercy. She vaguely thought, Maybe it will all turn out all right. Suddenly she was sure that everything would be all right. From time to time Felix came back to his glass of water on the bar and then ordered another beer. He said, 'You're not watching.'

'Yes, yes, I am watching,' she replied.

When Felix went to the bathroom, Buddy came over, stood next to her, and said without any transition, 'He's a silent one, your friend; you picked yourself a silent friend.' He nodded several times in affirmation, and Ellen stared at him, unable to answer him. 'You have to give him time, right?' said Buddy, going back to the pool table to wait for Felix. He then dropped three balls one after the other without a sign of triumph. The jukebox was playing 'Sweet Home Alabama' and 'I Can't Get No Satisfaction.' Unexpectedly the saloon door opened and warm, dry air came in, forcing its way into the cold, air-conditioned air. Ellen pushed the napkin under her wine glass aside, sucked on an ice cube, and lit a cigarette. She tried to concentrate on something, to concentrate on the fact that she was in Austin, in Austin in America in Nevada in the desert, in the middle of the Nevada desert and very far from home. She tried to concentrate on the fact that she was sitting at the bar in the Hotel International while Felix was finally putting down roots on this trip because he was playing pool with Buddy, putting out his cigarettes in the plastic ashtray on the edge of the pool table, and signalling Annie now for another beer. She tried to find in all this some sort of happiness or awareness or meaning, and then she lost track and started thinking of something else.

Ellen no longer remembers how long it was before the ghost hunter came back. An hour, two? She no longer recalls whether she spoke with Felix during that time. Felix and Buddy kept playing pool. Between rounds they stood next to each other at the pool table, leaning on their cues. Felix would say something that made Buddy laugh. Ellen wasn't sure whether she really wanted to know what they were talking about. She warded off the advances of two drunk Texans wearing silly cowboy hats and had a second glass of wine, inviting Annie to join her. Annie gave her change for a dollar, and she got up and went over to the jukebox. She had to pass between several fully occupied tables and for the first time realized quite clearly that she was the only woman here besides Annie.

She inserted the coins and took a lot of time to pick out 'Blue Moon' by Elvis, 'Light my Fire' by the Doors, and 'I'm so Lonesome' by Hank Williams—and then Felix was standing behind her, saying, 'Don't do that.'

Without turning around she said, 'Why not?'

Felix said, 'Because you don't know whether the others want to listen to the music you want to listen to.'

'Because you're afraid my choices might make me look ridiculous in front of somebody here,' said Ellen.

'Exactly.'

'I'm afraid of that too.'

It was true, she was actually afraid of that and had thought it over, but she still wanted to listen to Elvis and Hank Williams and the Doors. She pressed the start button and went back to the bar, without looking at Felix. Hank Williams sang to himself in his cracked, droning voice, and in the end nobody paid any attention to it. After the Doors finished—a choice that Ellen regretted in the meantime— Buddy and Felix stopped playing and came over to the bar. Buddy ordered another glass of wine for Ellen and beers for Felix and himself and said to Ellen, 'He plays well, your friend.' Felix blushed.

Ellen said, 'I know.' Then she didn't know how to go on and was briefly afraid that all three of them would now come to a dead end, that the expectations they had of each other would not be confirmed, that they would have to stand there together in silence. But Buddy pulled over a bar stool and began to talk with Felix about their games. They philosophized for quite a while about caroming and the American way of playing pool billiards, and Ellen was able to observe Buddy undisturbed. His dirty blue T-shirt with the name of some university on it, his baseball cap with no inscription, his very large hands, the scabby areas on some of his finger joints, the blue thumbnail, no ring, a narrow Indian band around the left wrist. His belly curving like a globe above his pants, the T-shirt stretching over it, the eagle on his belt buckle disappearing under it. Yet what was so familiar and calming about him remained invisible. Ellen thought, 'calming'.

It didn't seem remarkable when Felix and Buddy suddenly fell silent, and then she simply said, 'Actually we wanted to cross the desert in one day, but for some reason we got stuck here, in the middle of it.' And Buddy said, 'That happens.'

On the whole it was always Ellen who spoke with other people, asking, talking—not only in America but also back home, and in other places, always. Felix would just sit there, listening, not saying anything. Most of the time he sat leaning back, legs crossed; he would roll a cigarette, turning it around and around for minutes at a time, inspecting it at length, then light it and inhale deeply—a good cigarette, the best in the world. He would let it go out and gaze at it closely before relighting it. He would look up, sometimes at someone else, sometimes at Ellen; he would sit as still as a Buddha, weightless, his back ramrod straight, his shoulders thrown back. Some people were impressed by this silence, this wordless sitting and listening, thinking it wise and enigmatic, deep. Ellen did too.

On good days Felix would laugh at something that Ellen had said to someone else in his presence, and thereby give her a weak sign of his solidarity, his belonging. On bad days he wouldn't react at all. At rare moments he would—reserved, distant—say something; sometimes it was intelligent, sometimes completely incomprehensible.

He just about never asked any questions. Ellen had never heard him ask anyone anything, least of all herself. The question he asked Annie about the ghosts in the Hotel International had only been a ploy.

Back home, when they went out together at night she talked a lot, and he said nothing. They would sit down at a table in some bar, as a matter of principle always next to each other; that was Felix's custom. At first Ellen had considered it suspicious because she thought only people who have nothing to say to each other sit side by side. Later she got to like it; it seemed special and intimate. They would be sitting next to each other and Felix would be silent and Ellen would try to endure the silence. Then she would start talking after all and out of sheer helplessness she'd work herself into telling such sentimental, crazy stories that both of them would eventually burst into tears. Felix sitting next to Ellen would simply start to cry, soundlessly. Ellen had to cry too, a little, and could then console him by stroking his face again and again. That was the ritual. Ellen knew that it was like a compulsion, getting him to cry and then being able to console him. A senseless undertaking.

In America, on this trip from the East Coast to the West Coast and back they had sat like that night after night, in national parks, in motels, in rented cabins on the banks of American rivers, and Ellen had started repeating herself, doing awkward variations on significant things. She couldn't think of anything any more, and actually she didn't want to talk about anything any more either. She had started asking Felix questions, and Felix had refused to answer. They spoke less and less, until Buddy pulled up a bar stool and sat down next to them in Austin, Nevada.

He was the first human being in weeks who had spoken with them, who had made Ellen sit up and concentrate, to formulate answers to his simple, purposeful questions. Buddy said, 'What kind of a trip is this you're on?'

And Ellen said, 'Once across America, from the East Coast to the West Coast and back.' A sentence she had wanted to say all this time because it sounded so terrific, only there hadn't been anybody who had wanted to hear it. Buddy said he had never in his life driven from the East Coast to the West Coast and back. To be exact, he'd never been out of Austin, Nevada. The way he said it was too matter-of-fact for

Ellen to have reacted with surprise or disbelief. He wanted to know how they lived back home in Germany. It must be 'an unusual life'.

'It's not unusual,' said Ellen. 'A lot of people live like that. They travel and look at the world, and then they come back and work, and after they've earned enough money, they're off again, to someplace else. Most of them. Most people live like that.' She told about Berlin and about life in Berlin. She tried to describe it, the days and the nights. Everything seemed a bit confusing to her, mixed up and pointless. 'We do this and we do that,' she had the feeling she couldn't describe it properly. Earning money, sometimes doing one thing, sometimes another. To be on the go all night feeling more and more euphoric, and then other nights when they went to bed at ten, tired, worn out, despairing. A group of friends. A kind of family. Open-ended? Forever? She tried to find something that could be compared with life in Austin, Nevada, life the way she imagined it here. She wasn't sure whether there could possibly be anything comparable, but Buddy seemed to understand this too. He wanted to know how they earned a living, their jobs. Ellen pointed at Felix, she wanted him to say the beautiful word describing his work, and Felix did say it, slowly and softly: 'Bicycle mechanic. A bicycle mechanic.'

Buddy thought that was terrific. He said a bicycle mechanic in Austin would have all the town's bicycles repaired in two hours, once and for all. But in the rest of the world you could stay busy with this trade a good long while. Seriously and thoughtfully he said, 'In China, for example, how would it be if you went to China as a bicycle mechanic?' And Felix's face lit up and then fell again. Ellen wanted to tell Buddy that it could be disastrous to talk with Felix about utopias, about mere possibilities. Any 'What if' and 'You might' made Felix suddenly grow weary and depressed. Maybe it's only since he's been with me, Ellen thought. She was actually amused at the idea for a moment.

'What are you laughing about?' Buddy wanted to know, and Ellen shook her head.

'I can't say.' She leaned forward and without thinking put one of her hands on Buddy's heavy, round knee. 'Excuse me, I wasn't laughing at you.' She said, 'I'd like to know about your life, what you do in Austin, Nevada.'

And Buddy said, 'The same things you do.'

Judith Hermann

Years later Ellen still stops sometimes—while she's washing the dishes, on the stairs with the mail and newspapers under her arm, at the streetcar stop, or looking at a timetable—and thinks of Buddy in Austin, Nevada, about his life there. She wonders what he might be doing at that very moment. She's sure that he still lives there, that he hasn't left. There would have been no reason for him to leave. She isn't surprised that Buddy unexpectedly comes to mind; it isn't strange to think of him, to think of someone with whom she spent one night in a bar—no more and no less. In an unspectacular way her life seems to be connected with his.

Buddy had taken off his baseball cap in the Hotel International, put it back on, and asked Felix to roll him a cigarette. Unimpressed, relaxed, he had watched Felix for quite a while as he rolled the cigarette. He said he was born in Austin thirty-two yeas ago, went to school there, later to high school in Ely, then briefly to Las Vegas where he worked as a temporary waiter, then back to Austin. His mother still lived here, in the last house on the main street going toward Ely. His father was dead. He himself lived a bit farther out in the desert. He had married the girl he fell in love with when he was sixteen years old, but he wasn't any more. He hesitated briefly; they were still together. Some things just aren't that easy to say.

He was now working for the state, for the highway maintenance department, and so on. You could call him a construction worker; he repaired the highway and inspected it regularly for damaged stretches and danger spots, that was all. Well-paid work; he could put up with it; he liked being out in the open, in the desert, between the towns. He looked at Ellen and Felix and said, 'You got any kids?'

Ellen shook her head. Possibly Felix didn't understand the question. Buddy said, 'Why not?' He had a way of asking questions, a way of speaking—without emphasis, not subtle, not oratorical; he didn't imply anything and didn't dramatize—Ellen found that good.

Ellen said, 'I don't know. I haven't thought about it, I mean, of course I want a child, but not now—I think that's how it is,' and Buddy nodded slowly and ponderously.

'I have a kid, a son, he's three years old now,' he said, then looked at Annie, who was sitting on her stool behind the bar and who had been listening, motionless all this time. Ellen saw him look up and had followed the direction of his eyes, but then at the last moment she didn't look at Annie. Annie laughed; Ellen had no idea about what. She had noticed the hesitation, the short hesitation in his interconnected, calm sentences, and she said, 'The girl you married, is she the mother of your child?'

Buddy answered almost indignantly, 'Of course she is. Who else should it be.'

And Ellen said half playfully, 'Is she beautiful?'

Behind the bar Annie again burst out laughing. Buddy said she had once been beautiful. She had been very beautiful; now she wasn't beautiful any more; she was ugly and fat. He said, 'She is so fat that you can only photograph her from an airplane.' Ellen was no longer sure he was serious. He said she had lost her beauty once and for all, and maybe this kind of life was responsible for that, life in Austin, or life in general; whatever, he still loved her, if only because she was the mother of his son. He said, 'I love her because she is the mother of my son.' And the sentence lay there between them for a long time until Ellen turned to Annie and asked for another glass of wine.

'You set your heart too much on what's been said, on sentences, on possible meanings,' Felix had once said to her. After Austin? Before Austin? Ellen isn't sure any more. In any case, she didn't contradict him. She still remembers that Buddy's sentence seemed dangerous to her because it contained a question, unspoken. But the look Buddy gave Annie seemed even more disquieting. She thought, I'd die if Felix ever looked at me that way. Annie slid the glass of wine toward her, filled to the brim with ice cubes. The bar had emptied out. On the dark street outside the saloon door on the dark street, drivers were starting their cars, whirling up dust. Only a few people still sat at some of the tables. Annie switched off the light over the pool table. Buddy raised his beer bottle and clinked it against Ellen's wine glass, 'To your trip and a safe return home. To you.' Felix had finally finished rolling the cigarette for Buddy and handed it to him. Annie came over to them from behind the bar, gave Buddy a light, and stayed there, leaning over with half-closed eyes. Buddy inhaled in the cautious, surprised way of people who smoke a cigarette once a year, then he gently blew out the smoke. He said, 'If you don't have a child, then you don't know, for instance, what it's like to buy your child a pair of little blue Nike sneakers.' He gave a short laugh and shook his head.

Judith Hermann

Ellen said, 'What's it like?'

And Buddy looked past her out into the street, squeezed his eyes shut, and said, 'Well, it's like this—it's hard to describe, but it's nice. These sneakers are so small and tiny and perfect, a perfect copy of a real sneaker.' He looked at Felix and said, 'Right?' Felix nodded. 'You buy these tiny sneakers, blue and yellow with sturdy laces and cushioned soles in a perfect little shoebox, and you take them home to your kid and put them on for him, and he runs off in them. He simply runs off in them. That's all.'

He took another pull on the cigarette, then gave it back to Felix who took it and went on smoking it. Buddy leaned back and was going to say something—Ellen was sure something completely different—and then the door next to the fireplace very slowly creaked open, and the fat ghost hunter stepped out.

'There's amazingly little time,' Ellen said to Felix afterwards, 'amazingly little time for things, for such moments, and sometimes I'm glad it's like that. It keeps me from losing control. From saying idiotic things. It keeps me from yielding, from total surrender.' Felix doesn't really let her know whether or not he understood.

The fat ghost hunter came into the room as though she had been waiting on the other side of the door. She looked no different than she had—how many?—hours ago; her hair wasn't messed up and her skirt wasn't torn, but she was covered with dust and cobwebs, and there was something solemn in her face, something at the same time sad and triumphant.

She walked across the room toward the bar with dignity, made a slight bow, and with an exhausted, satisfied and conclusive gesture she put her recording equipment down on top of the bar. Without asking, Annie poured her a glass of whiskey, which she drank in one long draught. Buddy brought over another bar stool and slid his over to Ellen, making room between himself and Felix.

The ghost hunter pulled the plastic camera attached to the leather strap over her head and handed it to Annie, who carefully, as though it were made of glass, put it down next to her on the bar. Then she sat down on the high stool like a fat, dressed-up child, drank another whiskey and started hiccuping. Ellen had to laugh, and the ghost hunter gave her a friendly nod. They sat like that for quite a while, quietly, next to one another; all the other customers had left; the air conditioner droned, and water dripped into the sink. Annie leaned her head on her hands, you couldn't see her face. The fat ghost hunter smiled. She pointed to her carryall, and Buddy pulled it over and handed it to her. She took a well-worn album out of the bag.

She said, 'I'll show it to you if you like,' then, not waiting for an answer, she opened the album. Ellen, Felix and Buddy bent over it, Annie looking over Buddy's shoulder. There were colour photos, postcard size colour photos; and though they were in plastic covers, they were wrinkled. They showed living rooms, stairways and cellars in dim half-light, and on each photo you could see in some corner a silvery stripe, a little shimmer, the reflection of a lamp or an out-of-focus head in a double exposure. There were intimate looks into bedrooms, clothes closets and kitchens, and Ellen would normally have said, 'Those were simply defects caused by the film processing. Double exposures, reflections, dust on the lens, nothing more,' but that night in the bar of the Hotel International she didn't think so. She believed the fat ghost hunter, the seriousness and the conviction with which she pointed to the photos, unintentionally always covering precisely the crucial elements with her index finger.

Ellen looked at the ghost hunter from the side, her bright red, glowing cheeks, the strands of colourless hair falling over her sweaty forehead, the little beads of perspiration on her nostrils and on her upper lip. The smell she had exuded in the afternoon seemed to have gotten stronger and was now mixed with something else, with dust and wood and ghosts—Ellen thought resolutely—with whatever it was that ghosts smelled of. She had to laugh at that. She had the clear sensation that she was happy just then, very happy, feeling very light. Buddy returned her laughter, gently and softly, and the fat ghost hunter said, 'Yes, well, I really liked this one; you like some more, and some you like less.' She nodded and pointed with her index finger at a photograph in her lap, staring at it as if remembering something.

Then she raised her head and looking at Annie she said, 'Those ghosts up there—' she pointed briefly toward the ceiling and everybody looked up, 'those ghosts up there can't come to terms with life.' She cleared her throat exaggeratedly and went on, 'I have to come back, in any case—if possible. Is it possible?'

'Of course it's possible,' Annie said reassuringly. 'I'm quite sure.'

She exchanged a serious look with Buddy. Buddy got up and rubbed his face with his left hand; he finished his beer and began to put up the chairs.

Over his shoulder he said, 'Time to go home, time to go to sleep.' Annie wiped down the top of the bar, rinsed the last glasses and turned off the air conditioner. Ellen drank her wine slowly; she felt tired and peaceful; she knew she still had some time. The fat ghost hunter rocked back and forth on her bar stool, lost in thought, humming a tranquil melody. Felix rolled himself a last cigarette. Whatever Ellen had tried to concentrate her thoughts on hours before was here, sharp-edged, crystalline, fragile and clear.

The fat ghost hunter pointed to her plastic camera and said, 'There's one last picture left on the film, the very last one. Does anyone want to have his picture taken?'

And Buddy said, 'If you're going to take one, then take it of all of us.'

The street outside the Hotel International was still and dark, except for the neon light of the Budweiser advertisement; the sky was deep blue and wide and full of stars. 'How warm it is,' Felix said, speaking mostly to himself. The warmth was dry and dusty. Annie locked the saloon door. The fat ghost hunter set her camera on a post—the same post they used to hitch horses to in the old days, Ellen thought—and peered awkwardly through the viewfinder, all the while mumbling to herself. Then she clapped her little hands and called out, 'Line up!'

Ellen stood on the porch in front of the saloon door; above her was the sign with the crooked wooden letters spelling HOTEL INTERNATIONAL; to her left, the dusty window with the neon sign. She suddenly felt excited, almost exuberant. The others took their places next to her, in one row, Buddy, Felix, Annie. The fat ghost hunter pushed the only button on her camera, a little red light flickered on, she rushed out from behind the post, stumbled up on the porch, and squeezed herself in between Felix and Buddy. She counted, 'Five, four, three, two, one,' and Ellen, who knew that she would never get to see this photograph and who suddenly thought in amazement that this would be one of thirty-six photographs on a roll otherwise full of ghosts, reached for Buddy's hand. She held it tight; he squeezed hers in return, and Ellen smiled and was sure she was beautiful, confident, and full of power and strength. And before she could think about anything else, there was a flash, the ghost hunter yelled, 'Photo!' and then everything was dark again.

The following morning they woke up late. Ellen had a headache; Felix claimed he'd had a headache every morning ever since they came to America. They packed their things, loaded them into the pickup, smoked cigarettes that made them feel ill on the stoop in front of their room. The neon sign in the window of the Hotel International was turned off, the saloon door was locked. The Ford pickup stood in front of the motel, the Chrysler was gone. Lizards scurried over the walls, rustled in the unreal stillness.

It occurred to Ellen that they hadn't paid for their drinks yesterday, but when she went over to Annie's office to make up for that, she found the door locked, the venetian blinds down. Someone had removed the vacancy sign from the flagpole. They waited a while longer, but no one came and nothing moved, and then they climbed into their pickup and drove off, westward.

Today, when Felix and Ellen sit down to supper with their child, Felix sometimes repeats the sentence, 'And when we finish eating we'll tell you how your parents got to know each other.' It's a gag, a little joke, and Ellen has to laugh at it too, has to laugh every time, even though she thinks the joke is eerie and she doesn't really know what she's laughing about. The child is still too little to be told about it. Ellen wants to know what it will be like when she can tell him about it. She's looking forward to that time and she's afraid of it too. She'd like to tell her child that at the decisive moments of her life she was not quite conscious, unaware of their importance. She would like to say, 'You're here because Buddy in Austin, Nevada, told us we didn't know what it was like to buy sneakers for a child, a pair of perfect tiny sneakers in a perfect little shoebox—he was right. I didn't know and I wanted to know what it was like. I really wanted to know.' □

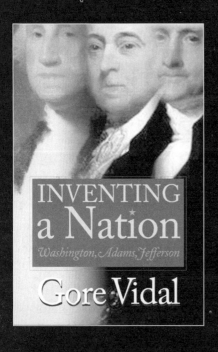

GRANTA

FARANGS

Rattawut Lapcharoensap

This is how we count the days. June: the Germans come to the Island—football cleats, big T-shirts, thick tongues—speaking like spitting. July: the Italians, the French, the British, the Americans. The Italians like pad thai, its affinity with spaghetti. They like light fabrics, sunglasses, leather sandals. The French like plump girls, rambutans, disco music, baring their breasts. The British are here to work on their pasty complexions, their penchant for hashish. Americans are the fattest, the stingiest of the bunch. They may pretend to like pad thai or grilled prawns or the occasional curry, but twice a week they need their culinary comforts, their hamburgers and their pizzas. They're also the worst drunks. Never get too close to a drunk American. August brings the Japanese. Stay close to them. Never underestimate the power of the yen. Everything's cheap with imperial monies in hand and they're too polite to bargain. By the end of August, when the monsoon starts to blow, they're all consorting, slapping each other's backs, slipping each other drugs, sleeping with each other, sipping their liquor under the pink lights of the Island's bars. By September they've all deserted, leaving the Island to the Aussies and the Chinese, who are so omnipresent one need not mention them at all.

Ma says, 'Pussy and elephants. That's all these people want.' She always says this in August, at the season's peak, when she's tired of farangs running all over the Island, tired of finding used condoms in the motel's rooms, tired of guests complaining to her in five languages. She turns to me and says, 'You give them history, temples, pagodas, traditional dance, floating markets, seafood curry, tapioca desserts, silk-weaving cooperatives, but all they really want is to ride some hulking grey beast like a bunch of wildmen and to pant over girls and to lie there half-dead getting skin cancer on the beach during the time inbetween.'

We're having a late lunch, watching television in the motel office. The Island Network is showing *Rambo: First Blood Part II* again. Sylvester Stallone, dubbed in Thai, mows down an entire regiment of VC with a bow and arrow. I tell Ma I've just met a girl. 'It might be love,' I say. 'It might be real love, Ma. Like Romeo and Juliet love.'

Ma turns off the television just as John Rambo is about to fly a chopper to safety.

She tells me it's just my hormones. She sighs and says, 'Oh no, not

189

again. Don't be so naive,' she says. 'I didn't raise you to be stupid. Are
you bonking one of the guests? You better not be bonking one of the
guests. Because if you are, if you're bonking one of the guests, we're
going to have to bleed the pig. Remember, *luk*, we have an agreement.'
    I tell her she's being xenophobic. I tell her things are different this
time. But Ma just licks her lips and says once more that if I'm
bonking one of the guests, I can look forward to eating Clint
Eastwood curry in the near future. Ma's always talking about killing
my pig. And though I know she's just teasing, she says it with such
zeal and a peculiar glint in her eyes that I run out to the pen to check
on the swine.

I knew it was love when Clint Eastwood sniffed her crotch earlier
that morning and the girl didn't scream or jump out of the sand
or swat the pig like some of the other girls do. She merely lay there,
snout in crotch, smiling that angelic smile, like it was the most natural
thing in the world, running a hand over the fuzz of Clint Eastwood's
head like he was some pink and docile dog, and said, giggling, 'Why
hello, oh my, what a nice surprise, you're quite a beast, aren't you?'
    I'd been combing the motel beachfront for trash when I looked
up from my morning chore and noticed Clint Eastwood sniffing his
new friend. An American: her Budweiser bikini told me so. I
apologized from a distance, called the pig over, but the girl said it
was okay, it was fine, the pig could stay as long as he liked. She called
me over and said I could do the same.
    I told her the pig's name.
    'That's adorable,' she laughed.
    'He's the best,' I said. '*Dirty Harry. Fistful of Dollars. The Good,
The Bad and The Ugly.*'
    'He's a very good actor.'
    'Yes. Mister Eastwood is a first-class thespian.'
    Clint Eastwood trotted into the ocean for his morning bath then,
leaving us alone, side by side in the sand. I looked to make sure Ma
wasn't watching me from the office window. I explained how Clint
Eastwood loves the ocean at low tide, the wet sand like a three-
kilometre trough of mud. The girl sat up on her elbows, watched
the pig, a waterlogged copy of *The Portrait of a Lady* at her side.
She'd just gone for a swim and the beads of water on her navel

seemed so close that for a moment I thought I might faint if I did not look away.

'I'm Elizabeth. Lizzie.'

'Nice to meet you, Miss Elizabeth,' I said. 'I like your bikini.'

She threw back her head and laughed. I admired the shine of her tiny, perfectly even rows of teeth, the gleam of that soft, rose-coloured tongue quivering between them like the meat of some magnificent mussel.

'Oh my,' she said, closing that mouth, gesturing with her chin. 'I think your pig is drowning.'

Clint Eastwood was rolling around where the ocean meets the sand, chasing receding waves, running away from oncoming ones. It's a game he plays every morning, scampering back and forth across the water's edge, and he snorted happily every time the waves licked over him, knocked him into the foam.

'He's not drowning,' I said. 'He's a very good swimmer, actually.'

'I didn't know pigs could swim.'

'Clint Eastwood can.'

She smiled, a close-mouthed grin, admiring my pig at play, and I would've given anything in the world to see her tongue again, to reach out and sink my fingers into the hollows of her collarbone, to stare at that damp, beautiful navel all day long.

'I have an idea, Miss Elizabeth,' I said, getting up, brushing the sand from the seat of my shorts. 'This may seem rather presumptuous, but would you like to go for an elephant ride with me today?'

Ma doesn't want me bonking a farang because once, long ago, she had bonked a farang herself, against the wishes of her own parents, and all she got for her trouble was a broken heart and me in return. This was when English was still my first and only language, and the farang was a man known to me only as Sergeant Marshall Henderson. I remember the Sergeant well, if only because he insisted I call him by his military rank.

'Not Daddy,' I remember him saying on many occasions. 'Sergeant. Sergeant Henderson. Sergeant Marshall. Remember you're a soldier now, boy. A spy for Uncle Sam's army.'

And for the first three years of my remembered life—before he went back to America, promising to send for us—the Sergeant and I would go on imaginary missions together, navigating our way through the thicket of tourists lazing on the beach.

'Private,' he'd yell after me. 'I don't have a good feeling about this, Private. This place gives me the creeps. We should radio for reinforcements. It could be an ambush.'

'Let 'em come, Sergeant! We can take 'em!' I would squeal, crawling through the sand with a large stick in my hand, eyes trained on the enemy. 'Those gooks'll be sorry they ever showed their ugly faces.'

One day, the three of us went to the fresh market by the pier. I saw a litter of pigs there, six of them squeezed tightly into a small cardboard box amidst the loud thudding of butchers' knives. I remember thinking of the little piglets I'd seen skewered and roasting over an open fire outside many of the Island's fancier restaurants.

I began to cry.

'What's wrong, Private?'

'I don't know.'

'A soldier,' the Sergeant grunted, 'never cries.'

'They just piggies,' Ma laughed in her stilted English, bending down to pat me on the back. Because of our plans to move to California, Ma was learning English at the time. She hasn't spoken a word of English to me since. 'What piggies say, luk? What they say? Piggies say oink-oink. Don't cry, luk. Don't cry. Oink-oink is yummy.'

A few days later, the Sergeant walked into my bedroom with something wriggling beneath his T-shirt. He sat down on the bed beside me. I remember the mattress sinking with his weight, the chirping of some desperate bird struggling in his belly.

'Congratulations, Private,' the Sergeant whispered through the dark, holding out a young and frightened Clint Eastwood in one of his large hands. 'You're a CO now. A commanding officer. From now on, you'll be responsible for the welfare of this recruit.'

I stared at him dumbfounded, took the pig into my arms.

'Happy birthday, kiddo.'

And shortly before the Sergeant left us, before Ma took over the motel from her parents, before she ever forbade me from speaking the Sergeant's language except to assist the motel's guests, before I knew what bastard or mongrel or slut or whore meant in any language, there was an evening when I walked into the ocean with

Clint Eastwood—I was teaching him how to swim—and when I looked back to shore I saw my mother sitting between the Sergeant's legs in the sand, the sun a bright red orb on the crest of the mountains behind them. They spoke without looking at each other, my mother reaching back to hook an arm around his neck, while my piglet thrashed in the sea foam. 'Ma,' I asked a few years later, 'you think the Sergeant will ever send for us?'

'It's best, luk,' Ma said in Thai, 'if you never mention his name again. It gives me a headache.'

After I finished combing the beach for trash, put Clint Eastwood back in his pen, Lizzie and I went up the mountain on my motorcycle to Surachai's house, where his uncle Mongkhon ran an elephant-trekking business. MR MONGKHON'S JUNGLE SAFARI, a painted sign declared in their driveway. COME EXPERIENCE THE NATURAL BEAUTY OF FOREST WITH THE AMAZING VIEW OF OCEAN AND SPLENDID HORIZON FROM ELEPHANT'S BACK! I'd informed Uncle Mongkhon once that his sign was grammatically incorrect and that I'd lend him my expertise for a small fee, but he just laughed and said farangs preferred it just the way it was, thank you very much, they thought it was charming, and did I really think I was the only *huakhuai* who knew English on this godforsaken Island? During the war in Vietnam, before he started the business, Uncle Mongkhon had worked at an airbase on the mainland dishing out lunch to American soldiers.

From where Lizzie and I stood, we could see the grey backs of two bulls peeking over the roof of their one-storey house. Uncle Mongkhon used to have a full *chuak* of elephants, before the people at Monopolated Elephant Tours came to the Island and started under-pricing the competition, monopolizing mountain-pass tariffs and staking their claim upon farangs at hotels three stars and up—doing, in short, what they had done on so many other islands like ours. Business began to sag after the arrival of MET and, in the end, Uncle Mongkhon was forced to sell his elephants to logging companies on the mainland. Where there had once been eight elephants roaming the wide corral, now there were only two—Yai and Noi—ageing bulls with ulcered bellies, trunks hung limply between their crusty forelegs.

'Oh, wow,' Lizzie said. 'Are those actual elephants?'

I nodded.

'They're so huge.'

She clapped a few times, laughing.

'Huge!' she said again, jumping up and down. She turned to me and smiled.

Surachai was lifting weights in the yard, a barbell in each hand. Uncle Mongkhon sat on the porch bare-chested, smoking a cigarette. When Surachai saw Lizzie standing there in her bikini next to me, his arms went limp. For a second I was afraid he might drop the weights on his feet.

'Where'd you find this one?' he said in Thai, smirking, walking towards us.

'Boy,' Uncle Mongkhon yelled from the porch, also in Thai. 'You irritate me sometimes. Tell that girl to put on some clothes. You know damn well I don't let bikinis ride. This is a respectable establishment. We have rules.'

'What are they saying?' Lizzie asked. Farangs get nervous when you carry on a conversation they can't understand.

'They just want to know if we need one elephant or two.'

'Let's just get one,' Lizzie smiled, reaching out to take one of my hands. 'Let's ride one together.' I held my breath. Her hand shot bright, surprising comets of heat up my arm. I wanted to yank my hand away even as I longed to stand there forever with our sweaty palms folded together like soft roti bread. I heard the voice of Surachai's mother coming from inside the house, the light sizzle of a frying pan.

'It's nothing, Maew,' Uncle Mongkhon yelled back to his sister inside. 'Though I wouldn't come out here unless you like nudie shows. The mongrel's here with another member of his international harem.'

'These are my friends,' I said to Lizzie. 'This is Surachai.'

'How do you do,' Surachai said in English, briskly shaking her hand, looking at me all the while.

'I'm fine, thank you,' Lizzie chuckled. 'Nice to meet you.'

'Yes yes yes,' Surachai said, grinning like a fool. 'Honour to meet you, Madame. It will make me very gratified to let you ride my elephants. Very gratified. Because he'—Surachai patted me on the back now—'he my handsome soulmate. My best man.'

Surachai beamed proudly at me. I'd taught him that word: 'soulmate'.

'How long have you been married?' Lizzie asked. Surachai laughed hysterically, uncomprehendingly, widening his eyes at me for help.

'He's not,' I said. 'He meant to say "best friend".'

'Yes yes,' Surachai said, nodding. 'Best friend.'

'You listening to me, boy?' Uncle Mongkhon got up from the porch and walked towards us. 'Bikinis don't ride. It scares the animals.'

'*Sawatdee*, Uncle,' I said, greeting him with a *wai*, bending my head extra low for effect; but he slapped me on the head with a forehand when I came up.

'Tell the girl to put on some clothes,' Uncle Mongkhon growled. 'It's unholy.'

'Aw, Uncle,' I pleaded. 'We didn't bring any with us.'

'Need I remind you, boy, that the elephant is our National Symbol? Sometimes I think your stubborn farang half keeps you from understanding this. You should be ashamed of yourself. I'd tell your mother if I knew it wouldn't break her heart.

'What if I went to her country and rode a bald eagle in my underwear, huh?' he continued, pointing at Lizzie. 'How would she like it? Ask her, will you?'

'What's he saying?' Lizzie whispered in my ear.

'Ha ha ha,' Surachai interjected, gesticulating wildly. 'Everything okay, Madame. Don't worry, be happy. My uncle, he just say elephants very terrified of your breasts.'

'You should've told me to put on some clothes.' Lizzie turned to me, frowning, letting go of my hand.

'It's really not a problem,' I laughed.

'No,' Uncle Mongkhon said to Lizzie in English. 'Not a big problem, Madame. Just a small one.'

In the end, to placate Uncle Mongkhon, I took off my T-shirt and gave it to Lizzie. As we made our way towards the corral, I caught her grinning at the sight of my bare torso. Though I had been spending time at the new public gym by the pier, I still felt some of that old adolescent embarrassment returning again. I casually flexed my muscles in the postures I'd practised before my bedroom mirror so Lizzie could see my body not as the soft, skinny thing that it was, but as a pillar of strength and stamina.

When we came upon the gates of the elephant corral, Lizzie took my hand again. I turned to smile at her and she seemed, at that moment, some ethereal angel come from heaven to save me, an angel whose breasts left round, dark, damp spots on my T-shirt. And when we mounted the elephant Yai, the beast rising quickly to his feet, Lizzie squealed and wrapped her arms so tightly around my bare waist that I would've gladly forfeited breathing for the rest of my life.

Under that jungle canopy, climbing up the mountainside on Yai's back, I told her about Sergeant Henderson, the motel, Ma, Clint Eastwood. She told me about her Ohio childhood, the New York City skyline, NASCAR, T. J. Maxx, the drinking habits of American teenagers. I told her about Pamela, my last American girlfriend, and how she promised me her heart but never answered any of my letters. Lizzie nodded sympathetically and told me about her bastard boyfriend Hunter, whom she'd left last night at their hotel on the other side of the island after finding him in the arms of a young prostitute. 'That fucker,' she said. 'That whore.' I told Lizzie she should forget about him, she deserved better, and besides Hunter was a stupid name anyway, and we both shook our heads and laughed at how poorly our lovers had behaved.

We came upon a scenic overlook. The sea rippled before us like a giant blue bedspread. I decided to give Yai a rest. He sat down gratefully on his haunches. For a minute Lizzie and I just sat there on the elephant's back looking out at the ocean, the wind blowing through the trees behind us. Yai was winded from the climb and we rose and fell with his heavy breaths. I told Lizzie about how the Sergeant and my mother used to stand on the beach, point east, and tell me that if I looked hard enough I might be able to catch a glimpse of the California coast rising out of the Pacific horizon. I pointed to Ma's motel below, the twelve bungalows like tiny insects resting on the golden shoreline. It's amazing, I told Lizzie, how small my life looks from such a height.

Lizzie hummed contentedly. Then she stood up on Yai's back. 'Here's your shirt,' she laughed, tossing it at me.

With a quick sweeping motion, Lizzie took off her bikini top. Then she peeled off her bikini bottom. And then there she was—my American angel—naked on the back of Uncle Mongkhon's ageing elephant.

'Your country is so hot,' she said, smiling, crawling towards me on all fours. Yai made a low moan and shifted beneath us.

'Yes, it is,' I said, pretending to study the horizon, rubbing Yai's parched, grey back.

After *Rambo* and lunch with my mother and a brief afternoon nap, I walk out the door to meet Lizzie at the restaurant when Ma asks me what I'm all dressed up for.

'What do you mean?' I ask innocently, and Ma says, 'What do I mean? What do I mean? Am I your mother? Are you my son? Are those black pants? Is that a button-down shirt? Is that the nice silk tie I bought you for your birthday?'

She sniffs my head.

'And is that my nice mousse in your hair? And why,' she asks, 'do you smell like an elephant?'

I just stand there blinking at her questions.

'Don't think I don't know,' she says finally. 'I saw you, luk. I saw you on your motorcycle with that farang slut in her bikini.'

I laugh and tell her I have hair mousse of my own. But Ma's still yelling at me when I go to the pen to fetch Clint Eastwood.

'Remember whose son you are,' she says through the day's dying light, standing in the office doorway with her arms akimbo. 'Remember who raised you all these years.'

'What are you talking about, Ma?'

'Why do you insist, luk, on chasing after these farangs?'

'You're being silly, Ma. It's just love. You make it sound like I'm a criminal.'

'I don't think,' Ma says, 'that I'm the silly one here, luk. I'm not the one taking my pet pig out to dinner just because some foreign girl thinks it's cute.'

I make my way down the beach with Clint Eastwood towards the lights of the restaurant. It's an outdoor establishment with low candlelit tables set in the sand and a large pit that the bare-chested chefs use to grill the day's catch. The restaurant's quite popular with farangs on the Island. Wind at their backs, sand at their feet, night sky above, eating by the light of the moon and the stars. It's romantic, I suppose. Although I'm hesitant to spend so much money on what

Ma calls second-rate seafood in a third-rate atmosphere, Lizzie suggested we meet there for dinner tonight, so who am I to argue with love's demands?

When we get to the restaurant, Lizzie's seated at one of the tables, candlelight flickering on her face. Clint Eastwood races ahead and nuzzles his snout in her lap, but Lizzie's face doesn't light up the way it did earlier this morning. The other customers turn around in their seats to look at Clint Eastwood, and Lizzie seems embarrassed to be the object of his affections.

'Hi,' she says when I get to the table, lighting a cigarette.

I kiss one of her hands, sit down beside her. I tell Clint Eastwood to stay. He lies down on his belly in the sand, head resting between his stubby feet. The sun is setting behind us, rays flickering across the plane of the sea, and I think I'm starting to understand why farangs come such a long way to get to the Island, why they travel so far to come to my home.

'Beautiful evening,' I say.

Lizzie nods absent-mindedly.

'Is there something wrong?' I finally ask, after the waiter takes our order in English. 'Have I done anything to offend you?'

Lizzie sighs, stubs out her cigarette in the bamboo ashtray.

'Nothing's wrong,' she says. 'Nothing at all.'

But when our food arrives, Lizzie barely touches it. She keeps passing Clint Eastwood pieces of her sautéed prawns. Clint Eastwood gobbles them up gratefully. At least he's enjoying the meal, I think. On weekend nights, I often bring Clint Eastwood to this restaurant, after the tables have been stowed away, and he usually has to fight with the strays that descend on the beach for leftovers farangs leave in their wake: crab shells, fish bones, prawn husks.

'Something's wrong,' I say. 'You're not happy.'

She lights another cigarette, blows a cloud of smoke.

'Hunter's here,' she says finally, looking out at the darkening ocean.

'Your ex-boyfriend?'

'No,' she says. 'My boyfriend. He's here.'

'Here?'

'Don't turn around. He's sitting right behind us with his friends.'

At that moment, a large farang whom I can only assume is Hunter swoops into the seat across the table from us. He's dressed in a white undershirt and a pair of surfer's shorts. His nose is caked with sunscreen. His chest is pink from too much sun. There's a Buddha dangling from his neck. He looks like a deranged clown.

He reaches over the table and grabs a piece of squid from my plate.

'Who's the joker?' he asks Lizzie, gnawing on the squid. 'Friend of yours?'

'Hunter,' Lizzie says. 'Don't do this.'

'Hey,' he says, looking at me, taking another piece of squid from my entrée, 'What's with the tie? And what's with the pig, man?'

I smile, put a hand on Clint Eastwood's head.

'Hey you,' he says. 'I'm talking to you. Speak English? Talk American?'

He tears off a piece of squid with his front teeth. I can't stop staring at his powdered nose, the bulge of his hairy, sunburned chest. I'm hoping he chokes.

'You've really outdone yourself this time, baby,' he says to Lizzie now. 'But that's what I love about you. Your unpredictability. Your wicked sense of humour. Didn't know you went for mute tards with pet pigs.'

'Hunter.'

'Oh, Lizzie,' he says, reaching out to take one of her hands, feigning tenderness. 'I've missed you so much. I hate it when you just leave me like that. I've been worried sick about you. I'm sorry about last night, okay baby? Okay? I'm really sorry. But it was just a misunderstanding, you know? Jerry and Billyboy over there can testify to my innocence. You know how those Thai girls get when we're around.'

'We can talk about this later, Hunter.'

'Yes,' I interject. 'I think you should talk to her later.'

He just stares at me with that stupid white nose jutting out between his eyes. For a second, I think Hunter's going to throw the squid at me. But then he just pops the rest of it into his mouth, turns to Lizzie, and says with his mouth full:

'You fucked this joker, didn't you?'

'Please, Hunter.'

I look over at Lizzie. She's staring at the table, tapping her fingers lightly against the wood. It seems she's about to cry. I stand up, throw a few hundred bahts on the table. Clint Eastwood follows my lead, rises clumsily to his feet.

'It was a pleasure meeting you, Miss Elizabeth,' I say, smiling. I want to take her hand and run back to the motel so we can curl up together on the beach, watch the constellations. But Lizzie just keeps on staring at the top of that table.

I walk with Clint Eastwood back to the motel. It seems like we're the only people on that beach. Night is upon us now. In the distance, I can see squidding boats perched on the horizon, fluorescent searchlights luring their catch to the surface. Clint Eastwood races ahead of me, foraging for food in the sand, and I'm thinking with what I suppose is grief about all the American girls I've ever loved. Girls with names like Pamela, Angela, Stephanie, Joy. And now Lizzie.

One of the girls sent me a postcard of Miami once. A row of palm trees and a pink condo. 'Hi Sweetie,' it said. 'I just wanted to say hi and to thank you for showing me a good time when I was over there. I'm in South Beach now, it's Spring Break, and let me tell you it's not half as beautiful as it is over there. If you ever make it out to the U S of A, look me up okay?' which was nice of her, but she never told me where to look her up and there was no return address on the postcard. I'd taken that girl to see phosphorescence in one of the Island's bays and when she told me it was the most miraculous thing she'd ever seen, I told her I loved her—but the girl just giggled and ran into the sea, that phosphorescent blue streaking like a comet's tail behind her. Every time they do that, I swear I'll never love another, and I'm thinking about Lizzie and Hunter sitting at the restaurant now, and how this is really the last time I'll let myself love one of her kind.

Halfway down the beach, I find Surachai sitting in a mango tree. He's hidden behind a thicket of leaves, straddling one of the branches, leaning back against the trunk.

When we were kids, Surachai and I used to run around the beach advertising ourselves as the Island's Miraculous Monkey Boys. We made loincloths out of Uncle Mongkhon's straw heap and an old T-shirt Ma used as a rag. For a small fee, we'd climb up trees and fetch coconuts for farangs, who would ooh and aah at how nimble we were. A product of our Island environment, they'd say, as if it was due to something in the water and not the fact that we'd spent hours practising in Surachai's backyard. For added effect, we'd make monkey noises when we climbed, which always made them laugh. They would often be impressed, too, by my facility with the English language. In one version of the speech I gave before every performance, I played the part of an American boy shipwrecked on the Island as an infant. With both parents dead, I was raised in the jungle by a family of gibbons. Though we've long outgrown what Ma calls 'that idiot stunt', Surachai still comes down from the mountain occasionally to climb a tree on the beach. He'll just sit there staring out into the ocean for hours. It's meditative, he told me once. And the view is one-of-a-kind.

'You look terrible,' he says now. 'Something happen with that farang girl?'

I call Clint Eastwood over. I tell the pig to stay. I take off my leather shoes, my knitted socks, and—because I don't want to ruin them—the button-down shirt and the silk tie, leaving them all at the bottom of the trunk before joining Surachai on one of the adjacent branches. As I climb, the night air warm against my skin, I'm reminded of how pleasurable this used to be—hoisting myself up by my bare feet and fingertips—and I'm surprised by how easy it still is.

When I settle myself into the tree, I start to tell Surachai everything, including the episode on the elephant earlier that afternoon. As I talk, Surachai snakes his way out on to one of the branches and drops a mango for Clint Eastwood down below.

'At least you're having sex,' Surachai says. 'At least you're doing it. Some of us just get to sit in a mango tree and think about it.'

I laugh.

'I don't suppose,' Surachai says, 'you loved this girl?'

I shrug.

'You're a mystery to me, *phuan*,' Surachai says, climbing higher now into the branches. 'I've known you all these years, and that's the one thing I'll never be able to understand—why you keep falling for these farang girls. It's like you're crazy for heartache. Plenty of nice Thai girls around. Girls without plane tickets.'

'I know. I don't think they like me, though. Something about the way I look. I don't think my nose is flat enough.'

'That may be true. But they don't like me either, okay? And I've got the flattest nose on the Island.'

We sit silently for a while, perched in that mango tree like a couple of sloths, listening to the leaves rustling around us. I climb up to where Surachai is sitting. Through the thicket, I see Clint Eastwood jogging out to meet a group of farangs making their way down the beach. I call out to him, tell him to stay, but my pig's not listening to me.

It's Hunter and his friends, laughing, slapping each other's backs, tackling each other to the sand. Lizzie's walking with them silently, head down, trying to ignore their antics. When she sees Clint Eastwood racing up to meet her, she looks to see if I'm around. But she can't see us from where she's standing. She can't see us at all.

'It's that fucking pig again!' Hunter yells.

They all laugh, make rude little pig noises, jab him with their feet. Clint Eastwood panics. He squeals. He starts to run. The American boys give chase, try to tackle him to the ground. Lizzie tells them to leave the pig alone, but the boys aren't listening. Clint Eastwood is fast. He's making a fool of them, running in circles one way then the other, zigzagging back and forth through the sand. The more they give chase, the more Clint Eastwood eludes them, the more frustrated the boys become, and what began as jovial tomfoolery has now turned into some kind of bizarre mission for Hunter and his friends. Their chase becomes more orchestrated. The movements of their shadows turn strategic. They try to corner the pig, run him into a trap, but Clint Eastwood keeps on moving between them, slipping through their fingers like he's greased.

I can tell that Clint Eastwood's beginning to tire though. He can't keep it up much longer. He's an old pig. I start to climb down from the mango tree, but Surachai grabs me by the wrist.

'Wait,' he says.

Surachai climbs out on to one of the branches. He reaches up for a mango and with a quick sweeping motion throws the fruit out on to the beach. It hits one of the boys squarely on the shoulder.

'What the fuck!' I hear the boy yell, looking in the direction of the tree, though he continues to pursue Clint Eastwood nonetheless.

They have him surrounded now, encircled. There's no way out for my pig.

I follow Surachai's lead, grab as many mangoes as I can. Our mangoes sail through the night air. Some of them miss, but some meet their targets squarely in the face, on the head, in the abdomen.

Some of the mangoes hit Lizzie by accident, but I don't really care any more, I'm not really aiming. I'm climbing through that tree like a gibbon, swinging gracefully between the branches, grabbing any piece of fruit—ripe or unripe—that I can get my hands on. Surachai starts to whoop like a monkey and I join him in the chorus. They all turn in our direction then, the four farangs, trying to dodge the mangoes as they come.

It's then that I see Clint Eastwood slip away unnoticed. I see my pig running into the ocean, his pink snout inching across the sea's dark surface, phosphorescence glittering around his head like a crown of blue stars, and as I'm throwing each mango with all the strength I have, I'm thinking: Swim, Clint, swim. □

GRANTA

GOD'S COUNTRY
Luc Sante

UNIVERSALIST CHURCH GLOVER VT

1.

God's Country

1. *Burning Church, Glover, Vermont, circa 1910*
It is a wondrous thing that the American nation, in its third century, remains such a fortress of the righteous. Despite the vanity of scientific advances, the tinkling brass of the educated and the low vice encouraged by popular culture, the United States is still a country in which eighty-four per cent of the population believes in miracles (according to the latest Harris poll) and an equal number believe in life after death. While it's true these figures might be said to illustrate American optimism rather than sacred fervour *per se*—sixty-nine per cent believe in hell, but only one per cent think they will burn—there is no getting round the fact that America, uniquely among Western nations, considers itself to have a special relationship with God.

The full extent of American religious certitude has not always been visible to outside observers, and certainly not to those familiar only with the citadels of wickedness on the east and west coasts, but the current presidential administration has brought persons and tendencies and modes of discourse previously shrouded in provincial obscurity on to the world stage. An Attorney General who had himself anointed before taking office, Christians who support the Israeli nation because its victory will hasten the Second Coming, federally funded initiatives in support of virginity—such matters fascinate Europeans, for whom they are colourful grotesqueries, albeit with more than a hint of menace about them, but they can hardly surprise anyone who has made a study of the fortunes of enthusiastic religion over the course of American history.

2. *Unknown Man of the Cloth, circa 1910*
The future United States was settled by diverse bands of Europeans in the sixteenth and seventeenth centuries, the ones who cast the longest shadow being arguably the Puritans who founded Plymouth Colony in 1620. The Spanish and the French may have planted crosses and dedicated rivers and mountains and campsites to various virgins and saints, but they were Papists, their devotion earthbound and political. It was the Puritans who established the City of God in the Wilderness. At no time since has there been such a unity and concentration of fervour.

For true believers, everything since has been tarnished—by deism,

207

by worldliness, by sin. That is why nostalgia is such an important motif of evangelism. The first revival began in the 1740s, and revivals have occurred at intervals ever since, each with the intention of returning the nation to that Edenic state when divine and human laws were identical. The 'old-time religion' that the song declares is 'good enough for me' may, like Jerry Falwell's 'Old-Time Gospel', refer to a vague memory of childhood Sabbaths, but what it ultimately invokes is the world of the Pilgrims, even if the Congregationalist communion that is their legacy has little appeal for enthusiastically saved Christians today.

3. Baptism in Grand River, Missouri, circa 1910

About forty per cent of Americans describe themselves as 'born again', a designation that covers a great many separate creeds, even, these days, a certain strain of Roman Catholicism. But for the most part the reborn attach themselves to churches that descend from branches of Nonconformism. There are too many to name or count, and clarifying the distinctions between them is a task not many of their members could undertake.

Full-immersion adult baptism was at first the mark of the Baptists, but it has spread, and there are by now many distinct Baptist conventions. The comedian Emo Philips has a joke about exchanging religious details with a stranger.

'Are you Protestant or Catholic?'

'Protestant.'

'Me, too! What franchise?'

'Baptist.'

'Me, too! Northern Baptist or Southern Baptist?'

'Northern Baptist.'

The conversation proceeds in this vein until Philips asks, 'Northern conservative fundamentalist Baptist, Great Lakes Region, Council of 1879, or Northern conservative fundamentalist Baptist, Great Lakes Region, Council of 1912?'

'Northern conservative fundamentalist Baptist, Great Lakes Region, Council of 1912.'

'Die, heretic!'

The various religion surveys cannot, of course, provide insight into why people attach themselves to one sect rather than another. It is

2.

3.

4.

hard not to believe that social pressures and conveniences easily outdo any theological considerations, and that the multiplicity of churches, like so many competing insurance companies or banks, is primarily a reflection of the Free Market.

4. *Revival Tabernacle, Elmira, New York, circa 1910*

The rise of enthusiastic religion in America was provoked in part by the increasingly class-bound structures of the established churches, and in part by the well-known deism of a majority of the Founding Fathers. (Thomas Paine wrote, 'My own mind is my own church.' Thomas Jefferson said, 'I do not find in orthodox Christianity one redeeming feature.' The Revolutionary War hero Ethan Allen, who famously claimed Fort Ticonderoga 'in the name of Jehovah and the Continental Congress,' went on to write a book called *Reason the Only Oracle of Man*.)

The major reason for its rise, though, was demographic. It began in the late eighteenth century in the West, which at the time meant west of the Ohio river or the Cumberland Gap, sufficiently distant from Unitarians, Universalists and readers of the French *philosophes*, but also, in many cases, far from churches of any sort. Farmers and loggers and trappers lived in remote settlements, were cut off from the world and engaged in back-breaking labour for meagre rewards. The revival which began around 1798 was wildly successful because it drew them together and provided a release for emotions that had few other outlets. This religion was no opiate—it was corn whiskey. Grown men could fall down and cry, or jump up and howl. The preachers translated scripture into their language, and offered sights and notions outside the constraints of frontier existence. The particular success of these meetings, soon unrepeatable, became another focus of the ingrained nostalgia of American religion.

5. *The Evangelist Ira Evans Hicks and Family, Toulon, Illinois, 1908*

Revivalism went through several cycles over the course of the nineteenth century. The blood-and-thunder effusions of Charles G. Finney, a man with eyes like a silent-movie mesmerist, took hold in the 1820s in a corridor of western New York State that was so successfully and repeatedly swept by holy enthusiasm that it was called The Burnt-Over District—it was also the birthplace of the Mormon faith, the home of John Humphrey Noyes's Perfectionist community and of William Miller's end-of-the-world sect, the hub of Fourierism and the mecca of the Spiritualist movement. The revivals took over a church, a barn or a tent for a week or more. They featured sermons that could last many hours, and public conversions accompanied by weeping and fainting and convulsing and crying out and running off into the woods, as well as much singing of hymns. They condemned the usual parade of vices: smoking, drinking and dancing in particular. Fornication was understood, but it could hardly be dwelt upon in detail. The cycles waxed and waned, depending on what no one would dare call fashion, with new upswings impelled by the appearance of charismatic performers.

6. The Chorus, Hicks-Scholfield Meetings, Toulon, Illinois, 1908
Dwight Moody, a large, rough-hewn man who migrated from the Connecticut countryside to Chicago, entered the revival business in the 1870s and immediately streamlined it. He was a businessman by nature, and his friends and contributors eventually came to include most of the great late-nineteenth-century entrepreneurs; his innovations mirrored theirs. Where most evangelists before him had reaped their harvests in rural areas, Moody worked the cities, staging mammoth events that could draw tens of thousands of people. He developed a formula that involved brief talks (where Finney, for example, had once sermonized for twenty-four hours straight) interspersed with musical numbers, and for the latter he found the sweet-voiced Ira Sankey, to whom he gave equal billing. This formula, including the partnership, would be repeated by preachers throughout the following century. Ira Hicks, a minor figure, followed it to the letter. His revival in Toulon, Illinois, in 1908 lasted a full two weeks. 'He does not make you mad, but he does make you laugh,' noted the local newspaper. 'He is an eloquent pulpit orator, a scholar, but he does not shoot above the heads of the congregation, but hits them square in the heart.'

By Hicks's time, revivalism had become a branch of show business, with a sideline in the sort of managerial philosophizing that nowadays has become a lucrative sector of the book trade.

5.

THE CHORUS
HICKS—SCHOLFIELD MEETINGS
TOULON ILLS.
AEWHITE PHOTO.

6.

The greatest men's meeting on record
Jan. 19, 1908.
Six thousand men listening to Billy Sunday's Hot Cakes.
Every man present felt the Heat.
Bloomington, Ill.
Copyrighted by C.U.Williams. 1908

7.

SEDALIA CHAUTAUQUA
BRYAN DAY JULY 18 1907

Thomas

8.

7. *Billy Sunday at a Men's Meeting, Bloomington, Illinois, 1908*
The man who brought evangelism into the era of vaudeville was a former professional baseball player named Billy Sunday, pictured here, appropriately, as a spot of white light. Sunday—that was his real name—embodied pep, the quintessential American quality of the early twentieth century, and he manifested it by remaining in constant motion on the stage. There are many existing photographs of Sunday in characteristic poses, for example standing on one leg with the other leg stretched straight back behind him while he points forwards. He was given to miming all the actions of a baseball game, including sliding into a base, and as he perspired he shed items of clothing—jacket, waistcoat, necktie, collar. Wherever he preached, he insisted that a tabernacle of unpainted wood be built for the occasion, with sawdust spread on the ground to deaden any noise but his. He was famous for his up-to-the-minute slang, notorious for the fact that many of his on-the-spot converts tended to sign false names and never made follow-up appearances in church. His theology was the simplest on record: he was against smoking, drinking, swearing and Socialism, and he stood for square shooting and good fellowship. Naturally, he became very rich.

8. *William Jennings Bryan at a Chautauqua, Sedalia, Missouri, 1907*
Until very recent times, the most prominent representative of God's army to have inhabited Washington DC was William Jennings Bryan, 'the old mountebank', as H. L. Mencken called him. Three times a losing candidate for the presidency, Bryan was originally best known for his advocacy of the unlimited coinage of silver—'You shall not crucify man upon a cross of gold,' was his deathless line. In 1925 he volunteered as principal attorney for the prosecution, in Dayton, Tennessee, at the trial of John Scopes, accused of having taught the theory of evolution in his science classes at the local high school. Bryan was a fundamentalist who argued that an article refuting evolution should be introduced into the Constitution. He won the Scopes case—it was later overturned on appeal due to a technicality—then dropped dead five days later. For decades afterwards sophisticates relegated anti-evolutionism to the dustbin of history, somehow thinking that time had chased it back into obscure Southern hollows. They little imagined that it would make

a major comeback, armed with elaborate logical sophistry, at the end of the century. A chautauqua, by the way, was essentially a secular camp meeting, a multi-day programme of open-air lectures and sing-alongs and dinner on the ground.

9. Religious Pageant, Buda, Illinois, 1909

My interest in the wilder currents of American religion is only partly explicable. I am a resident alien of many years' standing, an ex-Catholic unbeliever, and I have spent my adult life in or within a hundred miles of New York City. I have no direct ties with any aspect of the subject at hand, although I suppose there are subterranean links to the harsh and superstitious rural Belgian Catholicism imparted by my mother. My interest arrived in stages. First I fell for the biblical language and cadences that run through American literature, especially in Melville and Faulkner. Then I discovered a taste for religious country music and blues, beginning when someone played for me the DaCosta-Woltz Orchestra's 1920s recording of 'Are You Washed in the Blood of the Lamb?' and continuing on through Blind Willie Johnson, Washington Phillips, the Louvin Brothers and countless lesser-known performers whose sounds emerged from rickety churches in fields or in storefronts. Eventually I came upon the relevant imagery, as in these largely unstudied photographs made in the decade before the First World War and printed on postcard stock. They possess a stark beauty that is no more refutable than the shape-note hymns of the Alabama Sacred Harp Singers or the commanding periods of the King James Bible.

10. Unknown Preachers at a Banquet, circa 1906

Belief is as comforting to those who share it as it is terrifying to those who do not. Even for believers, though, the attraction of religion, American or otherwise, partly resides in the terror in which it has almost always consciously trafficked. That is why Universalism, for example, could only ever appeal to a tiny minority—its doctrine that absolutely everyone would be saved was just too easy and offered no opportunity for catharsis. Likewise, works of religious art can be extremely moving, but they fail if they merely soothe; it is in their mandate to account for the imminence of death. At least until the advent of Dwight Moody, the most successful revival preachers were

Tableau — HENSEL'S VISION SEPT. 24, 1909, Buda Ill.
J.L. Robinson Photo Buda Ill.

9.

10.

11.

those who could most vividly evoke the torments of hell, a much more significant aspect of the show than the comforts of heaven. For one thing, heaven could never be made to sound sufficiently perfect—hence the tiresome business of harps and clouds and gold and neoclassical architecture—whereas little effort was required to conjure up the unbearable. But the idea of hell can also give greater access to the unconscious, to those corridors that can best be opened through friction and tension. Religion in America has always been so much at war with pleasure because it is in direct competition with it, through opposite means.

11. *Unknown Preacher and Congregation, circa 1910*
Since the days of Dwight Moody, what I am calling the American religion has been working on two tracks. It wants to make sinners tremble and repent, and it wants to improve business by keeping everyone happily harnessed to their posts. The latter sort of rhetoric may have reached a certain apotheosis in the 1920s, when Jesus Christ was regularly invoked as the first booster, the first Rotarian, the guiding light of Realtors, and so on, but it is alive today, as a spur and as an alibi. The contrast between that sort of smiling pressure and the ancient, bottomless threat of damnation makes for a curiously disjointed system. It resembles a movie set: a bland, pastel-toned suburban ranch house with the fires of Gehenna raging below the floorboards. That, indeed, is not unlike the place where many Americans live now: a cocoon of narcotic, diffuse-lighted surfaces that rebuke the messiness of life and avoid mention of the messiness of death. As a result, everyone carries hell within themselves. □

MAGIC CIRCLES

The Beatles in Dream and History

DEVIN McKINNEY

In *Magic Circles* Devin McKinney uncovers the secret history of a generation and a pivotal moment in twentieth-century culture. Delving into concerts and interviews, films and music, outtakes and bootlegs, he brings to bear the insights of history, aesthetics, sociology, psychology, and mythology to account for the depth and resonance of the Beatles' impact. His book is also a uniquely multifaceted appreciation of the group's artistic achievement.

$27.95 / £18.95 new in cloth

THE HARVARD DICTIONARY OF MUSIC

Fourth Edition

EDITED BY DON MICHAEL RANDEL

This classic reference work, the best one-volume music dictionary available, has been brought completely up to date in this new edition. Encyclopedia-length articles by notable experts alternate with short entries for quick reference, including definitions and identifications of works and instruments. More than 220 drawings and 250 musical examples enhance the text.

Belknap Press Harvard University Press Reference Library
$39.95 / £25.95 new in cloth

FREEDOM IS, FREEDOM AIN'T

Jazz and the Making of the Sixties

SCOTT SAUL

In the long decade between the mid-fifties and the late sixties, jazz was changing more than its sound. The age of Max Roach's *Freedom Now Suite*, John Coltrane's *A Love Supreme*, and Charles Mingus's *The Black Saint and the Sinner Lady* was a time when jazz became both newly militant and newly seductive, its example powerfully shaping the social dramas of the Civil Rights movement, the Black Power movement, and the counterculture. *Freedom Is, Freedom Ain't* is the first book to tell the broader story of this period in jazz—and American—history.

$29.95 / £19.95 new in cloth

HARVARD UNIVERSITY PRESS

US: 800 405 1619   UK: 020 7306 0603   www.hup.harvard.edu

GRANTA

MY FIRST EUROPEAN
Edmund White

Edmund White (right) with John in Bath, 1983

I belong to the last generation of Americans obsessed with Europe and intimidated by it. When I was a small boy in Ohio in the 1940s, America was simultaneously isolationist and truly isolated. There were no foreign films. There were almost no foreigners. No one drank wine or used garlic or even ate in courses. We were served just one heaping plate of overcooked meat and fried potatoes and boiled beans, then chocolate pudding. Those who drank stuck to whisky and water.

Travel to Europe was expensive and few people could afford it. For us 'Europe' was the symphony (all our conductors were foreign-born) and opera. We listened to the Texaco radio broadcast of the Metropolitan Opera every Saturday afternoon. During the intermissions Europeans with heavy accents and Hungarian or Russian names were asked in a quiz to list all the scenes in opera in which (A) the tenor falls in love with his aunt, (B) the heroine is buried alive and (C) a witch switches two babies at birth. The jokey knowingness of the foreign participants, the unusual deliberation and circumflexion and secret mirth in their voices, seemed exotic and superior to us.

We longed to visit Europe, even live abroad for a whole year. Europe was where we would raise our general level of culture. Europe was where we might at last have experiences, even sexual ones. We deplored but were privately intrigued by 'European snobbishness', since in Texas and the Midwest where I'd grown up the word *class* was never mentioned and if pressed we'd all have declared ourselves middle class. The idea that we might be excluded from a club or a party because of our low birth seemed maddening and exciting to us.

In the 1950s, Americans took extraordinary pride in the Marshall Plan. We were convinced we'd not only saved England and France, we also believed we'd single-handedly rebuilt the entire continent. We expected Europeans to be grateful ever after. Most Americans didn't realize how quickly and triumphantly Europe had emerged out of the war. As late as the 1970s, ignorant friends and relatives of mine would say, 'I feel sorry for those folks, still living in bombed-out ruins.' Like some ninety per cent of Americans they didn't have passports.

My first trip to Europe, for some reason, was to the Costa Brava in the mid-1960s when I was in my twenties. I guess I thought that sounded affordable and not as scary as Paris or London. My first lover, Stanley Redfern, and I flew to Paris, where our luggage was lost, and then we sprinted on to a waiting plane for Malaga. We hadn't made hotel reservations and in January the town was packed. A nice man who worked behind the desk at one of the hotels that turned us away offered us his mother's guest-room. It smelled of backed-up sewage and was next door to an outdoor movie theatre where people sat on folding wooden chairs half the night and listened to booming voices; from our window we could look down on the entranced, upraised faces strafed and submerged by alternating lights and shadows. Our luggage took a week to arrive. I made Stanley go with me to a bullfight even though we had to sit in the sun wearing our wool winter-suits. We were too poor to buy new clothes or to afford tickets in the shade.

We visited the Alhambra on a guided tour conducted in English. Two young gay Swiss guys came up to us (they'd taken our tour to improve their English) and told us that they just wanted us to know that they *approved* of our war in Vietnam. We were appalled and realized for the first time that we were being taken as Americans, as representatives of our national policy, and not just as Stan and Ed.

The luggage arrived on Stan's next-to-last day. We celebrated by taking a bus over to Torremolinos and going to a gay bar full of effeminate Germans in bits of jewellery and finery they could remove and hide when they walked home through the dark streets. I stayed on another week with Brookie, a pretty girl from my office, who insisted on wearing miniskirts everywhere in Malaga in Franco's Spain. We had big wolf-packs of young men howling behind us wherever we went.

At night the restaurants were thronged. Twenty-two members of the same family would sit around adjoined tables in a cafe and eat ice cream. 'Europe' (at least the bit of it we'd seen) appeared eternal, poor but well-dressed, fiercely macho, Catholic and so little subject to change that all four generations of a family could laugh heartily at the same jokes.

Even fairly sophisticated Americans back home repeated over and over again, year after year, the same few clichés about Europeans. The English were 'terribly British', wore bowlers, hunted foxes and had stiff upper lips. The French were blasé about sex, didn't bathe, studied existentialism and ate rotting cheese. They were all unpleasant. The Italians were merry souls who sped around on Vespas, picked up girls, read photo romances instead of proper books, had innate artistic taste and liked everyone. The Irish were dour, downtrodden, Catholics and problem drinkers.

After I moved to Paris in 1983 and stayed on for the next fifteen years I came to resent these ill-informed, primitive views. I noticed that American friends, especially New Yorkers, were irritated that the quality of life was so high in Paris and owed almost nothing to America. Americans would point out a McDonald's in Paris with glee, but they couldn't be persuaded that American eating habits had made few inroads in France.

And my American friends were puzzled when they discovered what the French admire about America: everything to do with cowboys; the delicious vulgarity of Las Vegas; the novels of Paul Auster and John Fante and the poetry of Charles Bukowski; jazz; anything 'alternative' from the Lower East Side; anything Zuni. The French knew next to nothing about American composers, including those who'd lived and studied in France such as Aaron Copland, Ned Rorem and Virgil Thomson. They knew nothing of our minor writers who'd celebrated Paris such as Kay Boyle, Djuna Barnes and James Jones. In front of Jones's apartment on the Ile St Louis there was no historic plaque nor would there ever be, though in the 1970s Gertrude Stein's Rue de Fleurus address was finally commemorated. The French knew much more about American B-movie directors than we did and lamented our lack of 'film culture'. We weren't sure we thought 'film' and 'culture' belonged in the same sentence.

So strong was the American myth about disagreeable Parisians that it could not be modified through experience. My American friends would spend ten days with me and go out every night to a companionable dinner with French friends, often at their homes, but I'd catch them telling someone back in the States that no one ever invites you to his or her house in Paris, that all Parisians are nasty whereas the people in the provinces are adorable. The opposite is the truth, since Parisians travel, like foreigners, speak languages, crave novelty and live by their wits, whereas no city could be more closed and self-sufficient than Lyon or Bordeaux, no bourgeoisie more smug than that of Lille.

Edmund White

Because I learned French after the age of forty I could never eliminate my accent, though eventually I became enough at ease in the language to be able to give five half-hour radio broadcasts in a row. Because of my accent, however, I've always elicited a smile; if we English-speakers find a French accent supercilious or sexy, the French think an American accent is either charmingly or irritatingly childish—*bon enfant*, as they say. As someone who stammered as a child, still gropes for words and has always been guilty of malapropisms in English, I welcomed a built-in excuse for similar flaws in speaking French. My accent always provided new acquaintances with a ready-made subject ('I think I detect a little accent when you speak,' the super-polite French would say. They would then always add, 'If only I spoke English as well as you speak French.') This scrim of foreignness through which I lived during my years in France made me more interesting than I was and as vulnerable as I felt. I didn't mind being *bon enfant*, even if the expression is lightly condescending.

As a homosexual growing up in Cincinnati and Chicago and Texas and Michigan in the 1950s, 'Europe' represented a benign and mysterious alternative to the beastly oppression we knew at home, a time in the States when we were persecuted by shrinks on one side and priests on the other and deliberately entrapped by the police, the three institutions that corresponded to the three prevailing interpretations of homosexuality: as mental illness, as sin and as crime.

Although we ourselves had no other available model, we still could dimly hold out for 'tolerance' or even 'decadence', and these qualities, piquant and somehow aristocratic, we located in 'Europe'. I remember when I was fifteen discussing Julius Caesar with Fred Mitchell, an abstract expressionist painter who taught at the art academy next door to my boarding school in Bloomfield Hills, Michigan. Mr Mitchell, a southerner in his thirties who thrived on ambiguity and the unspoken, told me with a little smile that Caesar had 'married' several of his soldiers and that 'people in Rome are still talking about it'. Imagine all that said in a nearly inaudible Tidewater drawl.

I found his comment electrifying because a respected artist and teacher was referring to my most shameful vice lightly, and as if it were the most recent gossip. Even more extraordinary, he was suggesting that Caesar (the boring author of *The Gallic Wars* which I'd had to translate in class) had an off-colour reputation that was being kept alive by the Romans of today. Europe, it seemed, was a place where homosexuality was joked about and rumours were passed down from one millennium to the next.

When I was sixteen I met a New Yorker in his thirties who was visiting Chicago. I understood that the man was married and therefore wouldn't be attracted to me, but a local queen I knew said, 'My dear, in New York they're very European.'

'In what way?'

'They're more bisexual. He might prefer women but on a cold night in a strange city he might bed a boy.'

I added bisexuality to my profile of 'the Europeans'. The same queen told me that Europeans insisted on anal intercourse. 'Oh yes, my pet, we're all suck queens but they don't think that's even real sex. They go all the way—they're *brownie* queens.' Of course I knew that American gays could be versatile sexually, but this information suggested that Europeans had hierarchized sex acts. They thought we were childish with our oral fixations, which my shrink had warned me about. Anal sex wasn't designed for five dirty minutes in the dark, which was usually all we had to work with; rather, it required a bed, careful positioning, hygienic foresight, a lubricant—above all it required privacy and time. It was more committed, more grown-up, and it represented a more total surrender for the passive partner.

The dream of Europe for an American gay in the Fifties was not only about our continental counterparts; it was also about the entire bric-a-brac of society. Most of us were anglophiles, read everything about the Queen's coronation, admired Auden and Britten; one of my friends bought his hat at Lock's and had his initials stamped in gold on the sweatband. Cologne from Penhaligon's, tea from Fortnum and Mason, shirts from Turnbull and Asser...

In the late 1960s, I would stay in London with a friend of mine, just a few years older, who came to represent for me gay London—and more profoundly the English middle class. John acted in musicals and plays but mostly earned his living by giving acting lessons. He was thoroughly imbued with the pantomime/musical hall tradition and took me to see two elderly drag artists who impersonated two elderly sharp-tongued cockney women. John knew and revered Noel

Coward with a deference unfamiliar to Americans of my generation.

He was a socialist and a republican; the depth of his hatred for the lazy, ugly, bloodsucking royals shocked me out of my anglophile fantasies. The mere mention of the Queen or Princess Margaret would elicit from him an angry snarl and a murderous mutter. He longed for a redistribution of wealth and took pride in the National Health Service. Once when we visited a friend of his who'd just inherited a fortune and bought a grand house in Mayfair, John said, as soon as we were back on the street, 'It's criminal for people to live like that.' He thoroughly approved of another friend who became a successful movie star but didn't change friends, pub or basement flat. Whereas we Americans admired success and smiled over a rags to riches story, John had more nuanced reactions. He followed politics carefully and read several papers a day.

He lived in a spacious flat for which he paid a curiously low rent on Marylebone High Street (he had to teach me how to say it, 'Marlbun,' with the correct accent). Like Nancy Mitford he insisted on 'curtains' not 'drapes', 'rugs' not 'carpets', 'writing paper' not 'stationery'. The flat itself was unheated. Astonishingly, he provided me with a hot-water bottle for my bed at night and we'd hurl ourselves into the kitchen as soon as we arose; it was the only warm room. At teatime he insisted we drink our tea before the ineffective fire in the vast, arctic sitting room. It was a necessary ritual. In America we had no such rituals.

He was resourceful in making his minuscule earnings go far though he had not an iota of ambition to earn more, if more work meant losing one hour of his precious free time. He introduced me to Bovril and Marmite. He'd prepare cauliflower cheese for lunch, bangers and beans for supper, though as often as not I'd invite him to a fancy new restaurant (I remember one run by a glamorous sex change who'd married a lord, another owned by John Schlesinger). In an expensive Italian restaurant I became so drunk I got up and danced a Highland fling all alone and knocked over the dessert trolley. I no longer drink.

If John was expert at paring cheese, he spared himself no pleasure. He was always finding cheap flights to the Greek islands or to New York, where he'd stay with me or a theatrical agent he knew. Sometimes the agent would ask all of John's New York friends to chip in to buy him an airplane ticket. In London he attended almost every play and musical, buying cheap balcony seats or getting complimentary tickets through his acting school or from friends in the production. He knew every bus and tube route and would never let me hail a taxi.

He had a mentality born of deprivation and rationing. If I bought him a tea or brought home groceries or just offered him a cigarette, he was punctilious about thanking me for the lovely treat. Whereas in America we thought nothing of raiding a friend's fridge, in England I quickly learned to respect John's calibrated meal planning. He made an orange drink from powder, he washed out tomato tins and used the tinted water for cooking something else. Even though I could vaguely remember wartime rationing in the States, for the first time I realized how wasteful we were back home, how thoughtless. Whereas we always left the light blazing and the central heat roaring when we went out in America, John would have resented even the extravagance of a pilot light if his Aga had had one. He was stoic about heat or cold, damp or discomfort, and never ever mentioned them.

In those years we saw Margaret Leighton in an ephemeral comedy about an English family who installed central heating, which caused their house plants to grow rampant with tropical exuberance and finally choke off every room. The only good moment came when the son's beloved, whose gender is indeterminate, asks Margaret Leighton if she has 'a little man' to make her lovely clothes. 'Yes, tiny...' Leighton said with icy nastiness. I found the whole play bewildering.

Whereas New York in the Sixties had almost no gay bars, since Mayor Wagner had closed them all in an effort to clean up the city for the World's Fair, London had dozens and dozens—everything from old-fashioned East End pubs full of working men and smoke to candlelit gay restaurants and bars on the King's Road, from leather bars (which seemed genuinely menacing back then) in Earl's Court to a suit-and-tie afterwork bar upstairs off Leicester Square. Everything in London—the licensing laws, the variable bus fares, the freeholds and the ninety-nine-year leases, the guineas and half-crowns and florins and shillings—seemed unnecessarily complicated, the silt of centuries, but with John at my side I could steer my way through these traps.

John didn't read much beyond newspapers and he didn't own a television. He lived for activities, a disposition that seemed unusual and exhilarating to me, sedentary and bookish as I was. He would make me tour Chiswick House and Hogarth's House, race through the National Portrait Gallery or the Tower of London, take tea on the roof of Biba's, complete with ponds and swans—and cruise Hampstead Heath at night. In warm weather we'd take the last tube out to Hampstead, walk up the long hill to the Heath and work our way down through forests and clearings, our prey on a cloudy night visible only by the pulsing of a cigarette or the glint off glasses or the shockingly near clearing of a throat. I remember picking up an Oxford boy and bringing him back to John's flat. We had to walk miles and miles to get home. In the morning, when I asked him if he wanted a 'scohn' (to rhyme with 'own'), he said in a languid drawl, 'I can't bear the thought I might know someone who'd fail to say "scon".' When I told another English friend that my mother always stayed in New York at the 'War-wick' Hotel, he whispered, 'You say that? I feel we're living in different worlds.'

In those days the image of Americans held by the English resembled the ones white Americans held about blacks—good in bed, good dancers, violent, lazy. We did seem to be less inhibited, to feel more at ease in our bodies. American gays, at least New Yorkers, were already beginning to work out. John, who was an adept of the Alexander Technique, thought that bodybuilding led to a grotesque distortion of the muscles, a way of creating top-heavy Michelin men. Each time he saw me I was a bit bigger and more muscled. 'All that's going to run to fat,' he'd hiss—correctly, as it turned out.

John had been in the air force and studied Russian in the services. He hadn't been to university but he'd studied every aspect of Russian language and culture to prepare him for a job in intelligence. I suspect he hadn't gone on because his officers had discovered he was 'queer'. (He didn't like the word 'gay', which for the English spoiled a perfectly good word, though Americans couldn't make a similar objection, since we never used 'gay' to mean 'merry'.)

He spoke a very posh English which, as a socialist, he refused to associate with the middle class. 'It's standard English, my dear,' he'd say, closing his eyes as if to indicate the discussion was over. 'I feel sorry for you people from the colonies with your bizarre mispronunciations—why, you pronounce *Mary*, *merry* and *marry* all the same way. No wonder you're so confused.'

He would fly into a rage at the very thought of American naturalistic acting of the Actors Studio variety and even wrote a book-length polemic against it, never published. 'Why, those slovenly fools can't walk or talk, they don't know how to fence or manage a train or even sit simply and gracefully. The Alexander Technique teaches us to say *no* to our bad habits—what you'd wrongly call *instincts*—and to rethink vocal production and the entire head-neck-spine relationship.'

He tried to 'sort out' my neck which over the years, as he predicted, has become arthritic and nearly paralysed. But the Alexander Technique, which requires months and months of one-on-one sessions and works only through tiny gradations, seemed quite alien to American rhythms. We believe in sudden conversions, weekend marathons, instant enlightenment. The notion of a technique that is built on small negations rather than one great affirmation made no sense to me as an American.

From his military background John retained a neat moustache, a dignified bearing, a lonely, slightly bleak independence. He was tidy, energetic, red-haired. If he was almost hypermasculine in repose, he'd wilfully added an overlay of high camp. He and I constantly spoke of every man in the feminine—in fact we never used a male pronoun or possessive from one day to the next. Everyone was titled 'Miss' (as in 'Miss Thing' or 'Miss Postman')—at the seaside we even once referred to 'Miss Wave'. We systematically suspected every man, no matter how podgy or uxorious, of being a flaming homosexual. We invented a fantasy in which I was a wayward young American heiress who'd been sent to London for John's instructions in deportment and elocution. He was always promising to turn me into a real lady. We exchanged dozens of letters in which we encoded all of our real experiences into this extravagant and fairly tiresome form of camp. Since it required constant translation of one thing into another even such a mechanical exercise kept us permanently self-amused.

In the Sixties gender substitution and archness were passé in gay America except in small towns and among older queens. I'd known a dim, provincial version of camp in Cincinnati in the 1950s. But for John who knew Noel Coward and had lived in a theatre milieu for most of his life, it was a living tradition. I suppose his ultimate point of reference was Lady Bracknell. Like her he pronounced 'girls' as 'gells'; I was one of his 'gells'.

With me he couldn't stop camping. It was sometimes a relief to run into one of his students or a literary friend of mine. Then he'd revert to his clipped military politeness, though when the others weren't looking he'd arch an eyebrow or purse his lips or bug his eyes for my benefit. I wasn't sure which tone was his real one and which the put-on.

American gays with their muscles, facial hair and lumberjack masculinity repelled and alienated John, who for me represented the last link to a gay past that always had one foot (a very light, well turned foot) in fantasy, that remained closeted out of necessity but took its revenge on dull normals by transforming all the men into women and all the women into enemies. His disapproval of the American butch style didn't keep him from being attracted to individual clones. But he was always quick to say, 'The minute I got that big man in bed he started whimpering like a little girl.'

He was also very romantic in a melodramatic way which struck me as vaguely 'period'. He told me that in the early Sixties he'd had a lover named Nigel for several years. They'd been on tour in Scotland in a big musical. On their day off John was driving them along the coast in a hired car. Nigel said, 'I'm leaving you, John. I've found someone else.'

John, in true staccato Coward fashion, said, 'Very well,' rolling the r, turned the wheel and drove them both over the cliff. They survived but were in hospital for months.

As John and I grew older I retired from the bar scene but John, still slim and handsome, went out cruising four nights a week, always looking for love. I imagine he was a very good lover—faithful, generous, devoted—if always slightly disapproving and nannyish.

American gays came to self-acceptance later than the English, and when it arrived we were already committed to the butch clone style, which excluded any excess of affection. John, however, had grown up on sentimental English wartime movies, on Shakespearean heroics and blockbuster musicals—three totally disparate forms that nonetheless shared a belief in exalted passion.

In London and especially in the theatre world, gay couples had lived out their loves discreetly and romantically since before the First

World War. All the Bloomsbury biographies and memoirs, for instance, attest to how well-integrated gay men were in straight literary circles: Forster, Keynes, Strachey—the whole buggery crowd in Virginia Woolf's generation. There was nothing comparable in New York. That some English gays had a niche and a style made them less susceptible, at least at first, to American machismo. In the same way the sceptical, combative style of English intellectuals ('What utter rubbish!') and the enduring English fear of sounding pretentious made them suspicious of American and French academic fads—or of all but feminism.

When I was nine in 1949 I accompanied my father to New York for the first time. He liked Asti's, a Greenwich Village restaurant where the waiters sang opera arias and where famous singers dined. I introduced myself to the bass Jerome Hines, and we ended sitting in his box the next night to hear him sing the role of the High Priest in *The Magic Flute*. We also befriended an English soldier who was eating alone at the next table.

I'd read Oscar Wilde and I assumed that because the soldier was English (my first!) he too must speak in constant quips and deliver polished epigrams. With my dull father and stepmother he sounded as tepid as they, but I felt that if I could recall one of Wilde's remarks he'd light up with recognition and deliver his own cascade of witticisms.

At last I got up my courage, interrupted my father, and said to the soldier, 'I know a widow who just buried her husband and her hair has gone quite gold with grief.' My father looked embarrassed at his sissy son's outburst. My stepmother knew perfectly well I'd never met a widow in my life.

The soldier looked genuinely repulsed. He winced with disgust and turned his attention to his chop.

I blushed bright red. I'd made an effort to communicate with my first European in a language—sophisticated and paradoxical—that I felt sure he would understand and appreciate, but he didn't get it. He'd been sickened by my effeminacy and crazy interjection. Here was this other continent—wise and humane and devoted to virtuoso conversation—to which I was beaming a signal, but the message hadn't been picked up.

Edmund White

Now I realize that 'Europe' isn't a thing at all except in the eyes of Americans and certain Japanese, that it has no unified culture or shared interests except for the optimistic architects of the European Union, and that nothing at all will ever join Swedish technocrats to Muslim farmers in former Yugoslavia. Now I know that there are as many racists and dunderheads and violent criminals in Hungary or Germany, in Spain or in Greece as there are in the United States. Now when I contemplate the boy I once was mouthing an Oscar Wilde phrase to a crop-haired English major from Liverpool and counting on a sympathetic vibration bouncing back my way, I can only smile at my illusions. Perhaps Europe is nothing but an outdated American fantasy, a place that is tolerant but not lacklustre, scintillating but never cruel. □

THERE IS ANOTHER AMERICA.

'The anti-Americanism on the rise throughout the world is not just hostility towards the most powerful nation... It is, more often than not, a resentment of double standards and double talk, of crass ignorance and arrogance, of wrong assumptions and dubious policies. Whether our current leaders are capable of self-examination at a time of military victory may affect the planet for a long time to come.' —Stanley Hoffman, *The New York Review of Books*, June 2003

HOW SHOULD WE RESPOND TO AMERICA?

You are invited to join the debate as it is uniquely engaged in the pages of *The New York Review of Books*.

Now in its 40th year, the *Review* is widely regarded as the world's most distinguished intellectual—and yet accessible—magazine. Each fortnightly issue engages some of the world's sharpest minds in the most passionate political and cultural controversies of the day, and reviews the most engrossing new books and the ideas that illuminate them. Contributors include:

NEAL ASCHERSON MARGARET ATWOOD ALFRED BRENDEL IAN BURUMA JOHN BANVILLE NOAM CHOMSKY J. M. COETZEE JOAN DIDION UMBERTO ECO JAMES FENTON ELIZABETH HARDWICK SEAMUS HEANEY MICHAEL IGNATIEFF DORIS LESSING HILARY MANTEL JONATHAN MILLER LORRIE MOORE JOYCE CAROL OATES CHARLES ROSEN OLIVER SACKS SIMON SCHAMA JOHN UPDIKE GORE VIDAL

The New York Review of Books

FOR MORE INFORMATION, VISIT WWW.NYBOOKS.COM.

Caricatures of Bush, John Updike and Gore Vidal by David Levine

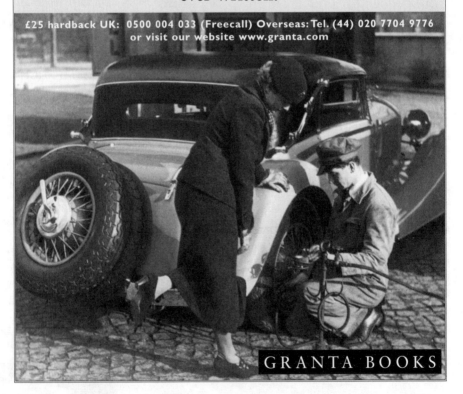

GRANTA

KNOWING FRENCH
Julian Barnes

Knowing French

Pilcher House

February 18, 1986

Dear Dr Barnes, (Me, old woman, rising eighty-one),

Well, so I read serious WORKS, but for light reading in the evenings, what does one do for fiction in an Old Folkery? (You will understand that I have not been here long.) Plenty enough 'Fiction' provided by the Red Cross. What about? Why! the doctor with the crinkled hair 'greying at the temples', probably misunderstood by his wife, or better still a widower, and the attractive nurse who hands him the saw in the theatre. Even at an age when I might have been susceptible to such an implausible view of life, I preferred Darwin's 'Vegetable Mould and Earthworms'.

So: I thought, why not go to the public library and go through all the fiction beginning with A? (A little girl once asked me: 'I understand about the Stag Brewery but what's the Lie Brewery?') Thus I find I have read many entertaining descriptions of pubs, and much voyeurism on women's breasts, so I pass on. You see where I am going? The next lot I come to is Barnes: 'Flaubert's Parrot'. Ah, that must be Loulou. I flatter myself that I know 'Un coeur simple' by heart. But I have few books as my room here is trop petite.

You will be glad to know that I am bilingual and pronounce a treat. Last week in the street I heard a schoolmaster say to a tourist, 'A gauche puis à droite.' The subtlety of the pronunciation of GAUCHE made my day, and I keep saying it to myself in the bath. As good as French bread-and-butter. Would you believe that my father, who would now be 130, was taught French (as Latin then was) pronounced as English: 'lee tchatt'. No, you wouldn't: not sure myself. But there has been some progress: the R is frequently rolled in the right direction nowadays by students.

But revenons à nos perroquets, which is my main reason for writing. I am not taking you up on what you say in your book about coincidence. Well, yes I am. You say that you do not believe in coincidence. You cannot mean this. You mean that you do not believe in intentional or purposeful coincidence. You cannot deny the existence of coincidence, since it happens with some frequency. You refuse, however, to attribute any significance to it. I am less certain than you, being on the whole agnostic in such matters. Anyway, I am in the habit, most mornings, of walking down Church Street (no church remaining) towards Market Green (no market either). Yesterday I had just laid down your book and was walking along, when what do I see, caged behind a high window, but a large grey parrot in its cage? Coincidence? Of course. Meaning? The beast looks miserable, feathers all fluffed up, coughing, a drip from its beak, and no toys in its cage. So I write a (polite) postcard to its (unknown) owner saying that this situation wrings my heart, and I hope when they get back in the evenings they are kind to the bird. Hardly am I back in my room when a furious old woman storms in, introduces herself, brandishes my postcard and says she will take me to court. 'Good,' I reply. 'You will find it very expensive.' She tells me that 'Dominic' fluffs up his feathers because he is a show-off. He has no toys in his cage because he is not a budgerigar and wd. destroy them if he had. And that parrots' beaks cannot drip because they have no mucous membrane. 'You are an ignorant, interfering old woman,' she flings at me as she marches away.

Now, this dissertation on parrots has impressed me. Mrs Audrey Penn is an educated woman, clearly. Having no other reference book to hand but my old college register, I idly look her up. There she is: Lady Margaret Hall, eight years junior to me, exhibitioner where I was top scholar, and reading French. (Not veterinary science.)

I had to write this to you as nobody else would understand the oddity of the synchronicity. But whether all this constitutes a coincidence in the fullest sense, I am not equipped to say. My fellow incarcerees here are either mad or deaf. I, like Félicité, am deaf. Unfortunately the mad ones are not deaf, but who am I to say that the deaf ones are not mad? In fact, though the youngest, I am Head Girl, because, through comparative youth, I am comparatively competent.

Croyez, cher Monsieur, à l'assurance de mes sentiments distingués.
Sylvia Winstanley

March 4, 1986

Dear Mr Barnes,

So why did you say you were a doctor? As for me, I am a spinster, though you are ungenerous to offer me the choice of only Miss, Mrs or Ms. Why not Lady Sylvia? I am Upper Clarce after all, 'senior county family' and all that. My great aunt told me that when she was a little girl Cardinal Newman brought her an orange back from

Spain. One for her and one for each of her sisters. The fruit was then unfamiliar in England. N. was grandmother's godfather.

The warden tells me that Dominic's owner is 'well thought of in the district', so obviously gossip is going the rounds and I had better keep my mouth shut. I wrote a conciliatory letter (no reply), and noticed when next I passed by that Dominic had been taken out of the window. Perhaps he is sick. After all, if parrots have no mucous membrane, why was his beak dripping? But if I go on asking such questions publicly, I shall have my day in court. Well, I am not afeared of the magistrates.

I have taught a lot of Gide. Proust bores me, and I do not understand Giraudoux, having a funny kind of brain that is brilliant in some areas and bone-stupid in others. I was supposed to be a dead cert for a First, the Principal said she would eat her hat if I didn't get one. I didn't (II, with Distinction in Spoken Language) and she took it up with the authorities; answer came that the number of Alphas was balanced by the number of Gammas; no Betas at all. See what I mean? I didn't go to propah school, and being a 'lady' didn't learn orthodox subjects, so at the Entrance Examination my essay on the maternal habits of the earwig did me more good than the 'educated' ones of the girls from Sherborne. I was a top scholar as I think I told you.

Now why did you say you were a doctor in your sixties when you obviously can't be more than forty? Come, now! In youth I discovered that men were deceivers ever, and decided not to take up Flirting until I came onto the Old Age Pension at sixty—but this has led me to a further twenty years of being—my psychologist tells me— an outrageous flirt.

Having done Barnes, I move on to Brookner, Anita, and blessed if she didn't appear on the Box that very day. I don't know, I don't know. THEY are certainly doing things to me. E.G. I say, 'If that is a right decision, let me see a stag,' choosing the most unlikely creature for that place. Stag appears. Ditto kingfisher and spotted woodpecker on other occasions. I can't accept that this is imagination, or that my subconscious was aware that these creatures were lurking in the wings. There would seem to be as it were a High Self that, for instance, tells an ignorant red cell to go and make a clot over a knife-cut. But then what is in charge of your high self and my high self teaching our blood to go and mend the cuts? On

'Hospital Watch' I noticed that they just rammed all the raw meat back into the hole and left it to remake itself into muscles on its own, and I had a very major operation three months ago, but all the bits seem to have come together in the right shape and done the right thing. Who showed them how?

Have I room on page for some parrot feathers? The Principal, Miss Thurston, was a rather graceless, horse-faced woman, twenty-four years my senior, 'assoiffée de beauté', and wore unsuitable picture hats in which she bicycled (Cambridge-style, basket behind). At one time we were very close, and planned to share a house, but she discovered, just in time, how nasty I am. One night I dreamed of Miss Thurston: she was dancing with joy; she had on an enormous hat with parrot feathers flying from it. She said, 'All is now well between us' (or something of the sort). I said to myself, 'But this woman was never PLAIN.' At breakfast I told my cousin, 'I am sure Miss Thurston is dead.' We look in the *Telegraph*—no obituary, as there would have been. The post comes—on back of envelope, 'As-tu vu que Miss Thurston est morte?' We visit other cousin; obituary and photograph in the *Times* newspaper. I have to add that I am not in the least 'psychic'.

I won't say I didn't mean to preach as I did. I am Head Girl here as the YOUNGEST and the most competent. Have car, can drive. As most of them are stone-deaf, there is little whispering in corners. Can I make a grand word for immense letter-writing (epistolomania?). I do apologize.

Best wishes, good fortune with your writing,
Sylvia Winstanley

April 18, 1986

Dear Julian,

I call you so with permission, and having been granted leave to Flirt; although Flirting with only a dust-jacket to go on is a new experience as you may imagine. As for why I chose to incarcerate myself in an Old Folkery when I can walk and drive and be cheered by the threat of law courts, it was a matter of jumping before pushed, or sauter pour mieux reculer. My dear cousin died, I was threatened with a major operation, and found the prospect of being Housekeeper to Myself until I conked out unappealing. And then there was, as they put it, an Unexpected Vacancy. I am a Maverick as you may have deduced and find the common wisdom just that. The CW states that we are all expected to remain independent for as long as possible and then succumb to an Old Folkery when our family can no longer endure us or we start leaving gas-taps on and scalding ourselves with our Ovaltine. But in these circs the OF is likely to come as a severe jolt, causing us to lose our marbles, mutate into cabbages, giving swift rise to another Unexpected Vacancy. So I resolved to transport myself here while still largely functioning. Well, I have no children and my psychologist agreed.

Now, dear Barnes, alas! The only book of yours you told me not to read was the only one available at the library. 'Before She Met Me' has been taken out eleven times since January, you will be fascinated to know, and one reader has heavily scored through the word 'fuck' whenever it occurs. However, he has condescended to read it all the way to the last 'fuck' on p. 178. I have not got so far yet. I tried a spot of raconterie at supper to the other deafs, but without success. 'I suppose,' I said, 'this book is about the Pleasures of the Bed.' 'Wot? Wot? Poddon? Poddon?' 'Plezzers! You know! nice comfy pillow, soft mattress, sleepy-byes.' So nobody thought this raconte-worthy. Well, I shall read it and no doubt learn a lot.

I am very cross, sore, etc., owing to excessive barrack-room rudeness from Warden's husband, ex-sergeant-major, whom I would fain have pushed backwards downstairs, but realized he was likely to be stronger. Let me preach some more to you, this time on the subject of Old Folkeries. When Nanny finally started going gaga, I investigated a number of such établissements. It does not raise the spirits to see, time after time, the same crescent of obedient biddies sitting in cheap armchairs while the Box blares at them like Mussolini. At one place I said to the Warden, 'What sort of activities do you provide?' She looked at me incredulously, for wasn't it clear the old deafs were already having as thrilling a time as mind and spirit could bear? Eventually she replied, 'They have a man who comes for games once a week.' 'Games?' I asked, seeing not many takers for the Olympics. 'Yes', she replied condescendingly. 'He gets them into a circle and throws a beach-ball at them and they have to throw it back.' Well: I made a remark about beach-balls to the Sgt-Major this morning but not surprisingly it was lost on him. The deafs and the mads here are

Julian Barnes

constantly afraid of Being a Nuisance. The only way of making sure you are not Being a Nuisance is to be in your coffin, so I intend to go on Being a Nuisance as a way of keeping alive. Whether I shall succeed or not, I don't know. This Old Folkery is working out exactly like something from Balzac. We disburse our lifetime's savings in order to hand over control of our lives. I imagined a system of enlightened dictatorship as approved by Voltaire, but wonder if such a government has or could ever exist. The wardens, whether by design or unconscious habit, are gradually eroding more and more of our spirits. The governing body are supposed to be our allies.

I was half-heartedly collecting 'sottises' for you; the one that annoys me most is the notion that in England we have something called 'the Summer' and that sooner or later 'it comes'. And then we all sit out in the garden after dinner being bitten by gnats. Granted 'tis about ten degrees warmer and you can go out after tea. The middle-aged all tell me that when they were young summers were red-hot and you wassailed on hay-wains etc. but I tell them that as I am quite thirty years older I remember perfectly well that May was a lousy month in their youth, and they have forgotten all that. Have you come across 'Les trois saints de glace'—I forget who they are, but they have to be past before you can have a proper— Latin—summer. I spent one May in the Dordogne and it rained all the time and they were beastly to the dog and showed me their operations and bread was only made once a fortnight so sucks to Aquitaine! I love the Drôme, though.

Book I haven't read: All Dickens
                              All Scott
                              All Thackeray
                              All Shakespeare except 'Macbeth'
                              All J Austen but one

I do hope you find a lovely gîte; I adore the Pyrenees; the flowers; and the little 'gaves'.

You see, I went round the world in 1935, before everything was spoilt. Also in a lot of boats, not avions.

You say, re coincidence, why not ask to see an armadillo or a snowy owl, that would test the power of intentional coincidence. I shall not rise to this, but will tell you that we lived in Putney back in XVI. Putney is next to Barnes.

Well, thanks a lot for writing. Now I'm feeling better, & the moon has come round the corner behind the pines.

Sylvia W.

Parrot D. back in window.

September 16, 1986

Dear Julian,

Your novel has proved educational, not on sex lines, but because your character, Barbara, has exactly the same slippery methods of discussion as our Warden here. Her husband is the acme of insolence to me, yet I know that if the word 'bloody' slips out I am totally sunk with the Gov. Bod., which approves of me so far. Yesterday I was on the way to the letter-box when the Sgt-Major accosted me and suggested it was an unnecessary journey. All the deafs and mads here give him their letters to post for them. I said, 'I may no longer be driving my car but I shall continue taking the bus into town and am well capable of tottering to the letter-box.' He looked at me impertinently and I imagined him steaming open all the letters at night and tearing up any which contained complaints about the Old Folkery. If my letters suddenly cease you may conclude that either I am dead or else under the full control of the Authorities.

Are you musical? Well, I suppose I am a bit, but, only because being clever and starting the piano at age six, I very soon got good at sight-reading, playing also the double bass & flute (more or less) so constantly asked to play church organs. Liked making terrific roarings on these instruments. (Not church myself. Think own thoughts.) I like going into town—always badinage in the bus or morris dancing in the shopping precincts with Brandenburg Concertos on a machine and proper persons playing violins with them.

I have read some more As and Bs. One of these days I shall tot up the number of drinks consumed or cigarettes lit, for padding purposes in novels. Also 'vignettes' of waiters, taxi-drivers, vendeuses and others, who play no further part in the story. Novelists either go in for padding or else for philosophizing, what we were told to regard as 'generalizations', chez Balzac. Whom is the Novel for, I ask myself. In my own case for someone of an undemanding nature who requires to lose herself between about 10 p.m. and bedtime. This may be unsatisfac, for you, I can see. Also, to be able to do this, it is essential that there be a character sufficiently like myself to identify with and, Maverick that I am, there isn't often.

Still, the As and Bs remain a cut above the monthly supply from the Red Cross. They seem to be written by Night Nurses in the long hours when they have nothing else to do. And the sole theme is desire for marriage. What happens after marriage doesn't seem to have struck them, though to me that is really the crux.

A Famous Person in the art world wrote in his autobiography a few years ago that he first grew to love women by falling in love with a little girl at his prep school dance. He was eleven at the time, and she was nine. There is no doubt at all that I was that little girl: he describes my dress, and it was my brother's prep school, dates right, etc. Nobody else has fallen for me since, but I was a pretty child. If I had deigned to look at him, he says, he would have followed me to the end of his days. Instead he chased after women all his life and made his wife so unhappy that she became an alcoholic, whereas I never married. What do you deduce from this, Mr Novelist Barnes? Was this a missed opportunity seventy years ago? Or was it a fortunate escape on both our parts? Little did he know that I was to become a bluestocking and not at all up his street. Perhaps he would have driven me to drink and I would have driven him to philandering, nobody would have been better off except the wife he thereby wouldn't have had, and in his autobiography he would have said that he wished he'd never set eyes upon me. You are too young for this kind of question, but it is the sort you increasingly ask yourself as you become deaf and mad. Where would I be now if two years before the Great War I had glanced in a different direction?

Well, thank you enormously, and I hope your own life is satisfac. and offspring all you wd. wish.

With love from Sylvia W.

January 24, 1987

Dear Julian,

One of the mads here has been seeing ghosts. They show themselves as little green flashes, in case you should wish to spot one, and they followed her here when she gave up her flat. Trouble is, whereas they were benign in their previous location, they have reacted to finding themselves incarcerated in an Old Folkery by playing the merry devil. We are each of us allowed a small refrigerator in our 'cubicles' in case of Night Starvation, and Mrs Galloway fills hers with chocolates and bottles of sweet sherry. So, what have the sprites been up to in the middle of the night but eating her chocolates and drinking her sherry! We all demonstrated due concern when this was raised—the deaf showing more concern, no doubt because they were unable to comprehend—and tried to offer condolences for her loss. This went on for a while, long faces being in order, until one day she came into Lunch looking like the Cheshire Cat. 'I got my own back!' she cried. 'I drank one of their bottles of sherry which they left in the fridge!' So we all celebrated. Alas, prematurely, for the chocolate continued to suffer nocturnal depredation, despite handwritten notes, both stern and pleading, which Mrs G took to leaving attached to the refrigerator door. (What languages do you think ghosts can read?) The matter finally went to the full assembly of Pilcher House one suppertime, with Warden and Sgt-Major present. How to prevent the spirits from eating her chocolate? All looked to Head Girl, who miserably failed the test. And for once I have to praise the Sgt-Major, who showed an estimable sense of irony, unless—which is perhaps more likely—he actually believes in the existence of the little green flashes. 'Why not get a fridge lock?' he suggested. Unanimous applause from Ds and Ms, whereupon he offers to go himself to B&Q to obtain one for her. I shall keep you au courant, in case this is useful for one of your books. Do you swear as much as your characters, I should like to know? Nobody swears here, except me, still internally.

Did you know my great friend Daphne Charteris? Maybe your great-aunt's sister-in-law? No, you said you were Middle Clarce in origin. She was one of our first aviatrices, Upper Clarce, daughter of a Scottish laird, used to ferry Dexter cattle around after she got her licence. One of only eleven women trained to fly a Lancaster in the war. Bred pigs and always named the runt of the litter Henry after her youngest brother. Had a room in her house known as the 'Kremlin' where even her husband wasn't allowed to disturb her. I always thought that was the secret of a happy marriage. Anyway, husband died and she went back to the family house to live with the runt Henry. The place was a pigsty, but they lived quite contentedly, getting deafer together by the month. When they could no longer hear the doorbell, Henry rigged up a car horn as a replacement. Daphne always refused to wear hearing aids on the grounds that they caught in the branches of trees.

In the middle of the night, while the ghosties are trying to pick Mrs Galloway's refrigerator lock to get at her Creme Eggs, I lie awake and watch the moon slowly move between the pines and think of the advantages of dying. Not that we are given a choice. Well, yes, there is self-slaughter, but that has always struck me as vulgar and self-important, like people who walk out of the theatre or the symphony concert. What I mean is—well, you know what I mean.

Main reasons for dying: it's what others expect when you reach my age; impending decrepitude and senility; waste of money—using up inheritance—keeping together brain-dead incontinent bag of old bones; decreased interest in The News, famines, wars, etc.; fear of falling under total power of Sgt-Major; desire to Find Out about Afterwards (or not?).

Main reasons for not dying: have never done what others expect, so why start now; possible distress caused to others (but if so, inevitable at any time); still only on B at Lie Brewery; who would infuriate Sgt-Major if not me?

—then I run out. Can you suggest others? I find that For always comes out stronger than Against.

Last week one of the mads was discovered stark naked at the bottom of the garden, suitcase filled with newspapers, apparently waiting for the train. No trains anywhere near the Old Folkery, needless to say, since Beeching got rid of the branch lines.

Well, thank you again for writing. Forgive epistolomania.

Sylvia

P.S. Why did I tell you that? What I was trying to say about Daphne is that she was always someone who looked forward, almost never back. This probably seems not much of a feat to you, but I promise it gets harder.

October 5, 1987

Dear Julian,

Wouldn't you think language was for the purpose of communication? I was not allowed to teach at my first practice school (training college), only to listen to classes, as I got the tu of the Passé Simple wrong. Now if ever I had been taught Grammar, as opposed to Knowing French, I could have retorted that nobody would ever say 'Lui écrivis-tu?' or whatever. At my 'school' we were mainly taught phrases without analysis of tenses involved. I have constant letters from a Frenchwoman with an ordinary secondary education who happily writes 'J'étais' or 'Elle s'est blessait' regardless. Yet my boss, who dismissed me, pronounced her French R's with that horrid muted sound used in English. I am glad to say all that is much improved and we no longer rhyme 'Paris' with 'Marry'.

I am not sure as yet whether the long letters I write have lapsed into senile garrulity. The point, Mr Novelist Barnes, is that Knowing French is different from Grammar, and that this applies to all aspects of life. I cannot find the letter in which you told me about meeting a writer even more antique than me (Gerrady? sp?—I looked for him in the library but could not find; in any case I shall surely have conked out before getting to the Gs). As I recall, he asked if you believed in survival after death and you answered No and he replied, 'When you get to my age, you might.' I am not saying there is life after death, but I am certain of one thing, that when you are thirty or forty you may be very good at Grammar, but by the time you get to be deaf or mad you also need to know French. (Do you grasp what I mean?)

Oh! oh! oh! for a real croissant! Yet French bread is made with French flour. Do they get that in your part of the world? Last night we had corned beef hash and baked beans; I wish I didn't love my food so. Sometimes I dream of apricots. You cannot buy an apricot in this country, they all taste of cotton wool impregnated with Austerity orange juice. After frateful scene with Sgt-Major I cut lunch and had a samwidge and knickerbocker glory in town.

You write that you are not afraid of dying as long as you don't end up dead as a result. That sounds casuistical to me. Anyway, perhaps you won't notice the transition. My friend Daphne Charteris took a long time a-dying. 'Am I dead yet?' she used to ask, and

Julian Barnes

sometimes, 'How long have I been dead for?' Her final words of all
were, 'I've been dead for a while now. Doesn't feel any different.'
   There's nobody here to talk to about death. Morbid, you see, and
not <u>naice</u>. They don't mind talking about ghosties and poltergeists
and suchlike, but whenever I get going on the real subject the Warden
& Sgt-Major tell me I mustn't scare the ducks. All part of my battle
against the tabooing of death as a subject—or Fear of It—and the
energy with which the medical profession tries to stop the dying from
dying, keeps alive babies born brainless, & enables barren women
to have artificial children. 'We have been trying for a baby for six
years'—Well! so you go without. The other evening we all got
double-yolked eggs—'Why? This is strange.' 'They are giving the
pullets fertility drugs to bring them into lay earlier.'
   What do I keep in my refrigerator, you ask? My purse, if you must
know, my address book, my correspondence, and a copy of my will.
(Fire.)
   Family still united? Yours? Any more children? I see you are doing
your Modern Father stuff well. George V used to bath his children,
Q. Mary didn't.
   V. best wishes, and succès fou to you,
   Sylvia

October 14, 1987

   Merci, charmant Monsieur, for the food parcel. Alas, the
combination of the GPO & the Sgt-Major meant that the croissants
were not as fresh as when they left you. I insisted on having a
General Distribution of this Lease Lend, so all the deafs and mads
got half each. 'Poddon? Poddon? Wozzit? Wozzit?' They prefer
floppy triangles of white bread toast with Golden Shred. If I pushed
the leftovers through the letter-box for Dominic—still in window—
do you think Warden wd have me gated? Sorry only postcard, arm
not good. Best wishes, Sylvia

December 10, 1987

   Barnes comes at about chest level, Brookner you have to get on
the floor. I do think her 'Look At Me' is a beautiful piece of tragic
writing, unlike 'King Lear' which I have just read for the 1st time.
Apart from some purple patches, plot and characterization total

250

balderdash. Emperor's clothes paradigm (word I've just learnt from crossword). Only postcard—Arm. V. best wishes, Sylvia

January 14, 1989

Dear Julian,

(Yes! Old Winstanley), Please forgive more senile garrulity. Also state of handwriting, which wd shame Nanny.

Fascinating telly of lion-cubs trying to eat porc-épic (why épic?—Larousse says corruption of porcospino which is obvious but why not épine instead of épic?). I am not really attracted to the hedgehog—I had a cattle grid at my cottage into which hedgehogs constantly fell. I found lifting them out by hand was the simplest way, but they are vermin-ridden and have inexpressive eyes, rather mean.

Foolish and senile of me to go on about your children when you say you have none. Plse forgive. Of course you make things up in your stories.

As I am eighty-four and still have an excellent memory I know it is inevitable that coincidences should occur, e.g. parrots, French scholars, etc. But then the Famous Art Person. And a month ago, I learned that my great-niece Hortense Barret is to go to university to read agricultural science. (We had Forestry in our day. Did you have Foresters? Earnest young men with leather patches on their elbows who lived in colonies near Parks Road and went off together for Field Work?) So the same week I am reading a book about hydrangeas and learn that the Hortensia may have been named after a young woman called Hortense Barret who went on the Bougainville expedition with the botanist Commerson. Enquiries reveal that there were however many generations between them, in and out of marriage, names changing, but the line was direct. What do you make of that? And why had I chosen to read a book about hydrangeas? I own neither pot-plant nor window-box nowadays. So you see, one can't attribute all this to Great Age and Good Memory. It is as if a Mind from outside—not my own unconscious mind—were saying, 'Take note of this: we have our eyes upon you.' I am agnostic, I may say, though could accept the hypothesis of a 'guide' or 'surveillant', even a Guardian Angel.

If so, what about it? I am only telling you that I get this impression of a constant dig-in-the-ribs. 'Watch it!' and this I find of signal use to me. May not be your pigeon at all. To me it provides evidence of educational intent from Higher Mind. How is it done? Search me!

As I am on the psychic belt I notice how evolution in the understanding of the Mind is progressing almost at the speed of technology: ectoplasm as much dated as rushlights.

Mrs Galloway—she of the fridge lock and the green sprites—'passed on' as the Warden likes to say. Everything passes here. Pass the marmalade, she passed such a remark, Did it Pass? they ask one another of their troublesome bowel movements. What do you think will happen to the little green flashes, I asked one dinner-time. Ds & Ms considered topic and eventually concluded that they probably passed on too.

Amitiés, sentiments distingués, etc.,

Sylvia W.

January 17, 1989

I suppose, if you are Mad, and you die, & there is an Explanation waiting, they have to make you unmad first before you can understand it. Or do you think being Mad is just another veil of consciousness around our present world which has nothing to do with any other one?

Do not conclude from Cathedral postcard that I have stopped Thinking own Thoughts. 'Vegetable Mould and Earthworms' in all probability. But perhaps not.

S.W.

January 19, 1989

So Mr Novelist Barnes,

If I asked you 'What is life?', you would probably reply, in so many words, that it is all just a coincidence.

So, the question remains, What sort of coincidence?

S.W.

April 3, 1989

Dear Mr Barnes,

Thank you for your letter of 22nd March. I regret to inform you that Miss Winstanley passed on two months ago. She fell and broke her hip on the way to the post-box, and despite the best efforts of the hospital, complications set in. She was a lovely lady, and certainly the life and soul of the party around Pilcher House. She will be long remembered and much missed.

If you require any further information, please do not hesitate to contact me.

Yours faithfully,

J. Smyles (Warden)

April 10, 1989

Dear Mr Barnes,

Thank you for your letter of the 5th inst.

In clearing out Miss Winstanley's room, we found a number of items of value in the refrigerator. There was also a small packet of letters but because they had been placed in the freezing compartment and then the fridge had been unfortunately switched off for defrosting they had suffered much damage. Although the printed letterhead was still legible we thought it might be distressing to the person to receive them back in this condition so regrettably we disposed of them. Perhaps this is what you were referring to.

We still miss Miss Winstanley very much. She was a lovely lady, and certainly the life and soul of the party around Pilcher House during her time here.

Yours faithfully,

J. Smyles (Warden)   □

THIS MONTH AT
WWW.GRANTA.COM:

MEET THE MAN WHO GOT INSIDE AL-QAEDA.

TAKE A TRIP (A BLACKLY COMIC VOYAGE) THROUGH SMALL-TOWN AMERICA, VIA THE INTERIOR LIFE OF ITS MOST NEUROTIC MAILMAN. LISTEN TO J. ROBERT LENNON READ FROM HIS LATEST NOVEL.

JOHN GRAY. "IS THERE," ASKS JASON COWLEY OF THE NEW STATESMAN, "A MORE CONSISTENTLY INTERESTING THINKER IN BRITAIN?" YOU DECIDE: READ A CHAPTER FROM "STRAW DOGS".

REMEMBER "WHAT WE THINK OF AMERICA" — GRANTA'S PRESCIENT AND NEWLY PERTINENT SPRING 02 ISSUE.

DO A BIT OF WINDOW-SHOPPING — PERHAPS EVEN BUY SOMETHING. EG: XMAS GIFT SUBSCRIPTION (50% IS A MEANINGFUL DISCOUNT)...

...and find out how to build a nuclear bomb. (It's worryingly easy.)

Julian Barnes's books include *The Pedant in the Kitchen* (Guardian Books) and *Flaubert's Parrot* (Picador/Vintage). 'Knowing French' will appear in his new short-story collection, *The Lemon Table*, to be published by Cape.

Tom Bissell is the author of *Chasing the Sea: Lost Among the Ghosts of Empire in Central Asia* (Pantheon).

Gardner Botsford served with the First US Infantry Division from Omaha Beach to Czechoslovakia. He was a senior editor at the *New Yorker* for many years. His memoir, *A Life of Privilege, Mostly*, is published by St Martin's Press.

James Buchan's latest book is *Capital of the Mind: How Edinburgh Changed the World* (John Murray), published in the US as *Crowded with Genius: The Scottish Enlightenment: Edinburgh's Moment of the Mind*. (HarperCollins).

Paula Fox is the author, most recently, of *Borrowed Finery* (Vintage/Holt).

Nell Freudenberger's short-story collection, *Lucky Girls*, is published by Ecco Press in the US and is forthcoming from Picador in the UK. Her story 'The Tutor' appeared in *Granta* 82.

Paul Fussell's latest book is *The Boys' Crusade: The American Infantry in Northwestern Europe, 1944–1945* (Weidenfeld & Nicholson/Houghton Mifflin).

Charles Glass lived in Lebanon from 1972–76 and 1983–85. His most recent book is *Tribes with Flags* (Picador/Grove/Atlantic).

Chris Hedges has been a war correspondent for nearly twenty years, covering Latin America, Africa, the Middle East and the Balkans. He is the author of *War Is a Force that Gives Us Meaning* (Public Affairs Press).

Judith Hermann lives and works in Berlin. 'Nothing but Ghosts' is the title story from her new collection, *Nichts als Gespenter*, published in Germany by Fischer Verlag and forthcoming in the UK from Flamingo. Her short story 'This Side of the Oder' appeared in *Granta* 74.

Adam Hochschild is the author of five books. His next, a history of the early British antislavery movement, will be published in autumn 2004.

A. M. Homes's recent short-story collection is *Things You Should Know* (Granta/Perennial). Her novels include *Music for Torching* (Doubleday/Anchor) and *Jack* (Granta/Vintage).

Chalmers Johnson is the author of *The Sorrows of Empire: Militarism, Secrecy, and the End of the Republic*, published by Metropolitan Books in the US and forthcoming from Verso in the UK.

Murad Kalam's first novel, *Night Journey*, is published by Simon & Schuster. He lives in Washington DC and is working on a second novel set in Cairo.

NOTES ON CONTRIBUTORS

James Kelman's most recent book is a collection of essays, *And the Judges Said* (Vintage). 'Man Walks into a Bar' is taken from his forthcoming novel, *You Have to be Careful in the Land of the Free* (Hamish Hamilton/Harcourt).
Rattawut Lapcharoensap was born in Chicago in 1979, raised in Thailand and now lives in Ann Arbor, Michigan. 'Farangs' is his first publication.
J. Robert Lennon lives in Ithaca, New York. His fourth novel, *Mailman*, is published by Granta Books in the UK and W. W. Norton in the US.
Jacki Lyden is a host and correspondent for National Public Radio. She is the author of *Daughter of the Queen of Sheba* (Virago/Penguin).
Todd McEwen wears a topcoat and lives in Edinburgh. His most recent novel, *Who Sleeps With Katz,* is published by Granta Books.
Darryl Pinckney is a regular contributor to the *New York Review of Books* and is the author of *High Cotton* (Faber/Penguin).
Martin Rowson's cartoons appear regularly in The *Guardian, The Times,* The *Daily Mail* and other publications. In 2001 he was appointed London's first Cartoonist Laureate by Mayor Ken Livingstone, for which he receives one pint of beer per annum. His maps of literary London appeared in *Granta 65.*
Luc Sante is the author of *Low Life* (Granta/Farrar Straus) and *Factory of Facts* (Granta/Vintage). He is writing a book about the picture postcard and prewar America.
Eric Schlosser is the author of *Fast Food Nation* (Allen Lane/Houghton Mifflin). His first play, *Americans*, has recently been produced in London and is published by Penguin.
Gary Shteyngart's novel, *The Russian Debutante's Handbook* is published by Bloomsbury in the UK and Riverhead in the US. His short story 'Several Anecdotes about my Wife', appeared in *Granta 78.*
Anthony Suau was born in the USA but has lived in Europe since 1987. *Fear This*, a photographic essay on how the Iraq war was seen from the USA, will be published by Channel Photographics. His most recent book was *Beyond the Fall* (Network Photographers/Liaison).
Studs Terkel's new book is *Hope Dies Last* (Granta/New Press).
Paul Theroux's most recent book is *The Stranger at the Palazzo D'Oro* (Hamish Hamilton/Houghton Mifflin). He is also a beekeeper in Hawaii.
Joel Turnipseed is the author of *Baghdad Express: A Gulf War Memoir* (Penguin). He writes a magazine column about the Asian board game, Go.
Edmund White's most recent novel is *Fanny: A Fiction* (Chatto/Ecco). 'My First European' is taken from his memoir-in-progress. A book of his essays, *Arts and Letters*, will appear in summer 2004.